Scars of Vietnam

ALSO BY HARRY SPILLER
AND FROM MCFARLAND

*Death Angel: A Vietnam Memoir of a Bearer
of Death Messages to Families* (1992; paperback 2012)

Support Programs for Ex-Offenders: A State-by-State Directory (2011)

*American POWs in World War II: Twelve Personal Accounts
of Captivity by Germany and Japan* (2009)

Pearl Harbor Survivors: An Oral History of 24 Servicemen (2002)

American POWs in Korea: Sixteen Personal Accounts (1998)

*Prisoners of Nazis: Accounts by American POWs
in World War II* (1998)

Scars of Vietnam

*Personal Accounts by
Veterans and Their Families*

HARRY SPILLER

McFarland & Company, Inc., Publishers
Jefferson, North Carolina, and London

The present work is a reprint of the library bound edition
of Scars of Vietnam: Personal Accounts by Veterans
and Their Families, first published in 1994 by McFarland.

LIBRARY OF CONGRESS CATALOGUING-IN-PUBLICATION DATA

Spiller, Harry, 1945–
　　Scars of Vietnam : personal accounts by veterans
and their families / by Harry Spiller.
　　　p.　　cm.
　　Includes bibliographical references and index.

　　ISBN 978-0-7864-6742-6
　　softcover : acid free paper ∞

　　1. Vietnamese Conflict, 1961–1975—Veterans—United
States.　 2. Vietnamese Conflict, 1961–1975—Psychological
aspects.　 3. Veterans—United States—Biography.
DS559.72.S65　 2012
959.704'38—dc20
[B]　　　　　　　　　　　　　　　　　　　　　　　94-33860

BRITISH LIBRARY CATALOGUING DATA ARE AVAILABLE

© 1994 Harry Spiller. All rights reserved

*No part of this book may be reproduced or transmitted in any form
or by any means, electronic or mechanical, including photocopying
or recording, or by any information storage and retrieval system,
without permission in writing from the publisher.*

On the cover: (top) Soldiers of the Fifth Marine Regiment
during the Battle of Hue, 1968 (National Archives and
Records Administration); (bottom) Vietnam Veterans
Memorial, Washington, D.C. Front cover design by
Rob Cheney (http://robcheney.com/)

Manufactured in the United States of America

*McFarland & Company, Inc., Publishers
　Box 611, Jefferson, North Carolina 28640
　　www.mcfarlandpub.com*

For Chad

Acknowledgments

For their assistance I wish to thank Barbara Randolph; Marion Carroll; Gary Smith; Terri Rentfro; Cindy Malley; Sherry Ing; Gene Ing; Linda S. Horn; Pat Wagnor; Carol Mitchell; Shirl; Lisa; Chad; the county recorder's offices in Pulaski County and Alexander County in Illinois and Cape Girardeau County, Scott County, Mississippi County, Iron County, Bollinger County, Madison County, St. François County, Ste. Genevieve County, and Perry County in Missouri; and the photo lab at John A. Logan College.

Contents

Acknowledgments	vii
Author's Note	xi
Introduction	1
Part I: The Missing Names	7
One: SGT. STEPHEN M. MALLEY	9
Two: SGT. MICHAEL E. BAUMAN	24
Part II: In the Twinkle of an Eye	47
Three: PVT. JOHN F. TERRY, JR.	49
Four: PFC. CLIFFORD D. COMBS	53
Five: PFC. LAWRENCE S. MILLS	67
Part III: Corpsman Up	73
Six: CPO HOMER YOUNT	75
Seven: PETTY OFFICER THIRD CLASS GEORGE I. ELLIS	81
Part IV: Leaders of Men	95
Eight: LT. RAY FULKERSON	97
Nine: CAPT. PAUL EBAUGH, JR.	110
Ten: CAPT. WILLIAM H. WALKER	121
Part V: Crossing Paths	135
Eleven: SGT. DONALD BUATTE	137
Twelve: SGT. LLOYD SCHWEIGERT	151
Thirteen: SGT. JOHN BUATTE	158
Part VI: Coming Full Circle	167
Fourteen: SGT. CARL A. MEYER, JR.	169
Fifteen: SGT. CARL E. MCCORY	177

Sixteen: CPL. GORDON W. HUCKSTEP	192
Seventeen: SGT. RONALD A. LOWES	200
Appendix	215
Index	221

Author's Note

The stories contained in this book are those of Marines, Navy corpsmen, and the families of these Vietnam veterans who lived in my recruiting area, which included Pulaski and Alexander counties in Illinois and Cape Girardeau, Scott, Mississippi, Iron, Bollinger, Madison, St. François, Ste. Genevieve, and Perry counties in Missouri. Generally I met them while on recruiting duty, either through enlisting the men or by delivering casualty notifications to their families. The exceptions are the two Navy corpsmen and one Marine, William Walker, whom I did not know until after the war.

The information about their experiences came from taped interviews, written questionnaires, official military documents, or personal documents given to me by the Marines, Navy corpsmen, or their families.

During the course of my research I have been approached by individuals who suggested I contact a number of Vietnam veterans or the families of veterans who completed their service with other branches of the armed forces. Although I do not tell their stories in this book, the reader and the families and friends of those veterans should understand that they are omitted only because I wanted to restrict the content of the book as exclusively as possible to those that I had experiences with while I was a recruiter.

My heart goes out to all those veterans and families who suffered during the Vietnam War and still suffer today. In order that they be recognized also, I have, however, included an appendix listing all Vietnam veterans from each branch of the armed forces within my 11-county area who were killed in action.

Introduction

In the 1960s, Americans' perceptions of world events tended to be shaped by the view that other nations and their leaders were cleanly divided into "good guys" and "bad guys"—an outlook that some political scientists and historians have called the Orthodox Theory. The theory grew out of the Cold War and events like the Soviet invasions of Hungary, Poland, and other European countries, all of which appeared to support the idea that the central foreign policy goal of the Soviet Union was world domination.

Further, the threat of communism was brought into the living rooms of Americans via the television. I can remember watching a short, fat, bald man with a large mole on his cheek on the evening news almost every night. He shook his fist and barked in Russian, then afterward often grinned, exposing a wide gap between his front teeth. I rarely knew what he had said, but I surmised that it had to be something sneaky; after all, I was a good guy and he was a bad guy.

The Russians had put *Sputnik* and the first man into space, confirming their threat. But no one event was more convincing that the communists were working toward world domination than the Cuban Missile Crisis. When Kennedy stood up against the Soviets only 90 miles from the U.S. shores it sparked the new commitment he spoke of in his inaugural address. People wore buttons that said "give a damn" and became committed to "ask not what your country can do for you, but rather ask what you can do for your country."

As a teenager my own patriotism was further strengthened by reading such books as *Guadalcanal Diary*, *The Bataan Death March*, *The Bridge Over the River Kwai*, *Merrill's Marauders*, *The Sands of Iwo Jima*, and *Normandy Beach*, and by watching Vic Morrow's television series "Combat." I had no doubt that my future lay in the armed services—I was just a little confused as to which branch of service I would join. During my high school years I joined each branch at least twice, in my dreams, depending on which movie I had seen or which book I was reading.

A few times during those years I slipped into an academic mood and decided that first I should go to college. That ended, though, when in my sophomore year my guidance counselor informed me that, "You best forget college. You could never handle the studies." Although I didn't realize it at the time, his decision was based more on the quality of clothes I wore than on my academic ability—I held a "B" average and never studied.

I joined the Sea Scouts and the Civil Air Patrol. At the organizational events I proudly displayed myself in my Navy or Air Force uniform, depending on the event, hoping the girls would notice me while I strutted around and dreamed of being home on leave from the service. Then my senior year in high school arrived and I heard that the Marine Corps had a new program through which it was possible to enlist immediately and leave to enter active duty as much as four months later. I scurried to the recruiting office to investigate.

I immediately decided to join the Marine Corps based on two powerful lures: the dress blue uniform, which speaks for itself, and the 120-day delay program, which no other branch had yet offered. I was in such a hurry to sign on the dotted line that I enlisted in February 1963 at the age of 17.

I had four months until graduation, and until I was to join the ranks of "a few good men." For the next 120 days my thoughts never strayed from my departure date of June 2, 1963—five days after graduation. I made a calendar on a piece of notebook paper and hung it on the wall in my bedroom so I could mark off each day. I talked about it at school, and when the final school newspaper of the year published a list of the graduating seniors' plans, mine read, "Harry Spiller, Career U.S. Marine Corps. Leaves June 2."

After going through MCRD San Diego and Infantry Training at Camp Pendleton, I was assigned to the 4th Marines in Hawaii. I spent a year and a half either humping the hills of the Hawaiian Islands or being dropped off in some remote jungle area on a survival course. We didn't have to worry about surviving a snakebite because there are no snakes on the Islands, but we did have to worry about shitting ourselves to death from eating so many guavas.

The first time I ever paid real attention to Vietnam was in 1964 when Da Nang air base was attacked by the Viet Cong. Americans had over 100 casualties. Four months later, to my surprise, I was sitting in an open field just outside of Phu Bai village in Vietnam. I spent my time in Nam playing good guy on patrols and ambushes, digging foxholes, sweating, staring into the night, and doing my share of American colonialism by destroying the dignity of a people that I did not understand nor care to understand. For answering the call of my country in 1965 I received a gross income of $1,989. That same year Sandy Koufax pitched for the Los Angeles Dodgers and was paid $125,000.

I returned to the States and was stationed at MCRD San Diego where my career had begun in the Corps. I was assigned to the Communications and Electronics Battalion, but after several months I got the itch to move on. I was no longer sure I wanted to make the Corps a career, but things were attractive. I was a sergeant, I was single, I had a 1963 Chevy convertible, and the re-enlistment bonus was tripled because the Corps needed infantrymen. I signed the contract in 1966 and was paid my triple bonus of $3,200. The same year Koufax retired from the Dodgers and signed a contract as a sports announcer, for a salary of one million dollars.

I was 21 years old and had been in the Marine Corps for three years and eight months when I stepped into the recruiting office at Cape Girardeau, Missouri. I was young for a recruiter since most Marines were not assigned recruiting duty until they had at least 10 to 12 years of experience.

I don't know precisely how many men and women I enlisted in the next three and a half years, but our office averaged 8 to 10 enlistees a month. I was effective at the job, four times receiving the quarterly award for enlisting the most people. I was recommended for a meritorious promotion to staff sergeant, and my commanding officer awarded me a meritorious mass when I left recruiting duty for never failing to make quota during my three and a half years.

I had one other assignment while I was on recruiting duty: making casualty calls to the families of those men wounded or killed in Vietnam. I did not know about this assignment when I asked for recruiting duty, but it wouldn't have mattered because after all the war was not going to last long.

I cannot put an exact number to the casualty calls I made. My meritorious promotion letter dated June 14, 1968, stated that I had already been involved with approximately 25 casualty notification calls and approximately 35 funerals, and before my tour was over some two years later there were many, many more.

As the war and the casualty count escalated, so did the violence at home. Martin Luther King, Jr., and Robert Kennedy were assassinated three months apart. The good guys and bad guys had become the doves and the hawks, black and white, men and women, vets and war protesters. The buttons people wore read "God Is Dead," "Stoned," and "Go Naked." Just as the country was changing, so was I. Almost daily I made casualty calls, and by now the men killed and wounded were those I had enlisted. I began to feel responsible for the lives lost. The Vietnam War was my war, and finally I lost heart. At the end of my enlistment I again had a calendar on the wall, but this time I was marking the days until I would be a civilian again.

When I was discharged from the Marine Corps in 1973, I threw my uniforms away, and for years I put the Vietnam experience deep inside. I didn't talk about it, and I didn't want to hear about it. I thought I had forgotten, but one night in 1983, I watched a television movie about the trauma of a young bride whose husband had been killed in Vietnam. In one scene of the movie the wife was working in her garden when officials came to her and gave her the news of her husband's death. For some reason the movie jolted my memory, and during the next few days I saw the episode over and over again in my head. Then I began to remember episodes from my own experiences; I tried once again to bury the past, but the memories were like a slow-burning fire that I could not put out. I began to write down my thoughts on legal pads, leading to the publication in 1992 of my Vietnam memoir.

While waiting for the publishing date of that book, I decided that it was time to return to the recruiting area where I had served. It had been 21 years since I had been in the many small towns scattered throughout southeast Missouri making speeches at the high schools about "a few good men" or delivering death messages.

The first stop I made was at the Mound City, Illinois, National Cemetery. As my family and I pulled through the black iron gate, the garden of stones was still. The morning dew was evaporating as the sun's rays moved slowly across the ground.

I looked across the cemetery lots as I heard my son Chad whisper to his sister Lisa, "This is where Daddy fought the war." We walked to the gravesite of John Francis Terry, Jr. Into the white stone worn from time was chiseled a weathered October 22, 1967. My memory of events rushed back to the relative who grasped, in desperation, the letter she had received from John the same day I delivered the death message: We must have made a mistake! She was still carrying the letter on the day of his funeral.

We drove across the Mississippi River into Missouri, and stopped at Charleston and Sikeston, and then drove to Chaffee. I remembered the house of the Dobbs family near the circle drive at the edge of town. As I drove past the house I was amazed that it looked much as I remembered it. I wondered if the family still lived there, if they were the ones who had placed the yellow ribbon fluttering now from the pillar on the front porch as a token of support for the troops in a different war—a support their son never got. I wanted to go to the front door and knock, to tell them that I was the Marine who had delivered the message, to find out how they were doing. I was reluctant, though, fearing that I might be dragging up painful memories.

We went to Oran, Marble Hill, Lutesville, and finally to the town that had more of an effect on me than any other during my tour on recruiting duty—Marquand. I parked in the Creek Rock parking lot in the center of

Introduction 5

town. The first thing I noticed was the three oak trees at the edge of the parking area—the location where I met with applicants when I came to town two decades earlier. As I looked around, it was as if those 20 years had been erased. The funeral home had been remodeled but was in the same location; the stores, covering less than a block, were all the same except for a beauty shop in place of the J.C. Penney catalog store; and the two-pump gas station still featured an attendant with country gestures, coveralls, and flip-billed hat that reminded me of Mayberry on "The Andy Griffith Show."

We walked to a monument on a street corner that was dedicated to the town's 23 men who had served and died in U.S. wars. "Twenty-three!" I exclaimed as I scanned the list of names.

"Shush," my wife Shirl whispered. "Someone might hear you." She was right—I had enlisted a lot of people out of this town.

We walked to the new convenience store across the street from the monument, bought some Cokes, and started to leave. I stopped the car by the bridge and stream at the edge of town to take a photograph, and was suddenly aghast as I saw the green sign with white letters which read, "Marquand 231." Back in the sixties when I had made so many casualty calls, I had thought that population sign read 980—but the number must have been only 98! I had enlisted at least nine that I could remember, and three of them were killed in action. Moments later I took the photograph and returned to the car. As we pulled away from Marquand that day I knew I would go back. I didn't know why or when, but I knew it.

We completed our trip, driving through Fredericktown, Ironton, Farmington, Flat River, Ste. Genevieve, and Perryville. As we drove through each town the memories grew stronger, and I wondered more about the men I had enlisted. What did they experience in Vietnam? How did the war affect their lives afterward? How did the families of those who lost loved ones in such an unpopular war manage to put the pieces back together, or did they? This book was born out of the desire to answer these questions.

The experience of writing this book has produced a kaleidoscope of emotions—from laughter, excitement, fright, sorrow, and pain to the realization that many of the true casualties of the Vietnam War have never set foot "in country," have neer been on a battlefield, have never received Purple Hearts, and will never have their names chiseled into a monument or a wall. They are ordinary Americans who unselfishly answered their country's call.

From the heartland here are 17 personal accounts from veterans and their families who have felt the scars of Vietnam.

PART I

The Missing Names

ONE

Sgt. Stephen M. Malley
(August 3, 1947–May 28, 1984)

Hometown: Mounds, Ill.; Marine Heavy Helicopter Squadron 463; Marine Aircraft Group 16; Door Gunner; Wounded in Da Nang, Vietnam, May 19, 1968.

This is an angel trap. If I caught an angel, I'd let her take me up to God to see my daddy.
STEPHEN MICHAEL MALLEY II
January 9, 1989

Stephen Michael Malley loved the outdoors—hunting and fishing in particular—but most of all Mike, as he preferred to be called, loved people. Born and raised in Mounds, a small southern Illinois farm town, he used to charm the elderly neighbors on McKinley Street with his sunny smile and the inquisitiveness of a growing young boy.

As he grew his charm grew also. He was popular in school and played his two favorite sports, basketball and baseball. He didn't care much for the academic world, but after graduation from Mounds High School in 1965 he signed up for a semester at Southeastern Illinois Community College. He didn't like it. One day in the summer of 1966 he walked into his house and informed his parents that he was going into the service. Mike's father wanted him to join the Navy, but instead, Mike enlisted in the Marine Corps on September 1, 1966.

After boot camp and several months of aviation school at Memphis, Tennessee, and El Toro, California, Mike's wish came true when he received orders for Vietnam. His parents, James and Mary, were sick with the news, but Mike wanted them to be proud of him because as Mike said, "It is a cause worth fighting for."

Mike arrived in Vietnam on April 3, 1968, and received orders to the

Marine Aircraft Group 16 located near Marble Mountain in Da Nang, Vietnam. He was there for one month and 16 days before he saw his first and only action in the war. On May 19, he and several other Marines were working on helicopters when they came under a heavy mortar attack. Mike ran for a bunker but didn't make it in time. He lay in the open field wounded and helpless until the attack was over.

The Malley family got the news by telegram. The telegram stated that he was in good condition with a positive prognosis and that the military had transported him to a naval hospital in Japan. The Malleys had no other information, so James wrote to Mike's commanding officer for details. In early June, James received a letter from Lt. Col. J.G. Walker explaining how Mike's injury had occurred and adding that Mike had been evacuated on May 20 to Da Nang Hospital, then to Yokosuka, Japan, for further treatment. The colonel told the Malleys that Mike was in good condition, that he was receiving the best medical attention a Marine could get, and that the colonel looked forward to Mike's return to the unit.

The Malleys were relieved to hear that their son was going to be fine. James and Mary were very proud of Mike, and James, confident that Mike would recover soon, paraded around town in his country club style and boasted about Mike's experience in Vietnam.

One day I stopped by the Mounds post office to fill the literature rack and James approached me with a photograph of Mike. He looked concerned as he handed me the picture. I took one look at the picture and knew that something had to be wrong. James told me that Mike was in good condition with minor wounds, but the man in the photo was wrapped in bandages from head to toe. If he was in good condition with minor wounds, I thought grimly, I would hate to see anyone in bad condition. I didn't voice my concern to James, though; after all, hospitals did get carried away with bandage wrapping from time to time, and anyhow I was no doctor. I reassured James that Mike was in the best of hands, and that I was sure he would be fine.

Months later when Mike returned home, the Malleys and the people of Mounds found out what really happened on May 19, 1968. Mike asked if he could say a few words to the congregation at his church, and the speech he gave would prove to be the one and only time that he ever gave details of the mayhem he experienced on the night of May 19, 1968. These are his words.

> I asked the pastor if I could say a few words here today. I think most of you know me. Most of my youth was spent as that of most young Christians. But after one semester of college, I joined the U.S. Marine Corps. Later I went to fight for my country. On the nineteenth of May, I was shot in the leg and chest. My company were all pinned down by mortar fire. When the men were able to go out to get me, two men laid next to me dead and the other had lost an ear.

I had been hit eleven more times.

I think that ninety-nine percent of man's prayer is an unconscious act. As far as my own prayer, up until that day in May, I know in my heart I just went through the steps on the outside. But as I laid there that day and felt the warm blood of life flow from my body, I began to pray to God for the very first time.

A very short time passed and then my men had placed me in a safe sand bay bunker. Soon a man sat down beside me. He was a priest and had given to me my last rites. He spoke in a very soft voice. He said that I was going to be dead in a short time.

I was very weak, and could only say a word or two at a time without a short rest. Then I began to tell him what went on, as I laid out in the opening, wounded and close to death. I spoke to God and felt Him around me. I told him I knew the Lord was with me, and He would protect me from then on.

Mike Malley's wounds were much more severe than his family had known. He had multiple shrapnel wounds to the chest wall, left flank, back, buttock, abdomen, and lower extremities. While in Da Nang Hospital, he had a laparotomy performed when the doctors found that shrapnel had ripped through his stomach and liver.

Mike would never reveal to his parents the severity of his wounds because he did not want them to worry. When he wrote he was always positive and never complained. He was able to send them a tape on one occasion while he was in Japan and although he was weak, "It was a God's blessing to hear his voice," Mary Malley recalled, her eyes brimming with tears. "We worried so much about him. And when we heard his voice we felt that we weren't being told everything."

Finally, they received word that Mike was being moved to Great Lakes Naval Hospital. The day came and James and Mary drove to the hospital. As they walked into the hospital they promised themselves that they would not break down when they saw Mike.

"When we got into the hospital it seemed like everywhere we were sent we had to go a little further. Finally we walked into a large room. I was shocked. There were young boys everywhere. Arms off, legs off, and some of them were even in basketlike beds with no arms or legs at all," Mary said.

"I looked around the room and spotted Mike about the same time he spotted me. Needless to say neither James nor I kept our promise.... Mike was still very weak and had lost a lot of weight. His back was covered with little holes. It looked like he was shot with a BB gun all over his back. He had scars on his stomach and legs. He wouldn't talk about what happened to him, but we knew then that our suspicions were true—we had not been told how serious his wounds really were. We stayed for a week and went to see him every day and then were told that Mike was going to be sent to California for treatment. That was the last we were to see of Mike until he came home."

When the Malleys received the news that Mike was coming home, they planned a party for him. Several of his friends were waiting to see him, but Mike rejected the idea. Entering a house full of friends, Mike went straight to his room with a mere "Hi," unable to talk to anyone. The short time that Mike was home was not a pleasant one. He was nervous, couldn't sleep, and was in continuous pain. Finally this condition forced Mike back to Great Lakes.

Doctors admitted Mike to the hospital with a complaint of pain and weakness in his left leg as well as diarrhea and pain from abdominal cramping. The doctors examined him and found that his chest wound was draining properly and his other wounds were healing as they should, but then x-rays revealed that Mike's body was still ridden with shrapnel; there were foreign substances still in his chest wall, back, arms, and legs. Mike was given codeine and several other prescription drugs for his pain. The doctors released him for a 30-day leave with orders to report to El Toro, California, to the air station.

Mike's condition was no better: he had further weight loss, constant pain, weakness, and diarrhea. Each time he went to the hospital he received more prescription drugs for the pain, but none improved his condition. Several months later, the physical evaluation board ruled that Mike was to retire with 30 percent disability because of the lacerations to his stomach and liver, ulnar nerve injury, and sciatic nerve injury resulting in weakness, hyperkeratosis, and hyperesthesia in the lower left extremity. On September 9, 1970, the U.S. Marine Corps retired Sergeant Stephen M. Malley for reason of permanent physical disability and sent him home.

The Malleys noticed a drastic change in Mike's living habits, a change that neither they nor Mike himself understood. He was constantly nervous and had to be on the move. He would stay up all night making frequent visits to the local restaurants. Once the restaurants closed he would just drive around town. He was in pain most of the time. Often a piece of shrapnel would work itself to the surface of the skin and his parents would take him to the local doctor who would remove the shrapnel, temporarily relieving the pain. He made more than 20 visits to the local doctor and another 32 visits to the veterans hospital in Marion and the naval hospital in Great Lakes.

In 1971, Mike landed a job at the Menard Penitentiary in Chester, Illinois, as a correctional officer. He worked at the job for almost a year, until he blacked out one day while driving home and crashed his car. The doctors refused to release him for medical reasons and he was forced to resign his position at the penitentiary.

In 1972, he returned to work at the prison as a counselor in the psychiatric ward. In less than a year the prison administrator asked Mike to resign because he could not cope with the prison environment.

Over the next three years Mike's condition worsened. He remained in constant pain, and now his condition was compounded by the effects of heavy doses of drugs. He took Dilantin, phenobarbital, and Tegretol in quantities of 200 mg per day under prescription by the Veterans Administration treatment policy of assembly line medication. His blackouts became more frequent, but regardless of his pain and anxiety Mike always remained supportive of his country and the effort in Vietnam. He expressed his thoughts in two poems he wrote in 1973, when once again he tried to pull his life together by furthering his education. Following is one of the poems that Mike wrote in an English literature class.

A MAN TODAY

Now that death is constantly near,
'Tis being dead I no longer fear.
Nor am I worried of failure or scorn,
But what kind of men this war has born.

What of the men with hair so long,
who burn their cards and chant their songs?

Who abuse the flag, we hold so dear,
Can it be death these men truly fear?

They are the men with spines so weak,
Who haven't been there, but choose to speak!

I know. I have been there, so I can say,
You're a sad excuse for a man today!

A short time later, Mike once again dropped college classes. This time it was not a lack of interest, but rather anxiety, pain, nervousness, and heavy drug intake that took their toll on his ability to concentrate.

In 1975, Mike tried working again. He landed a job at Union Carbide in Paducah, Kentucky, working at miscellaneous jobs. The heavy doses of drugs that Mike took for pain made him unable to perform adequately, however, and within six months he lost his job.

In 1977, Mike went to work for the state prison system as a trainee at Statesville Correctional Center. At 3 P.M. on February 4, 1977, he collapsed from an apparent epileptic seizure. Fellow workers rushed him to the Little Company of Mary Hospital by ambulance, and once again the prison administration asked Mike to resign.

Later in 1977, Mike went to work as a day counselor at the VA hospital in Marion, Illinois. Six months later Mike was in his office talking with a patient. He was in the middle of a sentence when suddenly a vacant expression appeared on his face for two or three seconds. His eyes rolled to the right and his head turned the same way, then his body stiffened for a few seconds and he began to jerk uncontrollably. He was rushed to the emergency room. Mike later resigned from the last job that he would ever hold.

For the next three years Mike would enter the hospital on the average of four times a month with severe headaches, more seizures, rambling speech, and daily regurgitation. He underwent hundreds of tests from CAT scans to spinal taps, but the result was merely a prescription for more drugs. At this point he was taking 200 mg of carbamazepine twice a day, 100 mg of phenytoin three times a day, 15 mg of thioridazine three times a day, 100 mg of Dilantin twice a day, 400 mg of Matrin four times a day, and 300 mg of Darvon three times a day. Each drug worked as a pain killer affecting the central nervous system, each with an individual effect and collectively with interactive effects, so it is not surprising that Mike became increasingly dysfunctional. He slurred his speech and walked around in a daze. He would sleep for hours, wake up, go somewhere for a couple of hours, then sleep again. He wrecked several cars because of his seizures and the effects of the drugs.

Mike still loved the outdoors and would sometimes grab a fishing pole and try to fish. One day while he walked along a creek bank, he was bitten on the leg by a cottonmouth. He walked around for over an hour unaware that he had been bitten by the poisonous snake before someone else fishing in the creek discovered that Mike needed immediate medical attention.

Mike still had a love for people, too, but the townspeople no longer looked upon him as affectionately. Mike often went to the local restaurants to be with people and talk, but many poked fun at him with taunts like "Why are you slurring your words, Mike?" or, "Kill any of them Viet Cong today, Mike?" One hot summer day Mike went into a local cafe in a heavy Marine Corps coat that he wore because of the frequent chills that he suffered as a reaction to the drugs. People laughed and snickered. "Another one of them Vietnam veterans come home smoking that dope," they whispered. "Hey Mike, ya cold? Better get over there and get some more of them Cong," one patron said as the people in the restaurant burst into laughter. Mike looked at them in silence, then got up and walked out of the restaurant.

In 1980, doctors declared Mike 100 percent disabled after they agreed that his central nervous system was completely dysfunctional. To compound the pain of his disability, his father James died of cancer around the same time. Mike's life seemed only downhill until January 1981, when Mike

From left: Terry Ditterline (Cindy's son from a previous marriage), Cindy Malley, Stephen Michael Malley.

stopped by the K&K truck stop for coffee and the waitress introduced him to Cindy Ditterline. Cindy, a fair complexioned redhead with deep hazel eyes, was overcome by Mike's gentlemanly manners. They talked for a while and Mike told Cindy that he wanted to dedicate a song to her. He played "Special Lady" on the jukebox.

They began dating that night. "We drove around a lot and mainly went to dinner," Cindy recalled. "We would go to Cape Girardeau to the Ramada Inn or to the Holiday Inn. Mike talked about Vietnam all the time. Either something that happened in Vietnam or about him going to the doctor.

Once in a while we would try to go to a movie. Mike would get so nervous that we would have to leave. We quit going because we were wasting our money."

On July 2, 1982, Mike and Cindy were married. They bought a mobile home and moved it onto his parents' property next to their home. Their days were never the same. Mike and Cindy would sleep for four hours, but then Mike would have to be up and moving for the next four hours regardless of the time. They went to local truck stops and diners. After coffee and a bite to eat, Mike would usually go outside to vomit; then they would head for home. The only other regular event in their lives was Mike's doctor appointments. "Regardless of what Mike's complaints were with the doctor the end result was always more pills," Cindy explained in a voice shaky with frustration. "He had been through detoxification several times, but then when he would go back to the VA for his pain or seizures they would put him right back on the pills again."

The happiest day for Mike was in January 1984 when he found out that Cindy was pregnant. "It started out with a home test," Cindy said. "It was positive so I called the doctor and had another test run. We went to the doctor and when he told me that I was pregnant, Mike stood up and started hooping and hollering. The office was full of people and I turned red as a beet. Mike was so excited he said that he was going to have it put in the newspaper."

Mike now had, as he said, "something to live for," but his health was deteriorating rapidly. He began to experience repeated thoughts and became delusional, angry, and belligerent, losing consideration for family and friends. He didn't always know what he was doing or saying. "Once I was in the living room and Mike walked up to me," Cindy recalled. "He had this weird look on his face and he told me that he was going to kill me. He said he was going to do it slowly. He raised his arm above his head and made stabbing motions to my chest. I said, 'Mike, what are you doing?' but he didn't answer. After a couple of minutes the weird look disappeared and Mike was just standing there as if he didn't know how or why he was standing there. He never knew that he had done any of it."

Mike watched television all the time and had a compulsion to watch war movies, but after watching one he typically became depressed. He became preoccupied with guns and knives and at one point got a passport to South America, saying he was going to train the people in villages to use guns.

In a delusion Mike told a doctor that he had been wounded while he was assigned to the Marine Special Forces. He said that while in a foxhole he was jumped by three men and was stabbed under his armpit and in the lower back. He indicated to the doctor that he had killed two of the men with his bare hands and the third with a knife.

Cindy had slowly reduced Mike's drug intake over the first year of their marriage, and now she was trying to find things for Mike to do. She told Mike she wanted to plant a garden, but he would have no part of it. He couldn't take care of a garden, he told her, and he wasn't going to let Cindy start one if he couldn't take care of it himself. But finally Cindy coaxed Mike into buying a tiller, and they broke a small garden, approximately eight feet square. Mike became an instant farmer. He would get up early every morning. Dressed in white bib overalls he would sit on the back porch and pet his dog, and then go to work in his garden. Proud of his work, he would go to the back window of his mother's house and tell her to come look at his garden. He began to talk about buying 10 acres of land and moving their mobile home to the farm. The new events in Mike's life excited him: he was going to have a baby and now own a farm. But Mike would never see either of his dreams come true.

It was April and Cindy, now five months pregnant, was becoming more alarmed at Mike's behavior. One day Cindy heard a thud in the bathroom and found that Mike had fallen backwards and hit his head on the corner of the bathtub. He was lying across the stool. Cindy pulled him up as well as a five-month-pregnant woman could lift 150 pounds of dead weight from the floor. She noticed that his nose was swelling. He was in a daze, but began to try to stand. Cindy and her brother helped Mike up and to the car. They drove him to the VA hospital.

A male attendant took Mike into his office. "You're taking street drugs, aren't you?" he snarled.

Mike sat in a daze silently glaring at the attendant sitting across from him.

"You're on street drugs and I know it. You're just another cop-out looking for benefits. Aren't you?" he yelled as he leaned across his desk and got face to face with Mike.

"He needs help!" Cindy screamed. "He just had a seizure!"

The attendant sat back in his chair as Cindy grabbed Mike by the arm and led him from the room. Soon after, a doctor examined Mike and released him—with another prescription for drugs.

On May 6, 1984, Mike had a seizure while he was sitting in his chair. According to Cindy he always had trouble urinating. "He had to concentrate and pass a little urine each time." On this occasion he had stayed up all night and watched the water in the creek behind the mobile home. The creek often banked during the spring and flooded the yard. "He told me to go on to bed about 3 A.M. I woke up and met Mike at the bedroom door. He had on his long pajama bottoms, looked to be in a daze and acted like he didn't know what was going on. He was sopping wet from the top of his legs up to his waist," Cindy explained. When Cindy asked him if he had been outside, Mike responded, "I don't know." He had vomited and lettuce leaves from salad had stuck to his pajama bottoms. He looked as if he was concentrating because he couldn't remember what had happened. Cindy said, "Mike, you peed on yourself."

"I don't know," he said.

"Did you throw up?" Cindy asked.

"I don't know," he replied.

Cindy went into the living room and looked at the chair. There was dried vomit on it. "Mike was very embarrassed when he found out that he had urinated on himself," Cindy recalled.

Mike was gradually becoming unable to think in a connected manner. He had periods of alternating depression and silliness that lasted up to two weeks, and then he would be okay for a while. His seizures became more like simple losses of consciousness. His medication nauseated him. He developed bulimia and would eat gross amounts of food (like eight grilled cheese sandwiches at one time), then vomit.

Cindy went to bed about 3 A.M. on May 28, 1984. She called out to Mike and told him that she wanted him to come to bed and hold her. Mike came to the doorway and told her that he was going through some papers and would come to bed in about 15 or 20 minutes. Cindy fell asleep. When she woke around 6 A.M., she realized that Mike had not been to bed. Cindy knew something was wrong. She went into the living room and saw Mike sitting in a chair, his arms and head dangling toward the floor. Scattered in front of him were his billfold, money, VA cards, and other billfold papers that it appeared he had been going through. Over to the left Mike had vomited. The vomit was covered with carpet cleaner. Mike's hands, fingers, face, and part of his toes were black. Cindy knew he was dead.

She ran to him and shoved him up in his chair. He stayed up, his eyes were closed. There was a curdle, like cottage cheese, on his lower lip. "You promised me you would stay here and help me raise our baby," Cindy screamed as she began beating on his chest. "You promised!"

Cindy ran to the phone and called an ambulance and Mike's mother, who came over and began patting Mike on the hand and calling out, "Mike, Mike, are you okay?" She picked up his billfold and put the papers back inside. Then she placed the billfold on the ottoman. The ambulance arrived and the ambulance attendants laid Mike on the floor. They cleaned the vomit from his mouth, began CPR, and gave him oxygen, then sped off to the hospital with him. The 36-year-old ex–Marine was dead on arrival.

Cindy's brother stayed with her the first night after Mike died. He was going to sleep on the couch, but Cindy couldn't sleep. She felt that her whole world had ended. She thought of Mike. She wanted to see him. So she asked her brother to call the funeral home.

The next morning Cindy's brother called and told the funeral director that Cindy wanted to see Mike. "We don't usually do that," the funeral director explained. "She needs to see him now," Cindy's brother insisted. They went to the funeral home. Mike was lying on the table with the sheet pulled up on him. "I noticed that they had embalmed him and I knew then that this was real. He looked so clean. He looked like he had just gotten out of the shower."

It took four days before they buried Mike and each day Cindy went to the funeral home to see him. Mike had not requested a military funeral, but Cindy felt that he should have one. Full military honors were given to Mike at the Mound City National Cemetery on June 1, 1984.

Cindy's friends stayed with her constantly. They helped her keep going. They kept her busy. She had a mobile home and a car to pay for, and a baby coming soon. Cindy's friends helped her gather the necessary papers to try to get veteran's benefits for her and her unborn child. She submitted Mike's medical records, the records showing that he was 100 percent disabled, and the death certificate.

On September 8, 1984, three months and eight days after Mike's death, their son Stephen Michael Malley II was born. Cindy was happy. She had given birth to an eight pound five ounce healthy baby boy. The child looked like his daddy and had replaced part of Cindy's emptiness. Yet, she longed for her husband. She constantly talked to Mike everywhere she went, and visited the cemetery daily. "I was obsessed. I don't know why I thought I had to be there to talk to him, but I did. The gates closed at five each night and no matter what I was doing I would stop and drive out to the cemetery. I would talk to Mike for a while and and then I was okay. I would go home and take care of little Mike."

In February 1985, Cindy got a real shock. She received a letter from the Veterans Administration stating that they were unable to establish that Mike's service-connected condition contributed to his death. Further, they said, the records did not show that Mike held a 100 percent service-connected rating for 10 years prior to his death. At the bottom of the letter an imprint read, "America's Veterans come first."

Cindy worried about the future. She had a mobile home and car to pay for and a baby to raise. Over the last six months she had used what little savings she had to pay the bills. Neighbors and friends urged her to fight for the benefits.

Cindy went to the Cairo, Illinois, veterans office to find out the reasons for denial. It didn't take long. On Mike's death certificate the doctor had recorded the cause of death as cardiopulmonary failure. The VA had seen no connection between Mike's heart failure and his service as a Marine.

Cindy went to the doctor and explained the problem. He was furious. He did not know Mike or Mike's medical history. In a letter to the VA, the doctor explained:

Stephen Michael Malley II

> The patient was pronounced dead about 7 A.M. on May 28, 1984. On the death certificate as the cause of death, I wrote "cardio-pulmonary failure." This is normal procedure for a patient with which I have no previous contact, even though some other condition caused that failure.

Family members, friends, and members of the local VFW wrote letters of support and telling about Mike's experiences and his life struggle after he returned from Vietnam.

Cindy took the papers and returned to the Cairo VA office to file an appeal. She soon encountered another obstacle—the VA representative. He had known Mike and didn't like him. In short, he told Cindy that Mike was nothing but a dope addict and didn't deserve anything. Neither did she.

The VA representative kept Cindy running back and forth to the VA office, filling out papers and more papers. When she would call him about the status of the claim, he would give her little more than a grunt for an answer. Finally, the receptionist in the VA office, who had always been sympathetic to Cindy's situation, put her in contact with another representative from Murphysboro, Illinois. Thirteen months after Mike's death, the VA notified Cindy that she and little Mike would receive benefits.

A couple of years passed and Cindy still longed for Mike. She continued her daily visit to the cemetery to talk with him. When a few male friends called and asked her out, she would get upset. "What is wrong with people?" she thought. "I belong to Mike."

Cindy began to have a recurring dream. In the dream, little Mike is a teenager. He wants a pizza and Cindy goes over to the local pizzeria to pick it up. She walks in a door and down a few steps. There are people standing around, and on the far side of the room is Mike with another woman. He turns around, looks at Cindy and then turns away. Cindy stands and watches him for a few minutes and then walks over to where the couple is standing. She interrupts them and asks to talk to Mike. She gets him away from everyone. "Mike, how is it you're here? You're dead," she says. "That's right, I'm dead," he replies. But only you and I know that. Nobody else knows that."

"Well, if you're dead and you can be here, then would you please come on home? We need you," Cindy says.

"No, this is my life now. And what you have is yours. We have our own jobs to do: mine is what I am doing and yours is what you are doing," Mike tells her.

Cindy had the dream over and over for about a year. She thought she was going crazy and went to a psychologist. He told Cindy there was nothing wrong with her. She was going through mourning. He explained that it would pass. "You're lucky," he told Cindy. "You're grieving at the right time. Often people don't react to a loved one's death for years. They bottle it up and try to forget. But always the grief will surface; it's just a matter of time."

Cindy began pulling her life together. Little Mike was growing like a weed. He often asked his mother why he didn't have a daddy like his friends. She tried to explain to the four-year-old that his daddy was in heaven. One day in little Mike's pre-school, the children were making string designs on paper. The teacher asked little Mike about the diamond and square shapes he had put together. "What is that?" she asked. "It's an angel trap. If I caught an angel, I'd let her take me up to God to see my daddy," he said.

Eight years after Mike's death Cindy sold her mobile home and bought a house five doors down from Mike's mom. You won't mistake where Cindy lives. The name on the top of the mailbox in large letters reads, "Mike Malley." And, you won't mistake the patriotism of the neighborhood. Every house along Bucher Road displays a yellow ribbon or an American flag.

Cindy has made several attempts to have Mike's name engraved on the Vietnam Wall in Washington. "He died as a result of wounds he received on the battlefield. It just took a few years longer. He deserves to have his name on the Wall," she says.

Stephen Michael Malley II's angel trap. In describing his design, the child said, "This is an angel trap. If I caught an angel, I'd let her take me up to God to see my daddy."

The government disagrees. "The Wall is in memory of those who died as a direct result of wounds received on the battlefield."

Cindy hasn't given up.

Cindy takes care of little Mike and makes crafts to help pay the bills. Little Mike has his daddy's dark complexion and dark hair. He also has a love for people, the inquisitiveness of an eight-year-old, and loves the outdoors just like his daddy. He knows nothing about the country or the war that has had such a devastating effect on his life. When I asked him if he had heard of Vietnam, he got a big grin, wrinkled his nose, and said, "No, where is that place at?"

He does have a wish though. He wants a daddy. Every Christmas he asks for a daddy. Cindy has tried to tell him that it just isn't that easy. After constantly hounding her, Cindy finally told him that he should pick one out and they would go from there.

He is still looking....

TWO
Sgt. Michael E. Bauman
(October 3, 1946–October 31, 1987)

Hometown: Ste. Genevieve, Mo.; Phu Bai, Vietnam; Auto Mechanic; Headquarters Battery, Fourth Battalion Twelfth Marines; Third Marine Division; Wounded on April 6, 1967.

> *I'm sorry, guys. I wish I could say it was April Fools', but I can't. I love you.*
> MICHAEL E. BAUMAN
> April 1, 1986

Michael Bauman grew up in Ste. Genevieve, Missouri, the oldest permanent European settlement in the state, located on the west bank of the Mississippi River, 60 miles south of St. Louis, Missouri.

Mike went to school at Valley Grade and High School. He was an average kid who liked football, baseball, hunting, and fishing. After graduating from high school, Mike studied auto mechanics at Technical School in St. Louis, Missouri.

In 1966, he joined the Marines to fight in the Vietnam War. He told his father it was the patriotic thing to do. Mike went through boot camp at San Diego, California. The Corps issued him a specialty number as an auto mechanic then stationed him at Camp Lejeune, North Carolina.

In December 1966, Mike received orders for Headquarters Battery, Fourth Battalion, Twelfth Marines stationed in Phu Bai, Vietnam. He had been there for two months when the Viet Cong made a big push in the area. Mike and his friend Doug took cover in a bunker when the attack began. A mortar hit the top of the bunker and exploded. Mike's eardrums ruptured. He couldn't hear. He looked around and watched the movement outside his bunker as if watching a silent movie. He then lay perfectly still as a Viet Cong came into the bunker and began shooting the dazed and wounded Marines. Mike felt a sharp pain in his lower leg as a bullet ripped through his skin. Suddenly the Viet Cong crashed to the ground as a Marine sergeant shot him, charged into the bunker, and began checking the wounded.

A couple of hours passed, the fighting was over, and evacuation of the wounded began. The bunker was so badly damaged by the explosion that Mike and the other Marines had to be taken out through the roof. Mike was taken first because he appeared more severely wounded than the others. He screamed with pain as he was lifted through the opening in the bunker. Several times while enroute to Da Nang he passed out, and doctors pronounced him dead three different times. Anger, pain, and sorrow came with the news that Doug, who was thought to be less severely wounded, had died.

I was at the funeral home in Ste. Genevieve checking on the funeral arrangements for John F. Shuh, who had been killed in action just a few days before, when I got the call about Mike. I took the information and hurried to his home to tell his parents Ed and Wilma Bauman. I told them that he had been shot in the stomach and his condition and prognosis were both serious. Ed, in an emotional state, told me that if his son died he wanted a glass coffin so his entire body could be seen. I was quick to inform him that we had the finest doctors in the world and that his son was in good hands.

Later we learned that the information about Mike's wounds was wrong. He had actually been shot in the leg and not the stomach. X-rays taken of his leg, however, did not show the location of the bullet. The doctors were concerned that Mike's leg would become seriously infected, and they amputated it below the knee. Later they found the bullet lodged in his back.

Several months later Mike returned home. Ed Bauman recalls, "We met him at the St. Louis Airport. He came with the leg on. He walked by himself over to the airplane hangar or whatever you call it. We met him at the door. We started on home and we stopped to get something to eat. He went to the bathroom. When he came out, he was carrying the leg under his arm. People were looking, but it didn't bother him. He said that it hurt him too bad to wear it.

"He never considered himself handicapped. A couple of times I tried to open the door for him and I would get a look that killed. He would get mad."

"He called one day from Cape after he started back to college and said that he found a horse that he liked. I said, 'Son, a man with a leg missing can't ride a horse.' He said, 'Well I bought it. I like it.' So he brought it home.

"One day he was riding the horse. Some men were building a swimming

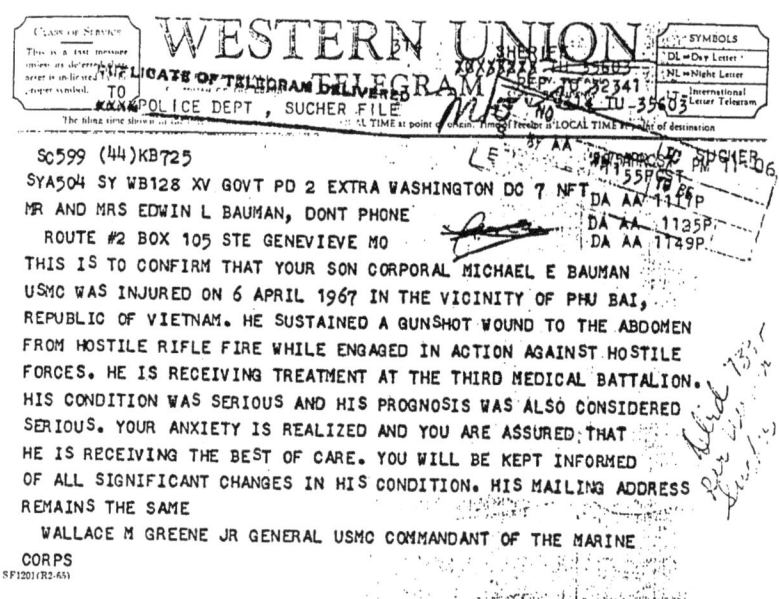

Telegram sent to Mr. and Mrs. Edwin Bauman notifying them of their son's injury.

pool across the road. They saw Mike go by and down this little dip in the road. When the horse came up the other side Mike wasn't on it. The carpenters ran down and found Mike sitting and holding his shoulder. They brought him up to the house and we took him to the doctor in Ste. Genevieve. He x-rayed his shoulder and said, 'Mike, the damn thing is broken.' Mike said, 'Well, I'm not going to the hospital.' The doctor asked if I could help with the cast. While he was mixing the cast, he asked Mike what had happened. Mike told him he fell off a horse. The doctor stood straight, shook his head, rolled his eyes, and said, 'I'll be a son-of-a-bitch! What in the hell were you doing riding a horse?'"

In 1970, Mike met Penny Thompson. Penny grew up with her two brothers in Cape Girardeau, Missouri. She graduated from Cape Central High School in 1965 and then enrolled at Southeast Missouri State College. Penny met David Dusik while attending college. After dating a few months, they were married. David joined the Navy with Penny's brother, and within a year the couple moved to the naval base at Norfolk, Virginia. Penny was 19 years old and pregnant when David began going to sea aboard the aircraft carrier *JFK*. Two months before their daughter Dava was born the Navy notified Penny that David died while in the Bahamas. She never learned the exact details of his death. The Navy told her that David was on leave and staying at a local motel in the Bahamas. He had sinus problems and had taken a couple of pills. He also had a few beers and supposedly passed out and fell off the balcony. Penny has always wondered about the incident, but as she said, "I was 20 years old, I was pregnant, and so I accepted it."

"I flew home and the first thing that I was hit with was that my father had a brain tumor and was dying. Six months later he was dead. I had a four-month-old and my mother to take care of.

"I met Mike on a Friday night. We were at a bar in Ste. Genevieve and he had a girlfriend. I told him to take her home and come back and he did. We partied the rest of the weekend at the Jour de Fête fest. We started dating regularly after that."

Mike was attending college at Southeastern Missouri State University. He was having a lot of trouble with leg infections so he was constantly back and forth from the school to the VA hospital in Poplar Bluff. The doctors would scrape the bone, send him home, and it wouldn't be long before he was back again.

Mike's sister remembers one incident when he went for an operation. "When we got there, Mike's bed was bloody all over. There was one spot on his leg, and you could tell it was supposed to be open. This doctor came down the hall, and we stopped to talk to him about it. He was getting ready to go out for the evening; he had his tuxedo on. He finally came into the room and just stabbed Mike's leg. Blood went everywhere. I told him never to touch Mike again."

Penny recalls, "In 1971, he had to quit school because he was missing so many classes because of his leg. He came back home and started managing a gas station. Shortly after that, he asked me to marry him and I agreed if he would have something done about his leg. I told him we couldn't be running back and forth for the rest of our lives to the hospital. He agreed, and we were married on July 3, 1971.

"For the next couple of years Mike managed the service station and went back and forth to the hospital for leg infections. I taught at Ste. Genevieve Middle School.

"Vietnam was always there because of Mike's wounds, but it had other effects as well. We had opposing views about the war. I didn't think the war was right. It was never declared and I never saw any reason for us to be over there. I just didn't think we should have been there. Mike always thought that it was a good cause. He wanted to see the movies about Vietnam when they came out. He would always ask me to go with him and I would, but not because I wanted to go. After the movies we would always end up in a fight. He always wanted to talk about how we were winning the war. And I always talked about how stupid and senseless the war was. We would go for a few days without talking and things would be okay again. Then another movie.

"Mike kept his promise and went to St. Louis to get an evaluation of his wounds. Several specialists from the St. Louis University Medical Hospital recommended that Mike have a hemipelvectomy—removal of his leg at the hip. They claimed that he would never have the problem with the infections again. Mike agreed and on Valentine's Day, 1972, they did the operation.

"Mike began to recover from the operation. Doctors prescribed really strong drugs for pain and infection. While he was recovering, the local county clerk, Doc Doyle, contacted Mike and persuaded him to run for State Representative. He came within a few hundred votes of winning. A short time later Doc Doyle died, and Mike was appointed to serve the rest of his term. In 1974, he ran for county clerk and was the youngest person in the state of Missouri to be elected.

"While Mike worked as county clerk and took care of Dava, I was teaching and had gone back to school to get my master's degree. One day I came home and found Mike sitting in a chair in the living room. He was holding a wastepaper basket and throwing up. I thought it was Coke because it looked brown and Mike drank a lot of Cokes. But he was really throwing up blood. By the time we got him to the hospital he needed three units of blood. The doctors found that Mike had bleeding ulcers from the prescribed medicine he was taking.

"Mike was released from the hospital within a couple of weeks. We continued with our lives. Mike had health problems, but would never let them stand in his way. I finished my master's. We had two children, Mathew in 1976 and Patrick in 1978.

"By now Mike's health problems became compounded. He had constant ear infections caused by the damage to his ears from the explosions during the attack in Vietnam. His hip would begin to jump at night from the severed nerve endings in his leg. He would often sit up all night so he wouldn't bother any of us. Sometimes he would have phantom pain. His foot would itch like crazy, but of course he had no foot. Mike was in pain so often that we went to the VA hospital in St. Louis to see if they could do something. There were all these foreign doctors and most of them couldn't speak English. When we did find one we could understand, we were told that they could operate on the spine, but there would be no guarantee that they wouldn't cut something during the operation. During Mike's last operation a kidney and testicle were cut accidently. There was no way we were going to risk another accident.

"For a while he took Valium. Bad stuff. He also developed high blood pressure.

"On Saturdays he and the boys would go to town, do their errands, and stop by a family bar. Mike would have a couple of beers, and the boys would play pool. They would come home around noon. We would eat lunch and then do whatever we had planned for the weekend. One Saturday in July 1984, I was stripping the paint off the cabinets in the kitchen. Mike came in and told me he didn't feel well. We decided he should go to the hospital, so I changed my clothes and took him to the emergency room.

"The staff contacted the doctor on call and told him that they thought Mike was having a heart attack. For some reason the doctor wouldn't come. They finally got a doctor who ran some tests. It was suggested that Mike go to St. Mary's Hospital. He did and a Dr. Davis checked Mike and found that he had had a mild heart attack. The doctors wouldn't admit that the cause of Mike's heart attack was from the medicine he took. They did say that the medication should be decreased. He was to take Coumadin for about three months and Inderal for at least a year. He did not need to be on Diltrayem and Nitro-Dur for the rest of his life. Those should be tapered as well. Too bad they hadn't realized that before he had his heart attack. Anyway, he was in the hospital for 10 days and would not let the kids come to see him. He was put on a diet, medication, and had his heart checked regularly.

"Mike continued his daily life as normal as possible, living with a lot of pain and frustration. The frustration was from the battle with the VA to get benefits for adaptive housing. Our house was old and had narrow doors. Mike got around fine, but I knew that in the future he would have to use a wheelchair. Let's face it, you can't walk around on your shoulders all your life. We couldn't get the approval from the VA because they kept sending us letters saying that you had to have an arm or leg missing. They were telling Mike that he didn't have a missing leg!

"January 8, 1986, Mike went to Jefferson Barracks for a checkup. They took x-rays and did a complete physical on him. A couple of weeks later they contacted Mike and told him they would like him to return for another checkup—they had lost all his records. He went back on March 26th.

"After the checkup, Mike returned home and began preparing for a trip to Kentucky Lake with several of his buddies. I was getting things ready for Mike when I noticed some large bruises on him. Really large bruises. I asked him if he had hurt himself, and he said he hadn't. He was taking high blood pressure medicine. I told him that it must be out of whack. He could be bleeding internally. I said, 'You really need to see a doctor.'

"Mike went to check it out. He came home just as I got in from school and told me that he had to go to St. Mary's Hospital for testing. I got a sitter for the kids. We got to the hospital about midnight. Mike told me to go home and get some sleep so I could go to school the next day. I was used to him being in the hospital so I went home. The next day I worked, and I had no intention of going to the hospital. I knew that they would run the tests throughout the day and wouldn't have the results till the following day. I was going to take the next day off and go find out what the problem was.

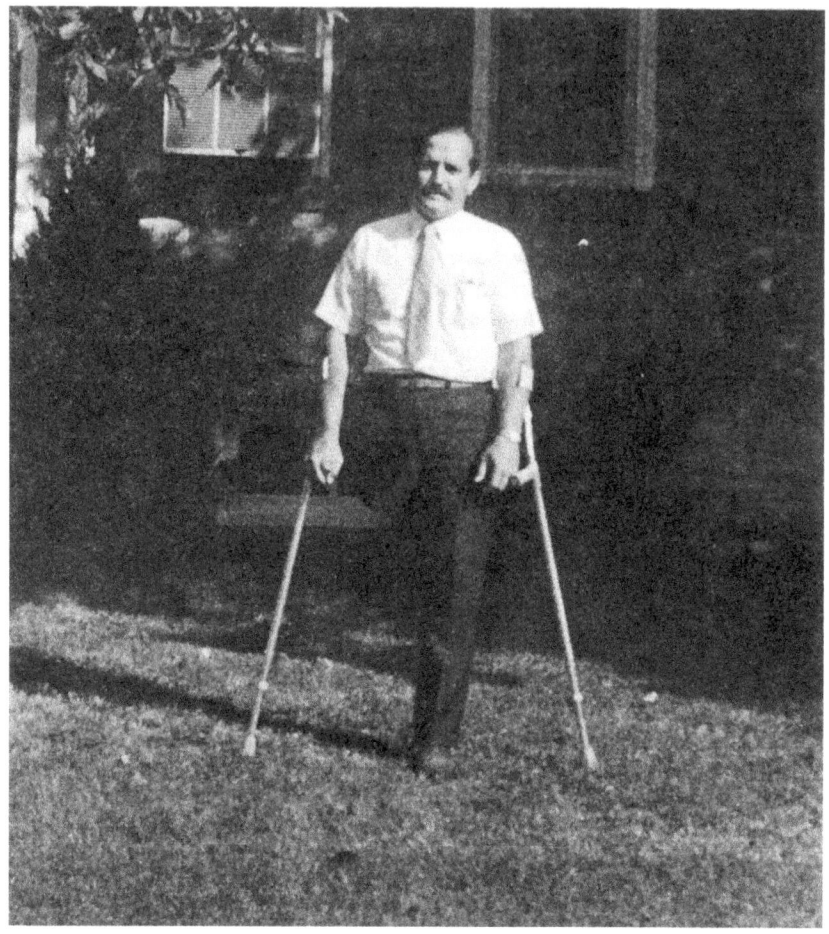

This photograph of Michael Bauman was taken shortly before he was diagnosed with leukemia.

Well, I got home from school that night (it was April Fools' Day by the way) and he called me and asked me if I was coming up. When I said I figured they hadn't gotten the test results back yet, he said, 'I think you better talk to the doctor.'

"I went to see the doctor, and he told me that Mike had leukemia. He said that Mike had almost died the night that he was brought to the hospital. He explained that if Mike had even brushed his teeth he would have bled to death. I took off from school, called his family, and went up to tell his Mom and Dad.

"The next day his sister and I went to the hospital and the doctor had explained it all to Mike. He wrote it down:

Sgt. Michael E. Bauman 31

Leukemia — Generalized disorder of blood cell production in which abnormal white blood cells accumulate in the blood and bone marrow.

Myelocytic Leukemia (also known as granulocytic or myelogenous leukemia) — The abnormal white blood cells are granulocytes or neutrophils, produced in the bone marrow.

"Mike had to have chemo treatments. I would go up on weekends and take the kids up on Sundays. After he completed the treatments, he would be allowed to come home. I learned how to give the chemo treatments and it used to scare me. He was still working, so he would get up, I would give him Benadryl and then I would start the antitreason. I had to mix it, and then had to clean the broziac to make sure there was no infection. Next, I would run it through the machine and make sure there were no bubbles. I found out later that you had to have a pretty big bubble to hurt him, but at the time I was scared to death I was going to run a bubble through his heart and kill him. Anyway I would complete the treatment, and he would get dressed and go to work.

"I took care of him all summer. Then one evening he had stopped at a restaurant while out of town and eaten dinner. He got home that night and was sitting on the couch when all at once he broke into a sweat. He started throwing up. Then diarrhea. Dava started screaming and ran out of the house. I called an ambulance and had him taken to the hospital. I couldn't find Dava anywhere. I couldn't leave the kids and I needed to get to the hospital. Finally, I got someone to stay with the kids.

"I went to the hospital thinking that he had food poisoning, but I was wrong. The leukemia had started all over again. He stayed in the hospital for more chemo treatments. I taught school and tried to have a normal life for the kids. As strange as it may sound, we did. Weekdays were normal except for Mike not being here. The kids were involved with school activities, but on weekends we were at the hospital. After Mike got the second round of treatments, the doctors harvested his bone marrow. Everything was going well. I had changed jobs from a fifth grade position to the junior high school.

"A couple of months passed and Mike had to get another blood test. He took the test and found out that the leukemia was back and that we would have to do a bone marrow transplant. We went back to the hospital with all the family members to see which member would be the best for supplying the bone marrow. They then told us the chances of the transplant working were slim, but it was the only chance he had so we tried. If you don't know anything about it, I can't think of anything worse. I don't think you could torture a person and do what this bone marrow transplant does to a person. But it was finally done.

"Mike had always been strong when he had the chemo treatments. He would tell me to go home and go to work—that he would be all right. I would go teach, come home at 3 p.m., drive up to the hospital, and stay till midnight. But this time it was different. Shortly after the transplant I went to the hospital and he told me not to leave. I didn't leave for four days. I had to go back to work because all my sick days were used up, so we figured out a plan. I would go up at 3 p.m. on Friday and stay till Sunday night and each of the other family members would take a weekday.

"As the days passed, the infection went into Mike's brain and ears. I couldn't believe what they would do to him. Mike would sleep during the day. And this one doctor wanted him awake. I was so mad. I asked the doctor if she ever stayed at night to see what they did. And I told her how one night they came in and woke him up 21 times. I asked her how she expected him not to sleep.

"The infection finally got so bad that he could not talk, and he could not respond. I went home and shortly after I arrived they called me and told me that Michael was dying. I drove back to the hospital.

"At about one o'clock in the morning Michael sat straight up in his bed, looked at us, then died. It was October 31, 1987. Halloween. And you know what was really strange, I have a brother and any time I have been in trouble in my life he has been there for me. We are just really close. He has a real sense of humor. When my husband died in Norfolk, my brother lived in Maryland and came down. He took me home. I did not expect it that day. But when I got up to the hospital I called him and asked him to go home with my kids, that I did not want them to be by themselves. He said, 'No problem.' I left the hospital around 2 a.m. I dreaded coming home because I knew I had to tell the kids that Michael had died. When I got home, I found out that Buz had already told them. Somebody had called him around 10 p.m. and said that Michael was dead. We don't know to this day who it was. The strange thing was that Michael didn't die until three hours after the call."

Penny won the first bout with the Veteran's Administration. Two months after Mike died she received papers approving an entitlement for special housing. It had taken four years to convince the VA he had a leg missing. But she lost the second round. Mike had been given a complete examination on March 26, 1986, just a couple of days before Penny had noticed the bruises and just four days before St. Mary's Hospital diagnosed Mike with acute leukemia. To this day, Jefferson Barracks has never sent results of Mike's exam or indicated that leukemia was ever found. Penny has never been able to get a response from the hospital.

She won round three. Penny applied for compensation for Agent Orange as the cause of Mike's death. She won and received a certificate of enrollment in the Agent Orange Veteran Payment Program and a check for $2,720.

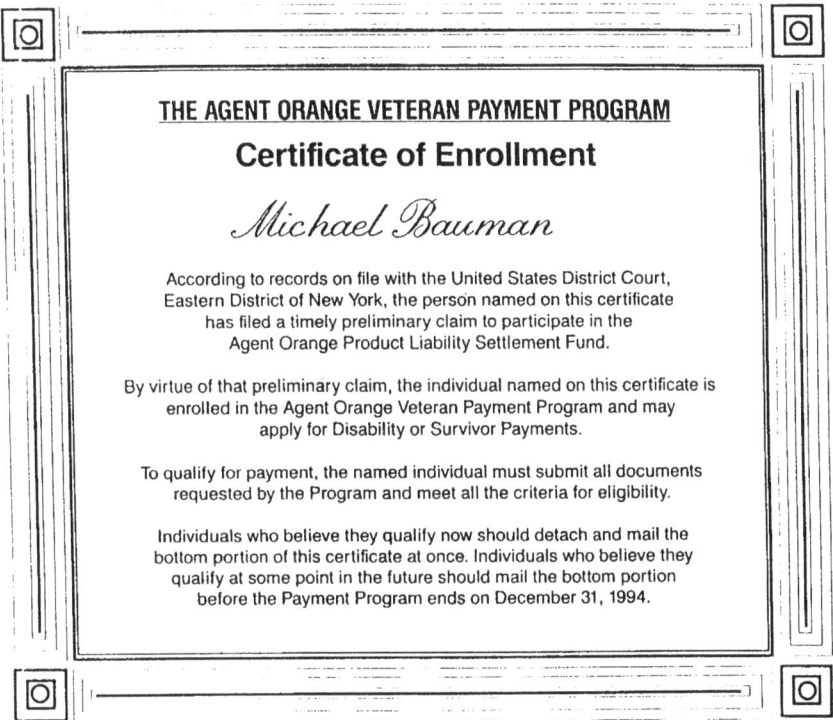

Michael Bauman's certificate of enrollment in the Agent Orange Veteran Payment Program.

She is still battling round four. "I want Michael's name on the Vietnam Wall in Washington. I just don't know if I can walk up to it. See, I haven't cried in a long time. Today I almost did. I'm not a crier, but I just don't know if I can walk up to the Wall. I think Michael's name deserves to be there. Or they need to have another wall right with it. He died from what happened to him in Vietnam. It just took him longer. This is what is happening 20 years later. They're still dying. Here is your effect. And there will be more every year.

"I told Michael a long time ago that if they ever had another Vietnam I would take my kids and go to Canada. Declare the war, fine, but not another Vietnam. One of the hardest things that I ever did was to sit through the Persian Gulf War parade. The bands were playing and the people were all excited. There was all this celebrating. They were all behind them. I wanted to say, 'Where were you when all the Vietnam vets came home?' If they were supported when they came home, maybe we wouldn't have so many of them screwed up in the head.

I : The Missing Names

DEPARTMENT OF THE NAVY
HEADQUARTERS UNITED STATES MARINE CORPS
WASHINGTON, D.C. 20380-0001

IN REPLY REFER TO
3040-2
MHP-10
2 2 MAY 1989

John C. Gegg
Commander V.F.W.
Post 2210
Ste. Genevieve, MO 63670

Dear Mr. Gegg:

This is in reply to your recent letter on behalf of the family of the late Sergeant Michael E. Bauman, U.S. Marine Corps, Retired.

We appreciate your concern for the Bauman family and understand their desire to memorialize Sergeant Bauman's name by having it inscribed on the Vietnam Veterans Memorial; however, this special Memorial which honors all Americans who served in Vietnam--is a special tribute to those who were killed in a combat or combat-related situation or who remain missing. An individual's name cannot be inscribed on the memorial, therefore, unless his death occurred as the direct result, or aftermath of wounds received in a combat or combat-related situation. Because Sergeant Bauman's death, however, tragic, was not directly attributable to the wounds he received in combat, regrettably, he does not meet the established criteria for inclusion on the Memorial.

Please assure Sergeant Bauman's family that, as Marines, we fully recognize and appreciate Sergeant Bauman's dedicated service to our Country and Corps during a difficult period in our Nation's history. We also appreciate his courageous sacrifice in the years thereafter, and truly regret that a more favorable response is not possible.

Sincerely,

A. E. EDINGER
Major, U.S. Marine Corps
Personal Affairs Branch
Human Resources Division
By direction of
the Commandant of the Marine Corps

Family and friends of Michael Bauman are trying to have his name inscribed on the Vietnam Veterans Memorial in Washington, D.C.

"If I had left the parade, it wouldn't have been right. These men didn't ask for the Gulf War, but Michael didn't ask for Vietnam.

"Why couldn't they have given that to Vietnam vets? It's too late for a parade, I'm sorry. Who cares about a bunch of paper falling out of a window? Where is your backing? Where is your emotion? Where is somebody to say we were behind you? I didn't want them there, but I sure had a respect for every one of them. They went."

Writings from the Bauman Children

I didn't know much about his pain. They kept me in the dark. He stayed up late at night, but I didn't know it was because he was in so much pain, I just thought it was because he couldn't sleep. Really the first time I ever saw him in deep pain was when he got a staph infection while working the flood down in Ste. Gen. He had put his hand in the water with all the cuts and he almost went into lockjaw. I stayed home from school for about three or four days because his hip would literally jump four or five inches. There was nothing you could do about it. I constantly had to run and massage it and give him medicine and rub him. I stayed home from school, I made good grades. I was expendable, I guess. I didn't have to make money, not that that was an issue, but Mom needed to be at work.

When he had his heart attack, I didn't think he was in that much pain. I was painting the house and he said, "Boy my arm hurts and I am having trouble breathing. I think I need to go to the doctor." There was no sign of pain. He said, "I think I need to get checked out." Then he didn't come home and he didn't come home. Then my uncle showed up and said that he had had a mild heart attack. He didn't make any big deal. In fact, I went to see him and he laughed and said, "No big deal. I had a real mild heart attack. We will just have to watch our diet."

As I got older (I was just 18 when he died), I was just beginning to get a realization of what was going on. I was signed up for the first semester of college and I was going away and I was trying to break that bond. Mom said, "You know your dad is in a lot of pain." He had leukemia by now. I said, "Yeah, I know, but he has lived with a lot of pain." Then it started to register. I never thought of pain with him. I mean, we played football together. I watched him play softball. He would pitch and hit and someone would pinch run for him. His arms were so massive from using the crutches he would hit the ball and someone would run for him. I saw him dive for a ball. Every Sunday in the summer we would barbecue, and he would play softball and football. He taught me how to throw a football. We would play catch constantly. I never realized. Things were normal except he just didn't have a leg. People would ask him about it and he would say that it got shot and turned bad and they had to take it off. Sometimes little kids would stare. That was the only time that you ever realized it. When we would ask, he would tell us a little bit, as we got older he would tell us a little more, and then finally he would tell everything. Never being bitter, nothing. The only thing he said was he was sad because they didn't take his friend first.

He was a very proud family man. When I graduated, and I was the only one he got to see graduate, our row was first. I was an honor student. We went to the podium to get our diplomas and he was the very first person

Dava Micheale Donze Bauman

out of 3,000 people to stand up and clap. The very first person. For me it was a very proud moment. I don't know if anyone else in the world noticed it, but I noticed it. He was a very proud family man, a very proud citizen. If he would see the controversy now over burning the flag, I think he would be in Washington demonstrating. He wouldn't stand for it a minute.

He was diagnosed on April 1. For that year we were back and forth to the hospital. Every weekend we went to the hospital. He was in remission for a year and Mom bought him a rose plant when he came home. He loved rose plants.

I didn't think anything was wrong yet. I knew that he had leukemia, but I thought that he had control of it. Then when he got the food poisoning, I ran out of the house and I couldn't come home. I just knew it was something bad. Someone said, "There is an ambulance at your house. What are you going to do? You need to go home." And I said, "I can't." It took them four hours to find me.

Finally when I went home they told me that they were going to take him to St. Louis and I needed to go see him before he went. I walked into the emergency room at Ste. Gen and I broke down crying. He said, "It's just food poisoning." I just kept crying and I told him that I thought he was going to die. I guess it was the breaking point for me. It all came together.

The leukemia came back. He stayed in the hospital for a while then he elected to have his treatments at home. We had a nurse that came in and taught us how to work the machine that you use. I administered chemotherapy. He had a broziac catheter that went into his heart and I gave him shots all the time. All the time. I was 16. I didn't think it was all that weird. I knew that it was different, but I still didn't think anything was wrong. I mean he was home. How could anything be too bad?

When I was in my first year of college, they told me he had a brain tumor. I was at school lifting weights with a brand new friend. She didn't know any of my situation. My uncle came in all teary-eyed and said, "We've got to talk." I told my friend I didn't think I would be back. We went and got a six pack of beer. Then we drove around Cape and the Jackson area and he told me what was wrong. At that point I knew my life had changed. This was my first year of college. I had only been in school for two months. He suggested I tell my teachers that I would be home next week. I told them that if I wasn't in school that meant my father had passed away. Most of them were very supportive. That Friday I came home. Mom told me Dad's white cell count went up, and that I didn't need to go to the hospital. I suggested we go shopping or something. So we went grocery shopping.

When we got back both of my aunts were sitting in the living room. They told us we had to go to the hospital now. Dad had lapsed into a coma. I stayed with the boys. And my Uncle Buzzy came up to stay with us. That night at about 10:30 my uncle and I got a phone call telling us it was all over. My Uncle Buzzy said, "Well, Mike was a good man. He fought long and hard. And the person on the phone said, "Yeah, but it's over." We thought that was it.

Mom had told me to let the boys go to the football game. Let them have their last night because their lives would be changed forever. I had picked them up at about 9:30 and they were in the basement. Uncle Buzzy said that we needed to tell them. We went to tell them. But it turned out that he hadn't died yet. We don't know who made the phone call. No one at the hospital called. No doctor called. Nothing. Up until he died they worked on him. He didn't die until 1:30 in the morning on October 31. He had said that he wanted to stay till Halloween. He would make it till then. He made it until 1:30. I had a big Halloween card to give him. I was going to take it up to him the next day.

I began having problems. I didn't sleep. I like to go to bed early and get eight hours of sleep. But I would dream. I would dream the most rotten dreams. I decided I wasn't going to sleep. I would go to bed at 3 A.M. and get up at 6 A.M. I had dreams for nine months. I didn't cry. I couldn't cry. I had to be strong for my mother and for my little brothers. Until one night my boyfriend and I went to Springfield. We started drinking and he said,

"You're going to let this all out." I said, "Oh no." I finally started crying and I cried for 24 hours.

After that I cried at everything. I'd get teary-eyed hearing "The Star Spangled Banner." I never cried. I look at life differently. Life is short and I have to live it now. I may not be here later. I might die at 40 or 41 like my dad did. When I returned to college, my friend asked me if there was anything she could do. I told her to make friends with her dad. She and her dad are closer than ever. I never got that chance. I was a teenager and I wanted to break free from home and in order to do that you have to argue. I argued with my dad and I broke free. Now I realized that I missed out on being real good friends with Dad. I am with Mom now. But, we could have really been good friends. I was headstrong and he was headstrong. Of course, he got his way more than I did. But we could have been really good friends. I feel sorry that he missed my brother's graduation.

He didn't get to see as many games of theirs. I feel they got cheated. I feel that they lost out on growing up with a great man, one who could have taught them love, compassion and caring. Values, values that he knew that no one else knew. They have been cheated. We have an okay life now, but it was not like it could have been. Nothing is like it could have been and nothing will ever be the same. Ever.

DAVA MICHEALE DONZE BAUMAN

When Dad first got sick, I didn't know what was going on. I didn't know the whole story. I got bits and pieces of it. I was 13 when he died. When he first went into the hospital, I was 11. I was kind of lost about it. All I remember is getting a message one afternoon from Dad. It was on April Fool's Day. He had leukemia. It said, "I'm sorry this isn't an April Fools, but it is a fact now I got to go."

The more I heard about leukemia the more I started investigating it on my own. That's what lead me into finding out about Agent Orange. So I read the stuff from the government which said that the Agent Orange wasn't what killed him. It will be a cold day in hell before you can convince me that it wasn't. I've done enough papers on it to find out about it.

When you live with someone that you see suffer from it, you have to find out about it. I had to find out what it was. Everything I read I had to read between the lines. As I see it, he was killed in Vietnam. He just didn't know it. He is the only one in our family who has ever been diagnosed with cancer. It seems kind of a coincidence that he was a veteran, he was in an area that was heavily spread with Agent Orange, and he said himself that he remembered seeing it spread. And then he dies from leukemia. They still say it is not caused by it. I think there is too much evidence there.

Mathew Michael Alexander Bauman

A lot of what I found makes you wonder what was running through the people's minds that were responsible for spreading Agent Orange. I mean the government did know that dioxin was in it. That's a fact. And the people who were controlling it knew that it was in there, but they spread it anyway, as dangerous as it was. Why? Maybe there was something else behind it. Maybe they thought that the information would never get out. My dad got sacrificed. When I used to do my research, I couldn't sleep. I would run it through my mind over and over. And I would think how could this happen. Why was it my Dad? Why anybody's Dad? The research was kind of hard on me at first, then I got conditioned to it. It doesn't bother me much anymore talking about Dad, about the hospital, and the leukemia. But at first, I couldn't even begin to talk about it.

There has been a lot of cover-up about Agent Orange. The information has not been released like it should have been. If all the information ever comes out, it's going to be a disaster. There will be a witch hunt by veterans' groups wanting to get payback from the government. It has affected so many people. There are at least 200,000 men that were confirmed as being sprayed by it. Those are the ones that are confirmed. There are many they don't even know about. And there are the people that don't even know what Agent Orange is. There are kids my age that don't ever think that their parents could have been exposed to it. Yet they don't know anything about it. I did a paper in class for competition and I caught people's attention when I said, "If your parents are Vietnam veterans, they may have a time bomb ticking inside of them, too." You could see the scared looks on some of their faces. Just the shock and the idea of "Oh, my God. This could happen to my Dad." I explained what happened to my dad and you could see the fear in the kids' eyes. It's a scary thought when you think about it.

My Dad never really talked about his experiences over there. The way he dealt with it. He just, I guess, felt betrayed. The vets went over there, fought for their country, and then came back and were looked at as outcasts. It was just hard for him to handle. He was about 19 when he went over there and served combat duty. He lost his leg, barely made it out alive, and then he comes back over here and is treated like a freak and an outcast. I think he dealt with it by not really talking about it. But I do know he still held onto a lot of memories from what happened over there. If you started talking about Vietnam, you could tell a difference in him right away. He would quiet down a lot or he wouldn't want to talk about it. I guess he was holding in a lot of feelings. I remember the first time I saw my dad cry. We were watching the movie *Uncommon Valor*. It dealt with MIA's in Vietnam. I was sitting on the floor. When it was over, I turned around to say something to him, and he was crying. That got me right there. When *Platoon* came out, he would always have to see it. That drove my mom up the wall. She would beg him not to go because she would always know what was going to happen. Both of them would always be in a lousy mood afterward. He would have to go see it though. I guess he thought it was good so people could get the story straight. He felt real strongly that people should know what went on over there. God forbid you ever say they lost the war over there. That was something he did not like to hear. He was always very proud of what he did over there. He was a Marine and they are as gung ho as they get. He was very proud. He was never ashamed of it. He would always say, we may not have won that war, but we didn't lose it. He believed they would have won it if they were given a chance. They were fighting too limited.

Mom thought just the opposite. She thought that it should have never happened. She and Dad would argue about it so I usually didn't bring it up.

I was always proud of Dad for being a Vietnam vet. I looked at him as sort of a victim of the leaders of this country. They dragged us into it. He volunteered to go, but he was still a victim of what happened. My Dad was always patriotic, and he decided to do what was right.

I still question why we ever did it. But he saw it as something he had to do. He was patriotic. If he saw the controversy over the flag going on and he was alive, he would probably march to Washington himself. You never said anything bad about this country to him. I guess that's why he volunteered. He never regretted it, even though he lost his leg and eventually got leukemia. You don't find very many people who feel that way. A lot of people I know regret what they did over there. But he never did.

One thing I do know. He never pushed us to follow in his footsteps and join the military. Even though what he did over there was his choice, he never wanted us to have to go through it.

For a long time I have thought about going into the service. But even though he didn't say it, I could tell he would do anything to keep me from doing it. He figured that he had gone through enough, and he didn't want us doing it. And when I really thought about it, I realized it wouldn't be a very smart thing to do.

I guess you could say that what happened is unfair. He went through enough hardships in his life fighting in the Vietnam War. Losing his leg. All the operations that he had to go through. The complications and infections he suffered through. His heart attack which was related to the drugs he had to take because of his leg. His ulcers. Then you look at it and you think that was enough. I mean he suffered enough in his life. And then he died from leukemia which was because of Agent Orange. It almost seems like an overkill. Why? Why did it ever happen? You know he had enough. Why wasn't it just left at that? He was a victim of it even before it all started. I'm very very sensitive when it comes to Agent Orange, Vietnam, and my Dad. You don't say anything about him. I lived with a man who served over there and I would have gone through the pain that he did. Living with him you could see the pain he went through. I have heard of people calling Vietnam veterans cowards for what they did over there. If anybody ever said that in front of me, they'd better be prepared for a fight because that's what it is going to come to. A sore point with me is to hear people say that Agent Orange never happened. After my Dad, I can't take that. I have too much of his blood in me to sit there and take that from anyone. I am very proud of what he did even if it did put him in an early grave. He did what he thought was right. I am proud of him for it.

My Dad was the kind of person that cared a lot about the people around him. He would rather do for others than for himself. I remember a couple of years back when we were having really bad floods in Ste. Genevieve. The town literally shut down. He knew a lot of people who lived near here that were really in trouble and he took off work and sandbagged from five in the evening until five the next morning. He came home and changed clothes and went back. He spent two and one half days down there. He just stayed there. He helped a lot of people he had never met before. He knew they needed help and he was more than happy to do it. He was told to go home and wouldn't because he wanted to make sure that the houses were safe. They ended up making him come home. He ended up with a staph infection from all the cuts he got from the sandbags. He did not complain once about it. He wasn't doing it for himself, it was for someone else. He just took it. Even after he got the infection he still wanted to go back down.

Many times he would sacrifice for things he wanted for us. If it came to his family or him, he wouldn't think twice. I can remember one instance that if he were here right now I would wring his neck for it. We used to own a farm and it was common practice to go with him to take care of the feeding. One day none of us wanted to go. We were too tired so he went by himself. Later that night we had a religion class and he came to pick us up. We got into the truck and he never said a word. He started home and all at once he crouched over and I thought he was going to die right there. We got about halfway home and he said, "I fell through the loft and I broke some ribs. I am going to be all right, but I want to get you home first." I said, "Dad, go to the hospital now." He said, "No, I'm going to take you home and you get your Mom." He never thought twice. He wanted to make sure we got home safe before he took care of himself.

I saw that man do things that people with two legs couldn't do. Nothing would stop him. If there was a difficulty, he would figure out a way to get around it. He never thought of himself as handicapped.

After he died, I questioned his wisdom. The way I look at it, he did what he thought was right. Even when he was on his last legs, as you might put it, he put up a hell of a fight. Just like he did through all of his life. The last few days he fought it. Even though he eventually lost the battle, he won the war you could say. He lasted. It was a fight. He put up a hell of a fight. I know that because I saw that a lot of times when I went to the hospital. There were many times when I would go in after he had had his chemotherapy and he would be throwing up blood and have a high temperature. He looked bad but he would never quit. He was a tough SOB to put it bluntly. He was a tough man, and you could see it the last few days. If you even said anything bad about the Vietnam War, he would probably have jumped off that bed and set you straight. Even in the condition that he was in, he would have probably set you straight. He was a fighter about it. Seeing him like that was hard for me. I was there a lot, but I never got to say goodbye to him. But I always knew that he loved me.

I remember the night he died. We were at a football game. My sister came running up to me and grabbed me and said that we needed to get home. When we got home, my uncle had showed up. He knew things were bad and he just wanted to be there. At that point, I had gotten to where I could handle anything. If anyone told me any bad news it just went right over the top of my head. It no longer fazed me. I got so accustomed to bad news. And I was numb to it. I couldn't stand being around everyone because they were so upset. I went downstairs. It was 10:30 P.M. exactly because I remember hearing the phone ring and looking up at the clock. I knew it was over even before anyone came downstairs. And I was just kinda sitting there waiting to hear it. I didn't even cry at first. It had already settled in. It wasn't shock because I knew it was coming. We just all sat there and talked about it. I was calm about it as far as everyone else was concerned. And then everyone left. I got to thinking about it and all of a sudden I lost it. I stayed down in the basement for a few hours and got it all out. I thought about what it was going to be like to live without him. It was real scary. The next morning I got up and it was business as usual. It didn't last long though. I can't show my emotions in front of other people. I don't like losing control. I got up, walked into the shop in the garage, and shut the door real quietly. I began to tear the holy hell out of that place. And when I finally calmed down, I started all over again. Then I cleaned it up. Afterwards I very calmly walked back into the house and sat down. I stayed calm all the way through the funeral. At the funeral when they opened the casket, I didn't look because I wanted to remember him the way he was. I have never regretted making that choice. I was still calm until the 21-gun salute and when they played taps. I lost it right there. To this day I can't listen to them. If I go to a veterans service, I will walk off if taps are played and come back afterward. I can't listen to taps.

It took me two and one half years to go back to his grave. But I felt a lot better when I did. I guess I realized that he was gone and that life does go on. I don't visit it very regularly. I believe you don't have to go to a grave to mourn. There is one thing that my dad loved. It was his roses that he used to grow. He used to grow some beautiful roses. When I go to the cemetery, I will cut the best one off, and lay it on his grave. Even though I realize he is gone, it is hard for me to go.

MATHEW MICHAEL ALEXANDER BAUMAN

[Here is an excerpt from a paper Mathew wrote during his senior year in high school:]

Alex's Dad had leukemia, or in basic terms, cancer of the blood. As his mom explained the situation to him, Alex could feel the draining sensation that overtook his body. It felt as if someone had punctured a hole in his heart and soul, and everything that he ever loved was rushing out of him. The one thing that stuck in his mind and still does to this day was the message that his Dad left for them as he left for the hospital, "I'm sorry, guys. I wish I could say it was April Fools', but I can't. I love you." So many nights he would lie awake and hear those words over and over again. Madness only seemed a step away. Alex soon began to realize that it was no dream, and that it wasn't going away.

His weekends became filled with trips to see his Dad in the hospital. Some trips were good, like the ones when his Dad would be well enough to go out in the little park outside the hospital, or where he could crawl up next to his Dad and just sit there and talk. Those are good things that Alex could remember. But there were still the bad days, days that to this day he still represses in the deepest depths of his soul.

But this time around the rules had changed. His Dad had been in two times before, and every time it seemed he was cured, he came out of remission and everything started all over again, like an out-of-control nightmare that was lethal. That's when the decision was made and there was no other choice, he had to have a bone marrow transplant. The idea almost drove Alex to hysterics. He knew it was dangerous, too dangerous, and in his words, "There's no way in hell they're touching my Dad. God help them if they hurt him." These became words that still drive Alex to angered fits.

Though he prayed to God that they would stop before they killed him, it was done. After the transplant, Alex's life became a long, hard road of heartache, disbelief, anger, and a long desire for answers that no one could give him. This road is one that he still follows today.

As is common with patients of bone marrow transplants, their condition will deteriorate to the point where there is no immune system. This is where the lengthy and dangerous road to recovery begins. It is also the stage which Alex's father is at.

As Alex enters the room, he can sense the tension that is given off. It is in everything around him, and it scares him to death. His father is sitting up in bed, something he can only do with the aid of the nurse. His eyes are in a drowsy, half-open stage, mostly from the lack of sleep, but also from the lingering painkillers which he so desperately relies on. His head is totally devoid of hair from the intensive chemotherapy that he had to endure. Alex gazes upon his Dad, and the only thing that he can think of is, "I love you, Dad." But even if he had said it, his father couldn't have heard him. He was delirious from the painkillers and was for the most part unconscious. As he stepped closer to his Dad, Alex could feel the ache in his heart, that just wanted his Dad to be well again. Alex took his Dad's hand in his and stroked it, marveling over how, even in such a weak state, they seemed so powerful. But what struck him the most was how similar their

Patrick Norman Edwin Bauman

hands were. This struck a chord in him, one that prayed that some day he could become half the man that his father was.

As Alex's thoughts meandered, he felt a slight squeeze of his hand, and looked up to see his father looking at him with a weak smile on his face. "How you doing, kiddo," said his Dad. As before, all Alex could think to say was, "I love you, Dad." Upon hearing these words, his father's eyes began to glow with a light that Alex had not seen in such a painfully long time. His Dad looked at him with a peaceful look of a man who knew his fate, but refused to fall to it. "There is so much that I want to tell you, I hardly know where to begin. But I want you to know, that no matter what ever happens, be it good or bad, you will forever live in my heart. I know I have growled at you in the past about little things, but never has there been a moment when I didn't love you with all my heart. Just stick to your guns, and we'll both make it through all right." Alex couldn't speak, he could only sit and look at the man who meant more to him than any person in the world. As he leaned forward to hug his Dad, his father slipped back into his delirium.

* * *

I visited Penny one Saturday in September as I was passing through. She was trying to rest up after a week of teaching the sixth grade reading class at the middle school and going to Patrick's football game the night before. She was proud. Ste. Gen had won the game against Charleston.

Penny had just gotten off the phone with Dava who is now 23. She had graduated from Southeast Missouri State and was job hunting.

Penny had not heard from Mathew in a while. He was in his freshman year at Southeast Missouri State.

Patrick popped through the door with a grin and a mirrored expression of his father. The grin quickly disappeared though when his mother informed him he would mow the lawn before he did anything else.

We sat for a few moments then Penny looked up. "You know," she said, "I complain all the time. I really don't have anything to complain about, but I am like a lot of other people, I'm always complaining. But after all that Mike went through and all that happened to him, I never once heard him complain. He didn't feel sorry for himself or ever regret that he served in Vietnam. He loved his country. He loved life. And he loved his family."

PART II
In the Twinkle of an Eye

# THREE
Pvt. John F. Terry, Jr.
(May 11, 1949–October 22, 1967)

Hometown: Cairo, Ill.; Infantryman; Third Marine Division; Quang Nam Province, Vietnam; Killed in Action October 22, 1967.

> *There are some things that history cannot teach us and among them is how to bear, without pain, the sending of our young Americans into battle and how to fill the aching void as we wait for news of their fate and how to console the wife, or the mother, or the little children when the news is bad.*
>
> LYNDON B. JOHNSON
> February 17, 1966

I pulled through the black iron gate at the Mound City National Cemetery on November 1, 1967, at about 12:15 P.M. I drove a few hundred feet down the narrow cemetery road and stopped in front of several rows of unknown soldiers' graves. A wintry breeze brushed against my face as I exited the vehicle and straightened my gold belt buckle and my dress blue uniform. I scanned the tract and located the gravesite on a crest in the northwest corner and then decided to stand behind the monument located in the center of the cemetery to play taps. I was volunteered for the task after our normal procedure of recruiting a high school band member had failed. I was nervous. It had been at least five years since I had played a trumpet and I wanted to make sure I was out of sight when I played.

I positioned myself behind the monument and approximately 30 minutes later a white hearse pulled through the gates followed by a column of cars. I watched as the Marines lined up behind the hearse and carried the flag-covered coffin to the gravesite. Jeanette Terry, Gail Terry and John F. Terry, Sr. took seats in chairs that had been placed in rows under a tent and in front of the grave. Jeanette had a look of despair as her last hope that the government had made a mistake was quickly coming to an end.

Just a month before John stepped on a booby trap while on patrol in Quang Nam Province, Vietnam, Jeanette had read a story in the local paper about the parents of a soldier in Vietnam who had received notification that their son had been killed in action. A week later the son called his mother on the phone and was shocked to find that the army had notified his parents that he was dead. Jeanette remembered that story on October 24, 1967, when I delivered the death message to her. She had received another message a couple of hours before I arrived. A letter from John telling her that he was fine. She grasped the letter with a grip of desperation and hope that we too had made a mistake—there had to be a mix-up.

"You're wrong. This letter is dated October 22. He wrote this and mailed it the same day you say he was killed," she insisted.

"No, ma'am. I'm sorry. There is no mistake," I told her. John Terry, Sr., suffering from an ailing heart and a severe case of asthma, sat in his chair leaning on a wooden cane and attempted to control his emotions. His 18-year-old son had fallen after being in Vietnam less than two weeks.

When the young Marine's body was returned 10 days later, Jeanette demanded that the funeral director open the casket so she could be certain that it was John. "I've heard stories about the government sending empty coffins home in other wars," she remarked. The capacious black body bag and neatly folded set of dress blues inside the casket were still not enough to convince her that it was John. She wanted the body bag opened. The funeral director pleaded with her to no avail and unzipped the bag. The decomposed body was unrecognizable, but Jeanette did confirm that a ring on the fallen young Marine's finger was John Terry, Jr.'s. Jeanette was almost convinced. There was a body and there was the ring. But a lot of rings look alike and, after all, she didn't really recognize him and she still had the letter.

Jeanette, grasping the letter John had sent her, listened as the Reverend Larry Potts read the passage. When he finished, he took a step back and bowed his head. The firing squad came to attention and fired three volleys over the gravesite. With each volley, Jeanette jerked. With each jerk the expression of hopelessness deepened. Then I brought the trumpet to my lips and played taps. As the final echos cleared the air, the family slowly made their way back to the car. I watched as they pulled away. The expression on Jeanette's face revealed that she had accepted the reality that John Terry, Jr., 18 years and 5 months old, was dead.

"It happened so quickly. He was there and then we heard he was dead," the Reverend Potts explained in a soft-spoken voice.

Potts, a tall, slender man had grayed in the temples since I had last seen him at John Terry's funeral 24 years earlier. One thing I immediately recognized when I met the reverend at the Cairo Baptist Church in January 1992 was that he had not lost a bit of his compassion for a family he had ministered to for several years. He watched John grow up, he watched a family stricken by hard times hold on to a flame of happiness by keeping their faith in God, and he finally watched that flame go out when that family was devastated by war.

John Terry, Jr. and his sister Gail were raised by their aunt, Jeanette Terry. Their father was a carnival worker who traveled a lot and their mother had taken off years before. Jeanette was very adamant about discipline. She was from the old school, and very headstrong. The Reverend Potts recalled the time that the Terry children went to summer camp. When they returned, Jeanette was upset because the children had had a good time. "Her last century old-school ways forbade such a thing at a church outing. She was very hard on them, but she loved them," Potts explained.

John grew up in Cairo. He had a paper route with the *Cairo Evening Citizen*, he was a member of the Cairo Baptist Church, he attended the Cairo public schools, played football for two years, and he played in the marching band as a drummer. In 1967, he graduated from Egyptian High School and joined the Marines at the age of 17.

"When he left here, it was like it was his chance to live. He was under such heavy rule at home. Then when the news came it was really traumatic," the Reverend Potts recalled.

Evelin Yandell, another aunt, remembers John as a loving boy who liked girls. "He and Gail had a hard time growing up. Jeanette loved them both very much. She provided clothes and the things they needed, but she was very strict. When Gail was in high school, Jeanette used to make her wear long underwear. 'She has to stay warm,' Jeanette would say. When Gail would leave for school, she would take the underwear off and hide them under the porch. We never did tell Jeanette.

"John was a good drummer and he used to play at concerts. He would call and ask me and my husband Paul to come watch him play. Jeanette was unable to go because of her mother who was bedfast. John's dad was in such bad health he couldn't go either. We filled in as his parents at those events and he seemed happy. He had his whole life ahead of him. His death was such a waste."

Gail wanted to escape the painful memory of her brother's death. As soon as she graduated from high school in 1969, she moved to Boston with her mother. She only stayed a short time before she disappeared. No one in the family has heard from her in over 17 years.

John Terry, Sr., already in bad health, gave up hope after his son was killed and died two years later in 1970.

Jeanette had many friends in the church and was an active member. She had a rough life. Her invalid mother had a stroke and was bedfast for nine years. Her brother was ill with asthma and heart problems. And she was plagued with ill health herself. But she still had a soft touch, occasionally teaching children's classes in church.

There were the good times with some laughter, but whatever flame of hope and goodness that was there went out when she received word that John had been killed. Within a couple of years both her mother and brother had died. Gail was gone. Jeanette was alone and became very bitter, withdrawn, and distrusting of the government. She was constantly grieving, to the point that she was physically confined to a wheelchair. She died in 1974.

A plaque in memory of John Francis Terry, Jr. hangs in the Cairo Baptist Church auditorium. It reads:

IN MEMORY
PVT. JOHN F. TERRY, JR.
MAY 11, 1949–OCTOBER 22, 1967

He was the only member the church lost during the Vietnam War.

I returned to the Mound City National Cemetery in 1992 and walked to the crest where John is buried. The 24-year-old solid white tombstone had faded with a light shade of green blend. At one time the only grave on the crest, it was now joined by two rows of 37 tombstones, marking the victims of a generation of war. Among the victims are Ronald E. Shoemaker, Richard William Jones, Mose C. Hundley, Ronald Dean Clark, William Joseph Johnson and Wiley Anderson, soldiers who never made it past their 19th birthday.

I walked to the car, turned and looked back. I thought about the many people who say we should put the Vietnam War behind us now. Forget about it, it's in the past. You think they are right, John, I thought. Yeah, I know, John, we can't forget. It could happen again. But some people aren't worried, John. After all, there is still plenty of room on the crest in this garden of stones.

FOUR

PFC Clifford D. Combs
(August 15, 1949–February 25, 1969)

Hometown: Marquand, Mo.; Infantryman; Gulf Company, Ninth Marines; Third Marine Division; Da Nang, Vietnam; Killed in Action February 25, 1969.

> *There is not a day passed since he has been gone that he doesn't go through my mind. But I just talk to myself and realize that I can't just sit down and dwell on it. I have to let it go as much as I can let go. But every day I think about him.*
>
> ELIZABETH COMBS
> January 13, 1993

The sun glistened against the town sign Marquand 98 as I turned off the state highway onto Route F. It was the first sunny day southeast Missouri had seen in 1993. It was also the first time in 23 years that I had taken this twisting two-lane route of curves, hills, and dips into two creek beds through the St. Francois Mountains and Mark Twain National Forest to get to Marquand, Missouri.

As I crossed the bridge over the Castor River at the edge of town, the sandy bottom reflected through the blue-green water. The river was low and a few small islands of sand were surrounded by small streams of water, rippling over the sandy river bottom. This area was solely inhabited by Indians until 1804 when white settlers, attracted by the beauty of the area, built the town of Marquand along the banks of the river. Just a few hundred feet off the bridge was the center of town. On the right was a large parking area covered with red river rock. Two streets run parallel to the lot with a post office, restaurant, grocery story, and a few other businesses situated along the far side of the streets. I parked my car in front of the war memorial at the corner of the parking lot. I walked up to the memorial and read:

This photograph of Clifford D. Combs was taken in the summer of 1968 shortly before he entered the service.

PROUDLY WE PAY TRIBUTE
TO ALL VETERANS OF THE MARQUAND AREA:
RANDELL ABRIGHT, EVERETTE BARRETT, JOHN F. GRIFFON,
CHARLES W. HOVIS, GEORGE C. JOHNSON, LESLIE A. JONES,
THOMAS G. WALLIS, NORMAL H. HENSON, STANLEY B. KLUCK,
JAMES A. REAGAN, TONY WESTON, CLIFFORD D. COMBS,
LAWRENCE S. MILLS, LEGAL T. BUTLER, WILLIAM D. MARSHALL,
ORVILLE DUDLEY, E.J. LORANGE, CHESTER E. THORPE,
CLYDE S. OSBORN, CHARLES F.M. UNDERWOOD, DEWEY W. ROBINSON,
THEODORE WESTBROOK, AND JOHN R. JOHNSON

I had enlisted two of the people inscribed on the memorial. A short time later, in 1969, I had notified and participated in their funerals. Now I was back to talk with their families — to hear their stories and what they felt.

I returned to my car and drove to Elizabeth Combs' home. Her house sat at the base of a forest-covered hill. A large pile of firewood took up about half of the front porch. As I walked toward the house, I noticed a man chopping wood in a yard across the creek. He stopped for a moment, looked up, smiled, then continued on with his work. I took a deep breath then knocked on the door. Immediately the door opened. A small thin woman with silver-gray hair stood with a smile on her face.

"Mrs. Combs, I'm Harry Spiller."

"Yes, Mr. Spiller, please come in."

I walked through the door and was standing in the living room. In the corner of the room a display of pictures sat on a small stand. One picture was of Clifford in his dress blue uniform. The other one of Clifford displayed a Purple Heart, Vietnam Service medal, Vietnam Campaign medal, and National Defense medal in each corner of the picture.

We reminisced for a few minutes then Mrs. Combs began telling me about her family. "I had four children, two boys and two girls. When Clifford, Dale is what he went by, got old enough he wanted to join the Marines. He enlisted in the summer of 1968. He took his basic training at San Diego, California. He wrote home a lot." She fumbled with some papers and handed me a couple of envelopes. "These are some of his letters when he was in training."

I opened the letters and began to read.

Aug. 4, 1968

Dear Mom and Dad,

Hi again. I am doing just fine. It is a little rough but I think I can stand it.

I just got back from lunch and I am tired. The food is pretty good but not like home-cooked meals.

The country is just beautiful out here but not like home. It sounds like I am homesick, doesn't it? Well I am. HA HA!

We get up at 5:00 o'clock and go to bed at 9:00 o'clock. I haven't hardly slept on these bunks. They are hard to me.

Well, Mom, I don't know for sure when I will get home. Some say after Xmas but I really don't know.

We have to go to church every Sunday, so this is Sunday, and we will have to go after we finish writing our letters.

Well, Mom, tell all of them I said hi. Okay. They don't let us write but once a week.

II : In the Twinkle of an Eye

Oh, Mom, if you ever have to get in touch with me, contact the Red Cross, because if you don't then I won't get to come home. That is if someone is really sick in the family.

Well, Mom, I have to go. So bye for now and write soon.

Here is my address.

Pvt. Combs C.D. 2502461
Plt 1056 1st PT Bn
MCRD
San Diego, Calif

Aug. 7, 1968

Dear Mom and Dad,

It has been a week now and I haven't heard from you all. I am on my free time now, and I have time to write you a letter.

They don't let us smoke much but I really don't mind. If you will, Mom, give Gilbert my address. Tell him it is like hell in here but that is life, I guess. I don't have much to say, but it is nice to write to you all. I have been here a week and it is not too bad. It is not like I had expected. You are on a time schedule all the time. You eat. Then you work. Then you eat some more then you work some more. Then it is time to go to bed. I go to bed but I don't get much sleep because we have to get up and have our racks made before roll call in the morning. Tell all of them I said hi and that I love them all. Tell Cleta to write if she has time because it sure helps to get mail in here.

It sure is hot out here but the weather is nice. But I don't think I would like it here.

Well, Mom, I guess I will close for now, so write soon.

Your son,

Dale Combs

Love you all

Tell Dad I have had the shit kicked out of me a few times. Okay. Ha Ha.

I finished the letters. "After he took his training," Elizabeth continued, "he came home for 30 days. That was in late December. While he was home, his father had surgery on his back so Dale got to stay home for a little longer. As soon as he got back, they shipped him overseas. He was there for one month and one day when he was killed. These are his letters from overseas," she said as she handed me a small stack of envelopes.

The air-mail envelopes were edged with red, white, and blue stripes with the familiar "free" written in the upper right-hand corner. The edges of the paper were light brown from aging. I began to read.

PFC Clifford D. Combs

Jan. 26, 1969

Dear Mom and Dad,

I hope everyone is fine. I am sorry I didn't get to call again before I left, but they wouldn't let us.

We are about to V.N. now and I am kinda scared, but I sense everyone here is scared a little. I sure have enjoyed my ride on the plane. We have been on it for 14 hours now, but time is going pretty fast.

We left on a Friday and now it is Sunday because we lost a day in time, if you know what I mean.

I have my PFC stripes now so on my letters put P.F.C. Combs. I sure am proud of it. I sure worked hard for that stripe. I sure hope I make rank fast here in V.N. I think I will.

I sure wish you could all see the pretty country out here in Hawaii. We are flying over the ocean now and it sure is pretty out there. One of these days I am going to take you and Dad and we are going to fly to some of these places. I know you and Dad sure would enjoy it.

Tell Ivan and Bunny I said hi. When I send you my address give it to Bunny because she said she would write to me. That is what I want most is to get a letter because a serviceman sure likes to get mail.

If anything happens, go to the Red Cross and they will get in touch with me. O.K.?

Tell Grandmom and Grandpop I said hi and that I love both of them and may God watch over them both. Have them pray for me that I may come back safely. I sure hope I do.

Tell Gilbert that I sent him a picture of himself. I hope he likes it. It only cost about $5.00 in all, but I think the world of Gilbert and I hope he makes it OK.

It sure will be a long time before I see you all again. I guess it will be about 13 or 14 months. That sure is a long time.

I guess I will be stationed up around the DMZ in V.N. They say it's not too bad up there. I sure hope not. Don't you worry yourself sick about me because I will be well taken care of over here.

Tell Cleta that I said hi and that I love her and all the family. Tell Bill I said hi. Give him a pitch for me. He is a good brother-in-law.

Kiss the baby for me and give him a great big hug.

I sent some of my clothes back home because they wouldn't let us take but 60 pounds of gear, so just put them with the other things I have.

Tell Kathy to keep her grades up and stay on the honor roll. I sure am proud of her.

I sure hope she doesn't have any trouble if she gets married before I get back. I wish she wouldn't think of getting married now. She should have a lot more fun before she ties herself down.

Take good care of the horse and the dogs. I have made you out an allotment. So you should get some money some time. It will be a while. You can use the money if you need it and don't be afraid to spend it because if I find out you need it and don't spend it, I will be mad.

Well, Dad, I hope you are in fine shape when I get back so we can hunt with the dogs and catch some raccoons.

Well, Mom, I guess I will close for now and write when you get my address. Bye for now and I will see you in about 13 months. Tell them hi.

With all my love,

Cliff PFC   HA HA

Feb. 2, 1969

Dear Mom and Dad,

How are all of you? Fine, I hope. I made it here OK. I am in Vietnam now. I have been here for about four days. I am in the rear and it is really great. I guess I will go out to the field the next couple of days. I am in a pretty good company. It is called Hell in a helmet.

I stayed in Okinawa five days and it was great. You can't believe the people, how they look. They are like miniatures (short) 4' 5" or so. I hope you can read this.

It has been raining about every day since I have been over here, but it isn't too bad.

I hope you got those clothes I sent home. I guess you got that picture of Gilbert I sent to you? How do you like it? Fine I hope. That was painted freehand by a man at Disneyland in California.

You and Dad, I hope are fine. There is not much action over here now so don't worry about me. I will be careful.

Tell Gilbert and Sis I said hi and for them to write me because I can't call home now so I am looking for his letter and yours. Tell Cleta to write if she has time. Send some cookies or candy if you can. I sure would like to have some.

Tell Grandmom and Grandpop I said hi and may God bless them.

I guess the horse is doing just fine. I hope so.

I am right close to the DMZ, about five miles from it, I think. The jungle sure is going to be rough.

Tell Gilbert to go back to where he got my K-bar and send me that sales slip so I can wear my knives OK. And send it to me.

Tell Kathy I said hi and that I love them. I hope she makes good grades this quarter. She had better.

Well, Mom, I have just about run out of something to say.

I hope you got my postcard that I sent to you.

Well, Mom, I guess I will close for now and write as soon as you can. Tell them all I said hi.

Will all my love
your son,
Cliff

I love you all.   I miss you very much.

Feb. 3, 1969

Dear Mom and Dad,

How are you all? Fine, I hope. I am just doing fine. I haven't done much since I have been here. I guess I will go to study tomorrow. It is just another camp. I guess I have moved ten times since I have been here. I sure get tired of moving all the time, but that is the way it goes, I guess.

I guess everything is all right back home. I sure hope so. If anything happens, go to the Red Cross and they will get hold of me. Okay?

I was on a working party today and I am a little tired. I guess I will go to bed after I finish this letter. All I did was haul lumber all day. It was kinda hard to handle.

I have made a lot of friends since I have been here. They sure know what they are doing. I guess I will learn from them what to do.

The weather over here is not too bad. I guess it could be worse, but I like it the way it is. It is not raining now, but I think it will before night is over with. It doesn't rain very hard. Just enough to make you mad.

Mom, we are a day ahead of you all. Today is Monday, and back home it would be Sunday. We are just a day ahead of you all and it is kinda hard to keep up with time in the States.

Hey, Mom, will you get Ray Davis' address and send it to me? Maybe I can see him while I am over here. I hope so.

Well, Mom, I guess I will close for now, so take care and write as soon as you can. I sure would like to get a letter. I have been over here a week and it sure is getting boring, if you know what I mean. I sure hope you can read this because I don't have much light to write by.

Bye, Mom. I will see you.

I love you all and tell all of them I said hi and that I miss them all.

Bye bye for now.

With all my love
your son,
Cliff

II : In the Twinkle of an Eye

Feb. 4, 1969

Dear Mom and Dad,

I guess I will write again because I don't have anything to do. I have just been sitting around for about a week and a half. It sure is getting boring. I hope everything is going OK back home. I guess I will get paid in March. I will be sending my money home in checks so if you need any of it you can cash them.

The pay in here is kinda messed up, if you know what I mean. I would have been sending home some money, but as things have been going I just didn't get paid over $25 at a time and I need all of it, but as soon as they start paying me you will get some money.

I hope I will get some letters before very long. I am just about to go crazy for something to read.

I guess Gilbert and Sis are doing okay. Have them write me a little so I can have their address. Tell them to write as often as they can. It sure is a little different over here because I can't call home like I used to. It sure makes a difference. Tell Cleta to write or send me her address. I sure would like to hear from them. I sure miss the baby a whole lot. I guess they are doing fine. I sure hope so.

I guess Cleta is going to have another baby. At least I think so because of the way she looks. I hope so. I may be mistaken, but I don't think so. HA HA. I guess Kathy hasn't gotten married yet. I hope she doesn't for a while. She sure is not old enough.

Did you get those pictures back that you had taken of me while I was home on leave? If you did, send me one. OK? I hope they turned out OK.

Well, Mom, tell all of them hi and that I miss them. I guess I will close for now. Write as soon as you can.

P.S. Tell Gilbert to send me the sales slip on that K-bar he bought me. O.K.? I will need it so I can keep my knives. I hope you can get it.

Well, bye for now. Keep up your spirits. I will be home in about 12 months. HA HA.

I MISS YOU ALL

(DON'T WORRY)

With all my love
your son,

Cliff

Feb. 11, 1969

Dear Mom and Dad,

How is everyone? Fine, I hope. I thought I would write and let you know that I am OK. I guess I will go out to the bush tomorrow. I sure hate to go.

It's not too bad over here. It sure is getting hot. It was about 80 today. It will get better tomorrow.

I guess it will be a long time before I get any mail. They say it takes about a month before you get any mail.

I have been over here three weeks on Feb. 15 and it is not bad. The only thing is that you don't have a place to take a bath.

I sure am dirty now. I guess I will take a bath in about a month. HA HA. It's really not funny!

I guess Gilbert is doing OK. I sure would like to hear from him.

I guess I miss everyone. It sure is lonely over here.

I hope you don't worry too much about me because there is no need to worry.

I hope Dad is doing OK.

I hope he doesn't sell the dogs because I want to go hunting with them when I get home.

I am writing after dark over here, and I can hardly see.

We don't have any light out here. I am still in the rear, and we still sleep in tents. We don't have any beds so we have to sleep on the ground. I guess I will sleep on the ground for the next 13 months.

Well I have to go, so bye for now and write. I love you all and may God bless you all. Tell them all I said hi.

(Bye)
    (Kiss, Kiss)   I love you all.

With all my love,
Cliff

Feb. 14, 1969

Dear Mom and Dad,

I hope everyone is fine. I am just doing fine. I have been out in the bush for three days now and it is not bad.

Today for chow we had hobo stew. It sure was good. We took our C-rats and put them all into one. It was pretty good.

I guess I will be out in the bush for about a month. I sure am dirty as you can see from the letter. Dirt is all over it. HA HA. I guess I will get a bath in a couple of days. (I hope!)

We're out of water, so I guess we won't get any more until tomorrow.

How is Dad? Fine, I hope. It sure is hot today. It is about 90 degrees.

Today is the 14th and time sure is going fast.

I sure will be glad when my time is over.

I thought I would write and let you know that I am all right.

I haven't seen any action since I have been here. I hope I don't see any for awhile.

Well, Mom, I hope this letter finds you all in the best of health.

I guess I will close for now because I have to go on hole watch in a few minutes.

Bye for now and tell all I said hi and I love them all. Kiss the baby for me when you see them.

Bye Bye.

With all my love,
Cliff

P.S. Tell Gilbert to forget about that K-bar slip. I found out that I don't need it. Tell him hi.

Tell Grandmom and Grandpop I said hi.

Feb. 23, 1969

Dear Mom and Dad,

How are you all? Fine, I hope. I haven't gotten any letters since I have been here because I got put in a different company. It is "G" Gulf Company. The rest of the address is the same. All you have to do is replace the "E" and change it to "G."

All I have been doing is just digging holes.

I am just doing fine, but it sure is hot over here. I got my first bath today for the first time in two weeks. I sure did need it.

I need a haircut, but as you know there is no place out here in the bush. They say we are going back to the rear in a couple of days so I will probably get one then.

I guess everyone is doing fine. I hope so. I guess Sis is getting along with her baby OK. I hope she doesn't have any trouble.

Tell Gilbert I said hi and that I miss him.

I hope Dad is doing fine since his operation. I hope he will put on some weight.

I hope it doesn't bother him too much.

I guess Kathy is still in school and making good grades.

Have Kathy go and tell her homemaking teacher that I said hi and that I am just fine. (OK?)

That knife Gilbert gave me sure comes in handy out here because the jungle sure is thick.

We are sitting up on a great big hill overlooking a valley and it sure is pretty. It is as green as the day is long. Just like summer at home.

But it sure is not home.

I am not homesick. (NOT TOO MUCH!)

Tell Grandmom and Grandpop I said hi and for them to give me a little prayer every once in a while. (OK?)

I don't want you to worry about me because I am just fine.

Tell Cleta I said hi and Bill I said hi and kiss the baby for me.

I guess my horse sure is getting big with her colt. I hope she has a mare colt, don't you?

I am going to buy a camera so I can take some pictures over here.

Well, I am going to close my letter because it is just about dark over here.

We are a day ahead of you and when it is Sunday over here it is just Saturday back home.
(It sure is funny.)

Well, Mom, I will see you before long, like about 12 months! HA HA.

Bye for now. I love you all and I miss you all very much.

To a very sweet mom!

With all my love
your son,
Cliff

(KISSES)

I finished the letters and looked over at Elizabeth. "I can't read his letters. I've tried, I just can't," she said.

The letter of February 23, 1969, was the last letter Dale wrote. Two days later Dale was killed in action.

"He was shot in the leg just below the knee and bled to death. It was at night, and he was surrounded by the enemy. The medics couldn't get to him, and he bled to death.

"We were at home on Sunday, and he had told me one time, he said, 'Don't pay any attention to anybody if anything ever happens to me because if anything ever happens to me there will be a Marine who will come and tell you.' Anyway, this one Sunday a Marine came. He came to the Baptist Church and said they were looking for us. They didn't have any idea that that was what it was. So anyway, they came out on Shetley Creek. The neighbor had gotten word that these Marines were looking for us. So he came on to the house, but he didn't tell us anything about the Marines or anything. He just stayed with us because he knew they were coming. So we wouldn't be by ourselves, I guess. The Marine came. He sat us both down and told us that Dale had been killed. We got the telegram later from Harold Meyers that he had been killed on February 25, 1969.

Clifford D. Combs as he appeared in his boot camp photo.

"We didn't get his body back till March 8. We had him out one night at the funeral home in Marquand. Bob Homan went to St. Louis to pick him up. When Bob got him to his place down here, he examined him. Of course, we couldn't see him then, but Bob told us that he had places on his leg where he had been wounded. He was just as pretty then in that casket as he was the day that he left. It snowed the day of his funeral. I don't remember much about the funeral other than what his grandfather told me. He said when Dale was home on leave he told him that he didn't believe he was ever coming back. But we didn't know that. Maybe Dale knew something that we didn't know. He was so young. He was only 19 when he was killed. When they had the 21-gun salute I got one of the shells they shot and I still have it today. The Marines were all nice. Anyway, we buried him in the Young Cemetery on March 9.

"My husband and I moved from Shetley Creek and bought this place here in August 1978. Then we were divorced in April 1979. I live by myself. I have a good friend here, Mr. McCurry, who stays with me. We get along pretty well.

"The rest of the family is just about like I am. My daughter thought that they sent him overseas sooner than they should have. She thought he should have had more training. I thought the Vietnam War was all uncalled for, but they had it and the boys had to go fight. I still think that it was something that shouldn't have been.

"Every day I think about him. There is not a day passes that he doesn't go through my mind, but I just talk to myself and realize that I just can't sit down and dwell on it. I have to let it go as much as I can let it go. But every day I think about him. You know something that has always really bothered me though was that Dale never got a single one my letters while he was over there."

Suddenly Elizabeth stood and walked into another room. A couple of minutes later she returned with a small box. She set it on the table and pulled out a stack of letters. All the letters were still sealed as they had been 23 years ago: February 8, 1969; February 11, 1969; February 13, 1969; February 14, 1969; February 18, 1969; February 20, 1969; and February 25, 1969. All were stamped "return to sender."

"He never got a one. They were all lost in the mail."

She reached in the box and pulled out four folded sheets of notebook paper. The sheets had browned around the edges from age. She handed them to me and said, "This is the letter that I never mailed. I was writing it the day the Marine came and told me that Dale was killed in action."

Marquand, Mo
March 2/69

Dear Son,

I will answer your letter. Very glad to hear from you. Sorry you haven't gotten any mail from home. As soon as you start getting mail, you let me know.

Everyone is fine over here. Daddy is doing real good. Him and Henry and Charlie and Arlie went fishing today. They thought they could catch some bass.

I guess you are doing OK. I bet you felt better now that you got a bath.

Cleta and William came up and stayed all night. Today is William's birthday and tomorrow the 3rd will be Cleta's. She will be 23 years old and William is 26. Those babies sure are growing. They just talk like grown-ups.

Gib and Ivan came down Saturday about noon. The women didn't come. They went back Saturday night. They are working on their bathroom. Gib bought him a heifer calf and they bought one together to make beef.

Grandma and Grandpa are just doing fine. They went somewhere in his car. Probably down to Jamie's. We gave the teacher your address. She said she would send you all some cookies but Kathy took the address one day and then the same day we got the letter where you changed companies. So I will send her another one tomorrow.

I think Charlie is going to rent Cleta's house. He and Daddy are going to work some together.

The weather sure is nice over here. It is just like spring. Dewey and Patsy were out the other night. They sure have a sweet baby. The baby sure does look like Dewey Wayne. She sure is getting big.

Gary Barrett passed for the army but Danny didn't pass.

Kathy is just doing fine. She went to Sunday school and church this morning. She goes to Mountain View Church. She had her letter changed up there.

Sis and Gib can hardly wait until their baby gets here. The horses and dogs are doing fine. Old Babe sure is getting heavy with her baby. We are not sure about old Sugar.

You said something about a camera. As soon as you start receiving your mail, Cleta said we would send you the camera we made those pictures with when you were home. One will probably cost a lot more over there.

FIVE

PFC Lawrence S. Mills
(May 20, 1950–April 11, 1969)

Hometown: Marquand, Mo.; Headquarters and Company; Twenty-sixth Marines, Ninth Marine Amphibious Force; Quang Nam Province, Vietnam. Killed in Action April 11, 1969.

> *To everything there is a season, and a time to every purpose under the heaven:*
> *A time to be born, and a time to die;*
> *...a time to kill, and a time to heal;*
> *...a time to weep, and a time to laugh...*
> ECCLESIASTES 3: 1, 2, 3

One month and two days after Clifford D. Combs was buried, the tragedy of war again struck the small community of Marquand, Missouri. On April 11, 1969, 18-year-old Lawrence Steven Mills went to the 7th Marines camping area located at the Quang Nam Province to watch a movie. After the movie he boarded a truck to return to his living quarters. While on the truck, an M-26 grenade exploded and Lawrence was killed as a result of fragmentation wounds to the head and body. The military suspected a young Vietnamese villager of throwing the grenade into the back of the truck, but the source of the grenade was never confirmed.

Larry, as his family and friends called him, was born in 1950 and grew up in Marquand. Clara, his mother, was in her forties when Larry was born, and by this time her four other sons and two daughters were grown. Larry's father Emmett died in 1954 when he was three years old, and Clara raised him almost as if he was an only child. "He was special to her," one friend recalled. "It was just the two of them and although Clara never said it, you could sense the closeness when you were around them." The family was poor and fatherless, but Clara, the strength of the family, constantly worked to provide for Larry. In 1961, Harry Mills, Larry's brother, died in an accident as a result of carbon monoxide poisoning. Once again Clara's strength pulled the family through another bad time.

Despite the tragedies that Larry experienced as he grew up, he was a loving child. As Robert Homan, a family friend, recalls, "He was a good kid. He grew up in Marquand and everybody liked him." Larry fished in the Castor River, hunted in the St. Francois Mountains, and played sports in the Marquand school system. He was a kid that wanted to be something in life. There were never many jobs for young men in Marquand. When he turned 17, Larry decided to enlist in the Marine Corps.

I met Larry at the parking lot in the middle of town in the summer of 1968. His eyes danced with excitement as we filled out the enlistment papers. The baby-faced youngster was full of enthusiasm as we pulled in front of his home. He shot out of the car and headed for the front door to get Clara.

"Mom, Mom, I'm joining the Marines! You've got to sign some papers."

Clara asked me several questions then reluctantly signed the papers. We talked for a few minutes, and I went back to the car. As I drove off, I waved to the 17-year-old enlistee who was standing in the doorway with a big smile.

Little did I know that in a few short months I would be returning to Marquand not as a recruiter to talk with a young energetic kid full of life and dreams, but rather as a pallbearer to bury a young man that in the twinkle of an eye had all his dreams snatched away by a senseless war.

In April 1969, the government returned his body home for burial. As Homan remembers, it was a total nightmare for the community. "It was a real sad thing for the people in town. Both of those boys grew up here and were well liked. They were good kids and to have both of them killed and only a month apart was difficult to take. It was really hard for the young kids to handle. Clifford and Larry both went to school here and all the school kids were real torn up about it."

Larry Mills was buried on a warm spring day in April 1969. For the second time in a month, I was at the Marquand Funeral Home, a place that I hoped I would never revisit. I wasn't the only one. Elizabeth Combs, who just one month earlier sat in front of her son's casket in grief, had returned to the funeral home to be with Clara.

Homan recalled that Clara kept saying, "He told me that he wouldn't be back. He said that he would die over there. I don't know why he told me that," she said over and over.

I remember carrying his casket from the funeral home to the hearse. As we stood at attention near the back of the hearse, I watched Clara as she stood looking at the casket. She was silent. She stood and stared at the casket, then turned and walked away.

Lawrence S. Mills

We drove out Route V to a country cemetery and gave Larry the full military honors of a fallen Marine. I presented the flag to Clara and quickly walked from the gravesite. When I reached the car, I turned and looked back toward the crowd of people. Clara and Elizabeth were standing in front of the grave, gripping each other like two broken dolls.

All of the fallen Marines had a military escort of the same rank that remained with the body until burial. Robert Homan recalls the Marine that escorted Larry. "I can remember the Marine escort that stayed here with us. We have a daughter. The Marine escort was the same age as she was, and he really liked her. At first, he was a total Marine. Everything he talked about was the Marines. He never gave any indication when he was here that it bothered him that much. He asked for an extension after the funeral, and he stayed with us for a few days longer. We went on a picnic down by the river, and he really enjoyed it. Later, he opened up and talked to us. He said that he got to where he couldn't go to the family homes and talk to the families about their boys being killed.

"He came back a couple of years later and wanted our daughter to go with him and marry him, but she wouldn't do it. When he came back, he was a different person. He was living in his car, he had real long hair. He wouldn't stay at the house. He would go down to the river and take a bath.

Lawrence S. Mills and his mother Clara, summer 1968.

He told me that he took a razor blade and cut his military shoes into shreds. He said that he had to polish them every time he went to a funeral, and he would never polish a pair of shoes again. We just didn't know how much it bothered him. I guess a lot of Vietnam veterans were that way. You would think that someone would have tried to help them with counseling or something."

    The years passed and Clara found the strength to carry on. In 1972, Clara lost another son to a drowning accident in the Arkansas River. Then in 1978 she lost a daughter to cancer.

"She had a hard life, but she dealt with her loss," Homan said. "She kept all of Larry's pictures and medals sitting on the TV. She would talk about him and what happened. When they brought the Moving Wall to Cape Girardeau in 1989, we wanted to take her down there to see Larry's name, but she wouldn't go. She always was a strong person. She had gone through so many things." On December 30, 1990, Clara died. She was 80 years old.

I don't know how many men from Marquand served in the Vietnam War, but I do know that I enlisted nine men in Marquand or the Marquand area. I stood at the gravesite of three of them. A fourth was killed, but the family had left the area at the time of his death. Marquand had more than its share of agony from the Vietnam War. Yet, the ties of its citizens have helped Marquand remain a stable community. Today Marquand has a population of 261. The school is still in operation, and the people work hard to ensure their children get a quality education. Angelica Uniform Group employs many people in the community. Other town businesses include a grocery store, a hardware store, gas station, two garages, a tree trimming service, a bank, and a post office. The Marquand Community Fire Department and ambulance service are vital to the area. They also have a Senior Citizen Housing Project and nutrition center to help the elderly.

They have cut two of the three trees at the edge of the parking lot where I met with many of the enlistees. But little else has changed since the 1960s. Clifford D. Combs and Lawrence Steven Mills have their names on a memorial in the center of town. Elizabeth Combs told me that in May 1993 Fredericktown was going to have a ceremony for a war monument they had built in recognition of area servicemen. "I'm glad they are doing it, but I like the one we have in Marquand. I'm proud of it."

PART III
Corpsman Up

SIX

CPO Homer Yount

Hometown: Patton, Mo.; Navy corpsman; USS *Sanctuary* Hospital Ship; Gulf of Tonkin, Vietnam; Tour of Duty, February 1969–February 1970.

> *"Chief, I am dying! Don't let me die," he begged as tears began to roll down his cheeks. A minute later his death grip released from my arm and the young Marine's arm crashed to the bed. He was dead. I went berserk.*
> HOMER YOUNT
> December 31, 1992

Homer Yount was born in Patton, Missouri, to Edgar and Gertie Yount. Gertie died when Homer was three years old and his father raised him. Homer grew up in the rural Missouri community and graduated from Patton High School in 1948. Shortly afterward, he became a teacher in the Patton grade school.

Homer was teaching first grade in Patton's one-room school house when he received his draft notice. He did not want to serve in the Army so he joined the Navy to avoid the draft. Homer went to boot camp at San Diego, California, then to hospital corpsman school at the naval hospital in Corona, California.

After medical school, Homer reported to Camp Pendleton where he trained with the Marines for six months. Then for the next several years he was stationed at various naval and marine bases in the United States and the Philippine Islands.

While he was stationed at the naval air station located in Pensacola, Florida, he met Hazel Stowe, a nurse at the base hospital. Hazel was from Lavonia, Michigan, and the couple dated for a while and were married at the base chapel on November 27, 1960.

Homer Yount aboard the USS *Sanctuary*, 1970.

In the early 1960s, Homer shipped out to MAC 11 Marine Airwing in Japan. The Vietnam War began to escalate and so did the demand for corpsmen. Homer returned to the States in 1966 for more medical schooling and field combat training at Camp Delmar Marine Base, California.

Homer and Hazel wanted to have children, but Hazel had medical problems that made pregnancy impossible. So while Homer was in training, they adopted their son Brett in March 1966. A short time later, Homer completed his training, and the family was transferred to South Carolina.

Homer enjoyed watching his son grow and enjoyed coming home each day from work to see Brett who was always waiting at the door. Just as things seemed to be settling into a routine the inevitable happened. Homer received orders for Vietnam.

In February 1969, Homer received orders for the USS *Sanctuary* stationed off the coast of Da Nang, Vietnam. He recalls reporting aboard the ship. "The very first month that I was there I was very busy being oriented to the ship. We had 600 hospital beds, but in an emergency we could expand to 1,000 beds for 12 hours. We had 30 doctors, 25 nurses, and 50 corpsmen on board. There was a triage room and four operating rooms.

"Besides orientation there were constant drills. General quarters, battle stations, fire drills, and condition Zebra which meant condition set for battle. I heard general quarters in my sleep.

"After a month, I was assigned duty on incoming wounded. I would wait on the flight deck for the choppers to come in. Once there was a helicopter that came in with casualties. The pilot landed and yelled out the window, 'I don't know what's going on back there. Will you check my gunner? I can't get him to answer.' I ran up and he was standing and leaning forward on the machine gun. His eyes were open, but he was dead. He had been shot through the heart.

"We would take the wounded below to the triage room. It had four beds. A doctor, nurse, and two corpsmen were stationed at each bed. The room is a sorting station. You take the ones that you have a chance to save, the others you do what you can for them. If somebody had an amputated arm, you would dress the wound and send them to the operating room. Then the ones that had no chance of survival, you did what you could. The whole operation in the triage room and operating room was traumatic. It was a combination of moans and screams from the wounded mixed with doctors, nurses, and corpsmen yelling 'Get an IV! Got a belly wound here! Clamp that bleeder! Snow him with morphine!' Many died in flight to the ship. We would prepare them for the morgue. Then wrap them in Glad Bags."

Homer began to suffer from depression. As he explained, "The problem on the ship was you were at extremes all the time. There would be periods where there were no casualties. During that time there was nothing to do." It was the first time that Homer had been away from his wife and son. "I was very lonely. But, so was everybody else. Then the other extreme was 18-hour days of sheer numbers of mutilated bodies."

"One night I had duty on incoming wounded. I was on the flight deck, and we got this young Marine. He had both legs amputated. How the corpsmen ever got tourniquets on those stumps I will never know because there were just about three inches of legs left from the hip. He had an M on his forehead which meant he was on morphine. So we took him in to triage. Fortunately, he was the only one. The doctor looked at the Marine and told me to start an IV on him. He turned to the other chief and told him to start blood. There was one other corpsman and nurse with us. The young man was responding. He was very, very happy. He told me, 'The doc in the field took real good care of me, and I know that you are all going to take good care of me.'

"The doctor began tying off the bleeders. There is an artery that goes down each side of the leg. He worked for a while and he said, 'I have tied off all the bleeders. I am going to release the tourniquets because I don't want to damage the tissues.' He released the tourniquets and blood began to spurt and gush everywhere. The kid grabbed my arm and looked me in the eye. 'Chief, I am dying! Don't let me die,' he begged as tears began to roll down his cheeks. A minute later his death grip released from my arm and the young Marine's arm crashed to the bed. He was dead.

"I went berserk. I started yelling and screaming. I was cursing God. I was cursing everybody. The doctor got ahold of me and just slapped the hell out of me. They took me into triage and brought in a replacement for me that night. About 15 minutes later, the corpsman tripped out. Then the nurse. Finally the doctor tripped out.

"The next day the doctor came into my quarters and asked me to assist him in doing an autopsy on this young Marine. 'I have got to find out why that young Marine died,' he explained.

"We were all still teary-eyed over this, but we went down to help him. The doctor x-rayed the body. There was a piece of shrapnel part way on the side of the artery inside his body and there was nothing that could have been done. He literally bled to death, and there was nothing we could do."

Homer went into a very deep depression. He found out later that they even had some of the corpsmen watching to make sure he didn't harm himself. One day the commanding officer of the ship came down and told him that he needed to see a doctor.

"I told the captain that there was nothing wrong with me," recalls Homer. "I knew I was depressed. I told him, 'I will hit rock bottom before I bounce back. And I will bounce back. I am in deep depression, and I am aware of that. So don't worry about me. I am not going to do anything foolish or ridiculous. But, if you don't mind, I do not want to go see this doctor because I don't want to have this psychiatric evaluation on my record.' The captain agreed.

"Finally, one Sunday morning we were in Da Nang. Two chiefs came into my quarters, pulled me out of my bunk, took me over to a club called the White Elephant, and began to pour beer down me. I passed out on my feet. Then I cried for three solid hours. When we returned back to the ship, the nurses, corpsmen, and crew were lined up and cheered me on.

"They had to carry me back aboard the ship. I woke up the next morning, and it was a whole new day. I was happy and it was as if nothing had ever happened.

"My behavior was not unusual on the ship. We had chiefs, nurses, and corpsmen that were on the ship for one week and were gone. Some may last three or four weeks then be shipped out. They just could not handle the stress. Often the stress was from nothing to do. Other times it was from the constant mayhem of dealing with daily casualties. As one nurse said, 'What can you do with a half dozen holes spurting with blood and half their insides blown away?'

"We got a lot of nurses that had graduated from Officer Candidate School and Nurses training. When they came on board, they were just like models. I saw some of those nurses coming off the ward because of the long hours and stress from the constant pressure of casualties. They were just tired and lonely and sick to death of trying to fix the mutilated bodies of young boys. When they left there, if they stuck it out, they were excellent nurses when they came back to the States.

"In May, I took over the medical supply department. I didn't deal directly from that time on with casualties. I started at six in the morning and worked to midnight each day. I ordered medical supplies. If we needed supplies right away, I would try to get them from Da Nang Hospital. I also had a phone patch into the Oakland Naval Hospital for certain supplies. Pan Am would fly them into Da Nang for us to pick up.

"I was scared the whole time I was in Vietnam. Our ship moved up and down the coast from Da Nang to the DMZ. I was always afraid that we would be fired at from the coast. In fact, the USS *Repose* would stop and have swimming call. They were fired on several times, but we never did stop. Every time I had to go on the beach and stay overnight to get supplies, I would get totally wiped out. One time a rocket came in and landed about three hootches down from the hootch I was sleeping in.

"Around the middle of September the war seemed to wind down, and there weren't as many casualties.

"Gypsy Rose Lee came by. The captain wished that he had never let her aboard. She drove all the kids crazy. She would prop up on the bed and reach her hand under the sheet. She had those poor guys going bananas.

"We had Bob Hope come aboard. Teresa Graves and Connie Stevens were with the tour. After the show, Connie was going on tour and meeting the wounded that could not be moved. There was this one kid that had been blinded by a napalm explosion. He had bandages on his eyes. Connie came by and took his hands and told him who she was. He told her he remembered seeing her in a movie and tears began to stream from beneath the bandages. Connie had to be carried to the helicopter, she fell apart.

"We used to go up and count sea snakes. That's when we got bored. But you never got the casualties off your mind. The smell from burnt skin, blood, and dead tissue was in your nostrils, hair, and skin. You could never really get away from it. Even if you weren't in the operating room.

"When I left the ship, there was a sadness. I was glad that I was going home, but I felt as if I was leaving something there. I don't know what but something.

"I came back to Albany, Georgia, when my tour was up. After watching the families moving around and watching the children who were disoriented by the constant moving, I decided that it was time to retire.

"I came back to Cape in 1972 and attended Southeast Missouri State University. I finished my bachelor's degree, and went into the master's program for guidance counseling. The schooling helped me a lot with the nightmares. I used to wake up in cold sweats for several years after coming home. I was having dreams about the experience with the young Marine who asked me not to let him die. I drank a lot when I came home. Then I got picked up for a DUI [Driving Under the Influence]. After that I straightened up. The incident with the young Marine still bothers me from time to time. But I try not to think about it.

"Vietnam is not something that I dwell on because if I get on something and keep it up, I make myself miserable. I did not think that it was our war, and occasionally I would ask myself what I was doing there. But I told myself that I had chosen to be there. I had made the Navy a career, and it was my job. I think the whole thing was political though."

Homer finished the master's program and went to work for the Meadow Heights School District in Patton, Missouri, as a guidance counselor.

His son Brett is 26 years old and works at a local music store in Cape. Hazel is a nurse at Southeast Missouri Hospital. Homer laughed, "I had to have someone who would keep me close to the profession."

Homer is a member of the Marine Corps League in Cape Girardeau and attends regular meetings.

"By the way," he said as we ended our conversation, "do you know Sergeant Wilkerson here in Cape? He is the Marine Corps recruiter. He is a good one. He is going to get six of my boys this year out of Patton. I don't know what's the matter with the other services, but he sure is a go-getter."

SEVEN

Petty Officer Third Class George I. Ellis

Hometown: Fredericktown, Mo.; Navy corpsman; Second Battalion, First Marines, First Marine Division; Khe Sanh, Vietnam; Tour of Duty, May 1968–May 1969.

> To George Ivan "Doc" Ellis
>
> While we were together in RVN you were in my highest regards—a professional working under the worst of circumstances. I've never forgotten your dedication to duty to care for "my marines." You are a true Marine. I hope that your children do not have to experience the horrors of man's treatment of his fellow man.
> PHIL LESLIE
PLATOON SERGEANT
July 19, 1992
>
> P.S. Thanks for patch'n my butt on October 3, 1968, and helping me back to the battalion CP [command post].

> To George Ivan "Doc" Ellis
>
> I am forever obligated to you for being my friend the past 25 years and for giving such faithful service in Vietnam! Please accept these words as partial payment of that debt. You are truly my brother and I cherish our relationship.
> Welcome home,
Semper Fi
LEWIS B. PULLER, JR.

Ivan Ellis and I sat down at the kitchen table to begin the interview. We were both shuffling with papers. I grabbed my tape recorder from my

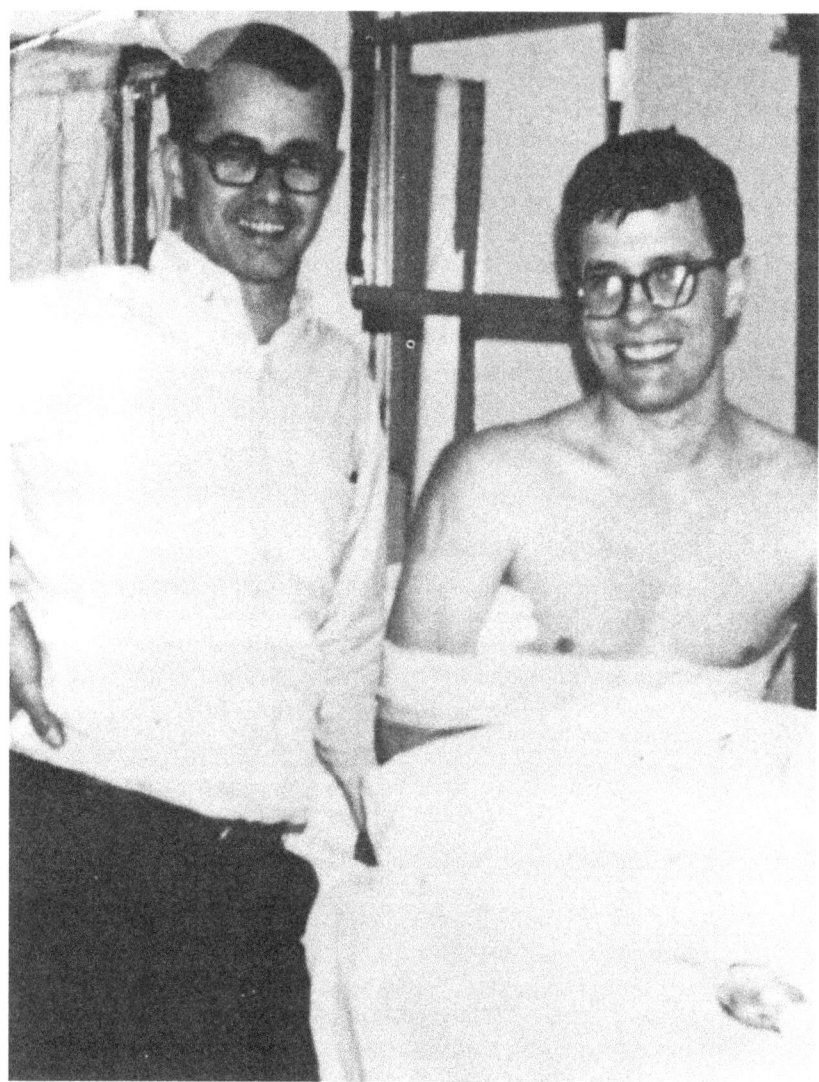

George Ellis during a 1969 hospital visit with Lewis Puller, Jr.

briefcase along with a notepad and a couple of information forms and placed them on the table.

Ivan reached across the table and handed me a hardback book, *Fortunate Son* by Lewis B. Puller, Jr. A photo of Puller in his wheelchair covered the front of the book. Both of his legs were amputated at the hips and part of one hand was missing. Obviously, Puller was lucky. He had survived the 155 howitzer that had ripped his body apart.

"I was his corpsman," Ivan explained. "It's a good book. You should read it," he said smiling.

"I'll do that," I said, handing the book back to Ivan.

The former Navy corpsman placed the book on the table and adjusted his dark-rimmed glasses as his smiling face turned to an expression of serious thought. His lips tightened as he rubbed his slightly thinned hair. He scooted his chair closer to the table, placed his arms on the tabletop, and looked me straight in the eye.

"I grew up in Fredericktown, Missouri, which is about 100 miles south of St. Louis. I went to Catholic schools growing up. Then I attended Kemper Military School in Bloomfield, Missouri, for two years. I enlisted in the Navy around December 1965 because I wanted to be in dental school. At that time Vietnam was going pretty good.

Dental technician and Navy corpsman go hand in hand. They needed Navy corpsmen, so when I finished boot camp at Great Lakes I was sent to medical school to be a corpsman. I was there for about a year. I was on a dirty surgery ward which was a ward for open wounds. You would see a lot of casualties from Vietnam. I had an opportunity to get trained in neurology.

"I got orders to go to Vietnam. We went to Camp Pendleton, and I was assigned to a DI [drill instructor] to learn how to make it in the field. From there we went to Okinawa.

"I was assigned to the Second Battalion, First Marines, First Marine Division at Khe Sanh. I was in Gulf Company, Third Platoon. A platoon has two Navy corpsmen. Khe Sanh had been under siege since about January 1968. They were under siege for several months. Everything was blown up. We lived in bunkers underground and had artillery coming in every day. We ran patrols out of there. We never had any contact. But the NVA [North Vietnamese Army] had forward observers in the hills, and they would always throw artillery in on them. Most of it came from Laos.

"We were at Khe Sanh for about two weeks, and then we went to Hill 552 which was south of Khe Sanh. We ran patrols out of there. There's a hill called 689 where the enemy was dug in at the base. We had a few Marines killed there.

"We got up to Hill 689 to help out. When we first got there, choppers were coming in and air strikes were coming in. It was spooky. One corpsman that I had not seen for a while was running around and he looked like hell-warmed-over. I asked him what was going on. Come to find out there were NVA dug in at the bottom of the hill. Marines were getting sniped at the bottom of the hill. There were dead Marines lying at the bottom of the hill. They wanted us to wait until it was dark and go down there and get the dead Marines. It didn't make much sense to me being a squid [nickname for corpsman]. Son-of-a-bitch, these guys are dead. We keep sending men down there, and they are going to keep getting picked off. Well, that evening our plan of attack was to go running down this hill screaming and yelling. I guess we were supposed to be psyching them out. We got into position, and we charged down that damn hill like we were crazy. We never did get any activity. We got the dead out though. We sat there for days without water or food. I can remember watching the Marines walking down the hills with body bags carrying the dead to the choppers.

"Up at Khe Sanh we had a lot of rat bites. We had a few psychological problems. Guys just couldn't take it any longer.

"In July 1968, we abandoned everything. Choppers came in and picked us up and we left. As we pulled out and flew over Khe Sanh, I watched them blow the airstrip up.

"We went to Dong Ha and ran patrols out of there. The terrain was completely different than any place that I had been. It was flatlands and sandy. It wasn't the big hills like at Khe Sanh. We had to watch the booby traps. But we didn't have any artillery.

"Later on our whole battalion was moved back to Da Nang. We were all relieved that we were back, but come to find out we were worse off than up north. We had a lot more booby traps and snipers than before.

"Our compound was about five clicks [kilometers] south of Da Nang. We ran patrols in three different areas there. One was across the two-cow bridge. We would run patrols in that area and guard the bridge. Across the road there were a lot of villages and we would run a lot of patrols. The third area was called the Rivera. That was between two/one compound and the Gulf of Tonkin. It was sniper infested. There were booby traps, a lot of VC and NVA in the area, and rice paddies to cross. It was nickel-and-dime stuff. A few wounded here and there. Maybe a kill once in a while.

"The Navy corpsmen are assigned to a combat company for six months. Then they are rotated out to a safer area for six months. Some guys would stay back at the battalion aid station. Some guys would go back to Da Nang at the Navy support hospital.

"While I was assigned to the field, we just kept losing guys—mostly from booby traps. We weren't running into the VC, but we just kept getting more casualties. The first and second platoons were put together as one platoon because we would lose guys but we weren't getting any replacements.

"When I got into combat in May, there were seven corpsmen attached to the unit. One of the other corpsmen finally refused to go into the bush. He was scared. That put more of a burden on us. By October 12 I was the only one left that wasn't wounded.

"I guess one of the most famous persons who joined our unit was Lewis B. Puller, Jr., Chesty Puller's son. He joined us in August 1968. Of course, being a corpsman, I didn't know who Chesty Puller was. The Marines around me started explaining who Chesty Puller was. The first part of October, Lewis joined our platoon. On October 11 we went on a battalion-sized raid. Lt. Puller was wounded, and they were the most dramatic wounds that I had ever seen. He lost both legs and six out of ten fingers."

Ivan quickly got up from the table and went into another room. Moments later he returned with a green metal box. He opened it and pulled out an old notebook. He began turning the pages as he muttered dates to himself. The edges of the pages had turned brown from age and one or two pages came loose from the binding. Suddenly, his finger pressed against the page as he looked up with excited eyes, "I found it. Here it is," he spurted. "I kept a daily diary while I was there." Ivan began to read:

1968, October 10, Thursday—Found out that Gulf 1 and 2 were going to the third Amtrac battalion and that we were supposed to go up there. The whole company would be choppered out at 0630 in the A.M. Well this burns us all up since it was around 2100 now and with the third Amtracs about six to seven clicks away. We started out the main gate and down the MSR, which is the Main Supply Root road, until we passed the first village and started crossing deep rice paddies. We crossed about a click worth of them and at places it was past my waist. At one point I had to hold up my camera and my rifle and smokes. We finally arrived there around 0100. It also rained on us a little on the way there.

1968, October 11, Friday—Dead on my tail and cussing, we rested there until the other two platoons came in. And then walked down to the LZ [landing zone] there and I ate some C-rats. We sacked out and had to get up at 0530. It started raining hard before that and I just threw my poncho around me and tried to sleep the best I could. Cold and soaking wet, we all packed up and walked down to the beach. My feet were so tired I could hardly walk. At 0630 on the nose, eight C-46s came in on the beach and we ran aboard. Gulf 3 was dropped off out of the leper village and just west of the French road. We were with the lieutenant and we finally got all the supplies together. Right off the bat three Alfa saw about seven NVA and fired but missed. They ran to the southwest and I think the other platoon might have seen them.

We then moved west in a line and stopped west of the village in the sand. About that time I heard a very loud explosion and heard someone call for a corpsman. I started running north where the explosion came from. Ron Rees lead the way by probing. We got about 100 feet from the accident and I saw a foot plus part of a leg attached lying in the sand. Upon arriving there I found out that it was Lt. Puller. Stein the HM2 found the second platoon was there. Puller's legs were completely blown off at about the knees. He was on his left side. Stein had given him morphine. The executive officer of the platoon was putting pressure on both iliac arteries. I tried to stop the oozing of blood but to no avail. I got some alfedmine and we started an IV. The lieutenant was conscious the whole time and talked, but he didn't know his legs were gone—maybe that just one was badly hurt. An emergency medevac [medical evacuation] was called and it didn't seem like it took long for it. With tourniquets on one leg, we put him on a stretcher that we had gotten from an amtrac and carried him to the area secured for the LZ. I walked along putting pressure on the arteries and got him aboard okay.

They said he must have stepped on a 105 round or about ten pounds of C-4. Watson was about three feet behind him and just got a little scratch on his hand. We looked for the rest of him and the rifle but found nothing. We buried his foot, etc., and sat up overlooking the village to the west. He hit the mine around 0800 I guess. We sat out in the rain until about 1300 until we got word to saddle up. The sun did come out long enough to dry my gear and clothes. We walked south on the high ground and then we all moved east and sat in some trees just below the French road. We were only about a click from the village I guess. We stayed there all night and it rained off and on.

Ivan slowly closed the diary. He took his glasses off and gently laid them on the table. He sat for a moment looking across the room in silence. He placed the diary back in the box and picked up his glasses. "You know what strikes me today about things like a Marine getting wounded, a Lt. Puller getting his legs blown off, or a guy getting killed out there is that as a rule all that stuff isn't forgotten about in your mind. But you put it in the back of your mind. You have to worry about that moment forward. You can't worry about this person was wounded or that person was killed. You have to worry about surviving now. I look in my diary when Lt. Puller was wounded October 11. I read in my diary October 12 and there isn't a mention of Lt. Puller. On October 13 I mention that I hope he is doing well, but the thing that is most on your mind is doing your job and saving yourself. You're not thinking about so-and-so being wounded. It's not like you're being callous. It's not that you have forgotten about them. The order of business is most important."

Ivan sipped his coffee, and then continued, "There was one incident back in August 1968. One of the hospital corpsmen that came over in country with me was killed in action on August 31, 1968. He was walking along a rice paddy with a radio operator and a claymore mine was detonated. A few days later Sgt. Leslie came up to me and another corpsman and was talking about this corpsman being killed. Evidently this corpsman was carrying a .45 pistol. This is a good sign to the enemy that you are either an officer, corpsman, radio operator, or somebody important. Sgt. Leslie told me to get rid of my pistol and get an M-16 and start looking like a Marine. From that point on I carried an M-16 rifle. The only difference was that I carried bandages in the magazine pouches instead of ammunition. I looked like a Marine.

"We didn't wear flak jackets or helmets at Dong Ha. We went out on a night patrol in August of '68. There was a full moon shining against the white sand. It was kind of spooky. You could see things but you couldn't see things. We had stopped for about five or ten minutes. I could see shadows and bushes moving. We had just gotten up and started to move out again, and we heard a couple of gunshots. We sat up in a three-sixty. One of the Marines on point was missing. A couple of Marines went out and found him and dragged him back in. He had evidently come up on a VC, and they had shot him in the face. All that night we had luminary for protection. It was a scary night not knowing what kind of force we were dealing with.

"On October 12, Charlie Tyner of Second Platoon Gulf Company had gone out on a patrol. He was on an amphibious tractor. Four Marines were on one amtrac and four on the other. They hit a mine and the amtrac just exploded. That got Charlie out of country. He wound up with burns on his legs and hands and lost a finger on one hand. I have stayed in contact with him and even today when he wears shorts you can see where his socks came to because of the different marks on his ankles.

"At this point I was the only corpsman out of seven that hadn't been wounded, and I had until December to get out of the bush. At this point we started losing more people to booby traps. It seemed like every day when we went out on patrol somebody was wounded or killed. We never got any rest at all. We were out all the time. In November, it got pretty nerve-wracking. Just no let up in activity.

"Talking to my platoon sergeant and Lt. Puller, they said they thought of me as being more of a Marine than a corpsman. As a matter of fact, they said that I was a better Marine than some of the Marines in the platoon. Puller said some of them were shit birds. You have to remember that at the time there was the draft. To me, 1968 was a very dramatic year.

"The radio man in our outfit was named Watson. We called him Red. We were pretty close. There was a black Marine corporal named Turner. He was squared away. If he had wanted me to go to North Vietnam with him in the middle of the night, I would have gone. I had the highest respect for him. Most of the Marines that I served with did their jobs.

"One interesting thing that our battalion did that I don't know of any other doing was a battalion-sized raid at the DMZ. It was a day operation. It was softened up by B-52 bombings before we went in. We never had any contact, but it was interesting.

"One of the things I remember about the nights in Vietnam was that there was never a night that was completely dark. There were always flares hanging on a parachute on the horizon somewhere.

"You prayed every day. You knew just about when you were going to go out. We would go out for two nights and three days. Those were bad times staying out in the boonies. I was scared every minute. I prayed a lot. Every step you take is closer to being back. You could come into certain areas, and you could sense that you were going to get ambushed. You sensed there were going to be snipers in there. Most of the time you were right. All of sudden you would hear the cracking sound of an AK-47. It has a distinct cracking sound. There is no other sound like it. When you heard it, chills would go through your body.

"On most of the patrols in Vietnam nothing ever happened. You were just scared to death and praying a lot most of the time. It was just nickel-and-dime stuff. Of course, when you first went out on the patrol, you sure as hell didn't know that. You were always 100 percent alert, but most of the time nothing ever happened.

"I read in a VFW magazine where one of the officers was saying that on most of the patrols nothing ever happened. It was what I had experienced. But I always heard about all of these major battles that went on; and I always felt guilty about not participating in any of them. Then when I read his story, I realized that most of the war was just as I had experienced. Patrol after patrol with little happening on any of them.

"When we were going to be out for three days, we would leave right after dinner and go out so many clicks. We would set up at dusk in a temporary position. After it got dark we would move out and go to our nighttime position. We would send out a squad or less on a nighttime ambush. As a rule they did not send a corpsman out, but I went out on ambushes several times. I did stand radio watches at night. Then once our ambushes came in, we would saddle up and continue the patrol.

"The thing that you were always scared of was being ambushed. In one incident we had been out for a day or so. It was in the morning, and we were coming into this opening. There was a tree line and some short paddy dikes ahead of us. We sensed that it was a good place to get hit. Just as we got out into the opening we started receiving automatic weapons fire. The column started moving into a rice paddy that had a paddy dike about chest high. Well, the whole platoon was behind us, and we had to make room for them coming in. The two guys on point, one who had only been in country for two weeks, started to climb over the dike and tripped a booby trap. We had two men down. I ran up there. They were not seriously wounded. Things were getting hot. We called in a medevac. I don't know about the other outfits, but we really had a lot of old equipment. Most of our medevacs were with the old C-34s, and they were really slow coming in. When they lowered the stretcher, you had to tilt the stretcher sideways to get the wounded in the thing. Anyway we had waited for a couple of hours. We found out later that the South Vietnamese had some emergencies so they got priority. We baked in the sun waiting on the choppers with the casualties. We got them on board and they did receive fire but they got out okay.

"When we ended up the three-day patrol, we had some villagers that were helping us get out to the main road. They were helping us so we would not get any sniper fire.

"A lot of times when we went in a village, kids would want to know where the boxy was. 'Boxy' in Vietnamese stood for doctor. Myself and a junior corpsman would doctor these kids. If we were going to run patrols out for two or three days or if we were just passing through though, I would never let them know that I was a corpsman. You couldn't trust them. They often gave the information to the VC. I was trying to look like a Marine. The kids used to get infected. One time a little girl had an infected earlobe. Minor stuff on the kids.

"We had gone to the Tu Cau bridge for two days of guard duty. There must have been another company that had engaged in a fire fight with the VC. The battle had gotten heated up pretty good. One of the Marines in our platoon had fired into a house in the village. He hit a little girl, who was about ten, in the arm. She got hit around the elbow and her arm was just hanging by a piece of skin. We patched her up the best we could and then got her back to our battalion aid station. She lived. The Marine that shot her never got over it.

"It seems like the corpsmen out in the bush had the supplies with us to take care of an immediate problem. We would call in a medevac quickly. We were about five clicks south of Da Nang. They had two hospitals with the best medical care. I believe Lt. Puller is alive today because of the hospital care that was quickly available.

"So many times people had foot problems. When it wasn't raining, we were in rice paddies. One thing that I never could understand was why the hell were we walking through rice paddies. Why not get on high ground and walk? My theory is that if you want to get from Point A to Point B, take the easier route. Besides, those rice paddies were full of human waste and really bad on our feet.

"When we were at Con Thien, we were going on a battalion-sized raid. I was the senior corpsman in the platoon and this junior corpsman outranked me, but I had more time in country than he did. He came up to me that morning and asked me where I wanted him. I told him to walk with the CP group. We started out like that. Later on that day we got to one of the checkpoints, and we got 11 rounds of friendly fire [accidental attacks by U.S. troops or allies] in on us. I jumped into a bomb crater. By the time they were able to get the firing stopped, the command group had gotten hit. The radio operator was killed and the junior corpsman got wounded. That just about took it all out of us that day. We were on a long march and then to have our people killed by our own was hard to take. I remember coming back into Con Thien and our butts were dragging. I had always said that as long as there was a Marine marching I would never drop out. But that particular day I was ready to drop out, and we were several clicks from

George Ellis in Con Thien.

Con Thien. There was a small shelter and there were some Marines there that were out for heat exhaustion. But I don't think I could have gone any further, my butt was really dragging. I stayed out there with the Marines while the rest of the battalion went on in, and they sent some tanks out to get us. We rode back on the tanks.

"At Con Thien we had heavy artillery coming in on us a lot. I remember one time we were sitting on six-by trucks, waiting to go someplace and heavy arty came in. We lived in underground bunkers because of the artillery coming in all the time. It rained a lot and our bunkers were always getting flooded. The only good thing about the rains was that we used them as showers. We didn't have showers. When it would rain, many times we would run out with a bar of soap and take a bath. It was miserable with the rain. It was wet and cold all the time. There was no way to stay dry.

"I remember another incident down in Da Nang. We had just come in off patrol and were sitting around the area. There was an Army observation helicopter flying around the area. It was a lightweight helicopter. The maximum it could carry was three people. They flew around looking for enemy activity. It had a bubble on the front and had skids. It was a 1950 helicopter. The back end of the helicopter was not closed in. Anyway,

Living quarters of Ellis in Con Thien.

these guys had spotted some enemy activity outside one of the villages. We had moved out very quickly. We were walking through a rice paddy that was about knee deep. An old Vietnamese man came running across the rice paddy. He was frightened and didn't know what was going on. This young Marine that was behind me told him to stop. The old man reached into his pocket to get out an ID, and the Marine got spooked and shot the old man. I remember turning and looking at the Marine just as he shot and seeing the bullet go through the old man and him splashing in the rice paddy. We picked up papasan and put him up on the rice paddy. He was shot through the stomach. The only chopper there was the operation helicopter. I told the sergeant that we needed to get the helicopter over there and put the old man on the skid. They could hold him on the skid until they got him to the hospital which was only a short distance from where they were. The chopper hovered over the dike. Papasan was put on the skid with this army guy holding his arm. When they took off, papasan was screaming. He was in pain and scared that he was going to fall off the skid. When we got back, the doctor told us we could have left him out there because he got shot through the liver. I felt like I had done the right thing because I was trying to help the old fellow."

I was listening to Ivan when suddenly three girls dressed in baggy pajamas burst through the basement door and raced through the kitchen. "Hey Jennifer, Jennifer, you girls will have to stay in the other room. I'm busy in here," Ivan ordered.

"Okay, Dad." The girls giggled as they disappeared into another room.

"Those were my daughters, Jennifer and Carrie. They had a slumber party last night," Ivan said grinning.

"How old are they?" I asked.

"Jennifer's 11 and Carrie is 9."

"Yeah, I know what you're dealing with. I have a daughter who's 12. She has friends over quite a bit."

Ivan laughed then reached for his coffee. He watched as the girls passed through another room. He looked down at the table for a moment then up at me. "That little girl getting her arm shot off, those kids out there getting hurt, that old man getting shot, at the time you don't think about that stuff. You put it in the back of your mind. But when you have kids, you're in civilian life, and you have a family, things like that start bothering you because that could be your kids. Old papasan could have been my grandfather. He was somebody's father and grandfather. The kids belonged to somebody, but at the time you don't think like that because at the time you're young. But you get older and wiser, and you realize that could have been my kid that got her arm shot off. It starts bothering you later on in life. Those memories start coming forward. It bothers you.

"The corpsmen were in the bush for six months and then back in a safe place. I remember very well the day that my replacement came in to relieve me and I came in out of the bush. It happened about the middle of December. One day you're in the bush, and the next day your replacement is there. You're not going to have to go to the Rivera or go on patrols again. That night I remember staying up all night. I stayed up with another corpsman and talked. I was so relieved. I never had so much burden lifted off my shoulders. I drank coffee all night long, and I had to work the next day.

"Right after that I went on my first R&R in Pinang, Malaysia. I was there for New Year's Eve. After coming back, I went to work in the hospital in Da Nang. Da Nang was pretty safe. We would get rocket attacks, but they were usually shooting at the airfield. In Tet 1969, some of the VC got into the area, but it was light activity. I worked in sick call. I remember one day I had the day off and was at the club having a beer. They came over the intercom and wanted the corpsmen to come to sick bay. You could hear the choppers coming in. They needed blood, any kind of blood. The club emptied, and they got 40 pints of blood for one casualty. They put 40 pints of blood in him, and it ran right out of him. He didn't make it.

"Sometimes when they would get a body for registration, I would have to go with the doctor for grave registration. That was an experience—going in and having to unzip body bags. I remember one body bag I unzipped there was only a torso. No head, no arms. There were body bags with guys that were burned. I don't know how those Marines that worked there every day stood it except that it was quiet and air-conditioned so you could get away from the humidity of Vietnam.

"One day I was sitting at the enlisted men's club drinking a beer with a corpsman. A friend of his was visiting, and I had never met this guy before. I had mentioned to him that I had gone down to grave registration, and one of the bodies down there was a corpsman. He had been in a chopper accident, and his body was all burned. I was talking about this, and this other corpsman became real quiet. He wanted more information, and I told him what I knew about it. Come to find out it was a friend of his who had been in Vietnam for a year. It was shit like that. You never knew who you were talking to.

"I came back to the States in 1969 and got out of the Navy. I came back to Missouri and finished my degree in biology at Southeast Missouri State College. I planned on going to medical school, but my grades were not that high. I kind of lost interest in it. I got a job at a grocery warehouse, Winter Out Foods. That was 19 years ago.

"I met my wife, Lucille Maune, the first year that I worked for Winter Out. She lived in an apartment next to mine and that is how we met. She taught school for ten years before we had our first child. She stayed home and raised our kids. We have three: Jennifer, 11; Carrie, 9; and Christopher, 4. This year she has gone back to full-time teaching at the Catholic school in Jackson, Missouri. She teaches the seventh grade.

"Things didn't bother me until the Vietnam Memorial was dedicated. There was something about that on television on November 11. My birthday is on Veterans Day, and I happened to be watching television when they started showing that. I just broke down—just broke down. That had never happened to me. I went into the bedroom, and I started crying. My wife came in and asked what was the matter. I told her, but I couldn't quit crying. I don't know why. It just happened. From that point on when I see the Vietnam Wall or anything like that, I just have to leave. That was quite a few years after the war. I had never had a desire to see the Wall. But last year I went on vacation out in Washington, D.C and I got together with Lt. Puller and Sergeant Leslie. All three of us got to see the Wall together. It was a traumatic experience.

"Lt. Puller was wounded twice in Vietnam. The first time he was wounded we were out on a night patrol. We were walking along and getting ready to set in for the night. It was in a sandy area and dark as could be. There were pine trees all around. There was a Marine in front of Puller, then Puller, and myself. We were nuts-to-butts, so to speak, and that

Marine tripped a booby trap. It blew him up in the air and he landed on an embankment. It knocked Lt. Puller back. I rushed down to the Marine, and he had a broken leg. That was one night we had to call in a nightevac. That was the first night we had ever used strobe lights. We called a chopper in, and we were going to pull in a strobe light. We got the Marine out. That night strikes me. Lt. Puller got a little scratch on his pinkie. I wrote him up with a medical tag for his Purple Heart. It was ironic to think that the next medical tag that was written up on him was a loss of two legs and six fingers. Purple Hearts are earned differently.

"Sometimes I read my diary that I kept in Vietnam. I want to pass it on to my son. As far as the Vietnam War goes, it seems like such a waste. At the time, most of us felt that it was the thing to do. They told us we had to go, and we went and did our jobs. But looking back on it, I don't know why we just didn't pull out. Surely those people were smart enough to know what they were getting themselves into. The military and the advisors just didn't want to lose face. But they could have saved a lot of lives if they had. You hate to admit that it was in vain. I don't know if I will ever admit that to myself. It is in the back of my mind, but I don't know if I will live long enough to admit it.

"There was one incident when I was in the bush around September. We were out on patrol and were getting ready to set up for the night. One Marine came up to me and said he had a terrible headache. I said, 'Well, wait until we set in, and I will give you some aspirins.' I gave him some, but that evening and night he started going into convulsions and making gurgling sounds. When you are set in for the night, you want everything as quiet as possible. The corpsman that was with me and I discussed the situation. We had two choices. We could call a nightevac in and get him out which was dangerous, or we could try to keep him as quiet as possible and get him out the next morning. So we elected to wait until the next morning. The next morning we called a chopper in, and it was a short trip to the hospital. He arrived DOA at the hospital. To this day I don't know why he died. It bothers me to this day. Because of my decision as senior corpsman not to call a chopper in, that guy died. I still stick by my decision because nightevacs are bad news. My decision cost him his life, but it might have saved a lot of lives.

"Other than the Vietnam Wall and seeing all the stuff on television around Veterans Day, I am okay, normal so to speak. I am as normal as anybody is going to be after going through something like that. I've got a great wife and three great kids so you couldn't ask for any more than that."

PART IV
Leaders of Men

EIGHT

Lt. Ray Fulkerson

Hometown: Cape Girardeau, Mo.; Artillery Officer; Second Battalion, First Marines; Khe Sanh, Vietnam; Tour of Duty, May 1968–1969.

My first night in Khe Sanh I slept in a trench. I had a Hershey candy bar in my front pocket. I woke up in the middle of the night with a rat chewing through my pocket, trying to get to the candy bar. That was my first lesson in keeping any kind of food off of myself.

LT. RAY FULKERSON
January 9, 1993

"My acquaintance with the Marine Corps came about by my not being able to complete college in four years. That reclassified me with the draft board. That was not predicated on grades, but it was predicated on having been in a church school and losing six hours of religion which was not transferable at Southeast Missouri State University. So as a result, I was looking for some branch of service that would afford me the opportunity to go ahead with my education. It just so happened that the Marine Corps was the only one that offered the platoon leaders class. I also had another reason. My brother, who is three years older than me, had gone through the platoon leaders class and was at the time serving in Chu Lai, Vietnam.

"I met with the Marine Corps recruiter and signed up in the Marine Corps Reserve and went to the platoon leaders class in the summer between my junior and senior years of college.

"I spent ten weeks in training. I met a friend at platoon leaders class from Baylor University by the name of Mike Dewlen. I returned and completed my senior year of college. I also got married to Sondra Ward during my senior year.

"In the fall of 1967 we went to Quantico, Virginia, to Officer Candidate School. I graduated from OCS in January 1968. I was put in a company with

Mike Dewlen and Mike Patterson. The three of us were sent to Fort Sill, Oklahoma, for artillery training. All three of us were married at the time. After completion of the ten weeks of training, all of us were going to Vietnam. Mike Dewlen made a comment that we should all take a life insurance policy out on one another because odds were that one of us was not going to make it. That didn't sit well with me because it was kind of tempting fate. So we thought better of that and didn't do it.

"I then went to Camp Pendleton, California, for two weeks of training in amphibious warfare. I never saw Mike Patterson or Mike Dewlen from that time on.

"I arrived in Vietnam by way of Okinawa in May 1968. I was immediately assigned to the First Marine Division Artillery and thought that I had escaped the confines of Khe Sanh. Parts of the Third Marine Division were up there. Immediately the artillery battalion was attached to the Third Marine Division, and I received orders to the Second Battalion, First Marines in Khe Sanh. I was attached to Echo Company as a forward observer.

"Before I went to Khe Sanh, I was sent south of Da Nang for weather acclimation. That was the first time that I came under fire. It was in the afternoon. We were located along China Beach at Fu Lock. We began to receive mortar rounds. What amazed me was that it was so much like being back in training at OCS. It was almost being play-acted as you watched the mortar rounds being walked in. Then reality set in, and I realized this wasn't a game. Their forward observer was trying to bracket us and send in a fire for effect. It seemed like minutes, but it took just a few seconds to get that changeover in my mind that now I was really in Vietnam. Fortunately, he wasn't a very good forward observer because most of the rounds that he called in for effect went into the South China Sea.

"I went to Quang Tri. I spent two nights with briefings. I thought back to an incident when I was in Okinawa. All of us lieutenants were in a barracks getting ready to go to Vietnam. We were like a bunch of kids not knowing what to expect. A grunt lieutenant that was on his way home from Vietnam came in, and we wanted to know what the key to success in Vietnam was. He said, 'If you can make it the first 60 days, then your odds of making it in Vietnam are very good.' That stuck in my mind. The next morning I boarded a chopper for Khe Sanh.

"I recall flying at tree-top level. It was the first time tht I had ever done that. I was extremely nervous and scared. I was watching the pilot and co-pilot. They kept giving each other thumbs up and thumbs down, and I thought that we were going to have some kind of mechanical trouble. Again the reality set in that the game was over and that I was going to be extremely fortunate if I were to survive this situation.

"I made my first real blunder when we landed at Khe Sanh. There was a lieutenant colonel on the chopper also. As we landed, the chopper didn't quite set down. He hovered about two or three feet above the ground and lowered the back ram down. When I turned around, everyone was gone, and I was trying to gather up my gear. This lieutenant colonel threw me off the chopper onto the ground and began kicking me across the runway trying to get me to the nearest bunker. Then when we got in the bunker, he politely informed me that I was not Stateside. This was not a scenic tour and that anytime an aircraft landed, artillery came in. Sure enough it did.

"My first night in Khe Sanh I slept in a trench. I had a Hershey candy bar in my front pocket. I woke up in the middle of the night with a rat chewing through my pocket, trying to get to the candy bar. That was my first lesson in keeping any kind of food off of myself.

"I was in Khe Sanh around the airstrip for about two weeks. Then I was sent to Hill 552 just west of Khe Sanh airstrip and Laos. We were an observation post. Hill 689 ran just to the south of us. Hill 689 took about 12 days of tremendous assault and sniper fire. I realized then for the first time that you could be close to the enemy, but not have any contact with the enemy at all. We lost about 40 Marines during that assault. Several of my friends from OCS were involved in that, and we were not over three or four hundred yards away. We didn't receive a single round.

"It was the first time I saw the enemy as a forward observer. I gained a great deal of respect for the enemy during that time because they had tunnels that they were working in. As we put artillery on one side of the hill, they would just run to the other side of the hill. When we would shift the artillery to the other side of the ridge, they would run back to the front side. It was like playing a game of cat and mouse. They were always one step ahead of us.

"We called in an air strike to try and burn them out and they continued to resist. We had an A-6 that came in and got a fix on a .50-caliber machine gun that had been hitting Hill 689. What amazed me was they had another .50-caliber on another hill and they triangled him as he came in and shot his wing off. We lost the aircraft, but the pilot ejected. The wind direction floated him to our side. They had very few weapons, but they had great control over their ability to use them. They seemed to be able to resist the great fire power we had.

"On Hill 552 it was just a matter of being on an observation hilltop. When they would impact rounds out of Laos into the airstrip, we would send directions to return fire.

"Corporal Brazer was in my forward observer team, and Lt. Cpl. Miller was my radio operator. Cpl. Brazer was one of the finest non-commissioned officers I ever met. I had always said, 'Don't wash your utilities' because every fire mission he had was written on his trousers. When he wanted to call a fire mission up, he just turned the calf of his leg over and called one in for the particular target. We became closest during the monsoon season. It was cold and rainy, just miserable. We actually huddled together man-to-man to absorb one another's body heat just to stay warm at night.

"Cpl. Brazer said the best way to handle rats is to put some food on the floor by your rack, and they would leave you alone. He had been there too long. When it would rain, rather than have a poncho thrown over you where you might get a little wet from the leaks in the poncho, he would go out and throw himself in a crater filled with water and sleep all night long. When incoming would come in, he got to the point where he would test it. If he happened to be taking a crap, he made no effort to get up.

"Capt. Egan was the company commander for Echo Company. He was a well-decorated Marine. He was a great combat Marine. He had learned the language. He taught me a lot about respect for the Vietnamese.

"We were on a patrol one day in the north. The Vietnamese were very pro. You didn't have to worry about the Viet Cong. When you went into a village, you didn't have to worry about booby traps. We made a tour through a village, and they were having some kind of celebration. We had to eat with them. I have a real sensitive stomach to things. Capt. Egan wanted me to eat with him. I didn't know the custom, but he did. I didn't know the custom was that if you ever emptied your plate that you needed more. My only guess was to get what I was eating down so I wouldn't throw it up and embarrass the captain. The village chief brought out some Vietnamese beer, Tiger Paw. It was warm. After getting the second plate down, Capt. Eagan sensed that I was having a hard time getting it all down. He leaned over and whispered that if I would just leave a little on my plate they would quit bringing the food.

"We had an incident at a road sweep in Khe Sanh. We went on a foot patrol about 3 A.M. to clear the road in front of the airstrip. About 5 in the morning we took a break. The sun was just coming up. The lieutenant in charge of the patrol had us fall out and take security positions. I was totally exhausted. I was lying in the road. The staff sergeant that had been assigned to me as a radio operator came over and said, 'Lieutenant, I don't want to tell you what to do but where you are sitting is a registration point for the NVA.' So I followed him to the other side of a B-52 crater. About the time that I sat down, 12 to 15 rounds came in the exact spot where I had been sitting. The lieutenant that was in charge gave orders to move out and start moving back toward the airstrip. That was the first time that I experienced the rounds on us without hearing the whistle. Lt. Cpl. Miller had the PRC-25 [portable radio]. He and I were running as fast as we could down the radio. We heard a shot, and we knew that it was on us. We both hit the deck and landed by a tree that was about two feet in diameter. Shrapnel was impacting on the left side of us. L/CPL Miller was on my right, and

I saw the concussion pick his body up and slam it back down to the ground. Before I could get my senses to ask him if he was all right, I looked up and he was about 25 yards down the road running like hell.

"We were at the point of evacuating Khe Sanh. Our mission was to evaluate Khe Sanh and all the surrounding hills and not let the enemy know it or leave anything that the enemy could use. So we were running truck convoys out of the area each morning. Sometimes we would have to run foot patrols before the convoys started, to make sure there were no mines. Other times, we would have to ride shotgun. One time we were on our way back to Khe Sanh with the convoy. There was a stretch of road that ran about a half mile parallel to the airstrip. To the left of the road were land mines put in by Marines and South Vietnamese in case of an assault or siege. Then to the right was the airstrip itself. At the end of the airstrip where the road began, we had what was called 'the run.' The run reminded me of a shooting gallery at a circus. As the ducks went across in front of you, you shot your rifle at them. If you knocked them down, you got so many points. The truck drivers would stop at the end of the road. One truck would start down the end of the road. Then about 200 yards down they would send another six-by. The road had been bombed and had a lot of holes in it. Once they started they couldn't stop because there were mines on both sides of the road. The trucks couldn't go backward because other trucks had already been dispatched. Since the NVA knew that, they would wait until the convoys got going and then they would call their forward observers up and start firing. All we could do was run as hard as we could for it. I can remember seeing artillery rounds hitting to my left. The closest I ever came to getting hit was a round impacted to my left. We all hit the deck in the six-by which had a metal bed on the side of it. I could hear the shrapnel hit the sides of the truck bed. As soon as we got where we could clear the road, we would jump off the truck and get in a hole or trench or anything that would give us cover.

"We moved back out to Hill 552. We had evacuated all night long. The last thing that I remember about Khe Sanh was that we woke up and the NVA had waited until the last truck had left and they blew it away. It was symbolic. They were telling us that they had had control of the situation all along. They did know when we were leaving. At that point they never fired another round. After the last truck was hit, the NVA transferred their weapons to the observation hills which they had never done before. Hotel Company was between us and the airstrip, and Gulf Company was on Hill 689. Helicopters came in and got the two companies off. Then we were the last company to leave. The NVA started moving their arty to the base of our hill. I can't understand why they did because we were completely exposed. But shortly after that the helicopters came in and evacuated us. We were flown into Con Thien.

"I had been in Khe Sanh for about three months. I had a great admiration for the grunts [infantrymen]. First of all, the living conditions were horrible. When we were on Hill 552, we didn't even have water to shave in. We took what water we had in one helmet, and we passed it around for everyone to shave in. All the water we would receive was what was helilifted in. They would drop a bladder of water on the side of the hill. Sometimes it would stay and other times it would roll all the way to the bottom of the hill. If it rolled down the hill, we would have to shoot it full of holes so the NVA didn't get it. Basically we had enough water to wet our lips. We were on two C-rations a day. We were under attack, had little food and no water to speak of. We bathed only every six weeks. It was so cold during the monsoon season that we had to sleep and cuddle to stay warm. Yet the relationship between the black and white Marines in the field and the relationship between the officers and enlisted men was unbelievable. We had tremendous morale.

"We were at Dong Ha just south of the DMZ. We pulled an operation in the DMZ looking for expected landing zones for NVA. That was the first experience that I had with the ARC light, or B-52 bombing raid operations. We were to fly in just west of Con Thien. We were the closest to North Vietnam. We were separated by a river that was about a hundred feet wide. We got on line. To our right there were Hotel, Gulf, and Fox companies — we swept the area. The division from the B-52s was unbelievable. A few NVA surrendered because the ARC lights had messed their minds up so badly. I always felt that our company was being watched over. That particular day mortars were coming in and all the other companies took casualties. We had none. We were under the command of Lt. Col. Poindexter. I didn't think that he was as aggressive as he should have been. His executive officer was Maj. Wright who had gone to Louisiana State University and had played football there. He was one of the finest officers that I ever saw. He was always concerned about the troops, always on the radio, always in command, always knowing what was going on. I remember the day we landed in the LZ it was extremely hot. The temperature that day had gotten up to 125 degrees. A lot of the men started falling out. Marines started drinking water out of the craters formed by the arc lights and got sick. Col. Poindexter was on the side of one of the craters with the rest of us, looking scared, while Maj. Wright was on top of the crater directing forces. We swept through. It took us about eight hours to sweep about 3,000 meters. We were supposed to be picked up by nightfall by choppers. As Marines will be, we were in one area for about an hour waiting for choppers. One of the Marines decided he wanted to go down in history as having been in North Vietnam so he swam the river, touched the North Vietnam shore, and swam back. His photo was taken on the shore. The choppers came in and again they were CH-46s. They lined up just parallel to the river that separated North and South Vietnam. There were six of them. The first two were filled up. It was questionable whether I was to get on the third or fourth chopper, but I ended up being the last one on the third chopper. We hadn't been in the air but a few seconds when an explosion ripped through the air. The fourth chopper had set down on a land-detonated mine. The NVA set it off. They had been watching us all the time. They waited till the chopper was full before they set it off. Everyone in the chopper was burned alive. We were out, but about half of the battalion was left at the DMZ. We flew to Con Thien. I never was so glad to get out of a place in my entire life after seing a chopper blown up right behind us. As soon as we landed, Capt. Woods from Gulf Company said we had to go back after them. I had a lot of mixed emotions about that. I didn't want to go. As it turned out, there was another officer there who overruled him. The rest of the battalion stayed at the DMZ that night. The next morning the tank battalion went up and got them out of the area.

"We rotated back south of Da Nang. We got the word that things were going to wind down. About one or two miles south of Da Nang around Christmas time, I got promoted into the Fire Direction Center as opposed to being a forward observer for infantry company. Any time forward observers called in a fire mission in a village area or the leper colony, permission for the fire mission was always denied. The VC knew that so they would hit us and then retreat to the villages. We sustained a lot of casualties, a lot more than we did up north from personnel mines and sniping. Even with the better living conditions of hot meals, hootches to live in where it was dry, refrigerators with cold beer and soda, this type of situation, the constant frustration of having someone hit without being able to do anything about it caused morale to go down tremendously. The blacks and the whites began to have trouble. The closeness of troops disappeared. When blacks met back and forth on truck convoys, they would use the symbol of black power with each other. You never saw that up north. I also noticed that a lot of blacks started refusing to go on patrols—some because their skin was unable to handle the climate.

"Because of all the frustration, there was a second lieutenant as a forward observer who called in a fire mission. As soon as I heard the coordinates, I knew he was going to be denied because the location was in the leper colony. They would give you clearance if you saw rockets fired because they didn't want the airbase hit. The next fire mission that came from the second lieutenant was with the same coordinates, but this time he reported rockets. I guess it was the Marine's intuition on how to get a job done because when he called in for a fire for effect he reported that he was walking them down main street. It was a German-sponsored leper colony. It almost caused an investigation by the top brass, but we had very little trouble out of that village from that time on.

"They used to pay the Vietnamese children for bringing in duds. We had a little Vietnamese boy come up with a dud round. The guards had been given so much money to pay them when they brought them in. I heard an explosion near the gate and I ran down there. This round had gone off and blew this little boy's arm off from the elbow. He was standing there with his arm off, and this Marine guard had caught one piece of shrapnel in his chest. You could see it just below the skin. We called a medevac. They were treating the little boy and put him on a stretcher. The corpsman told the Marine that he needed to go with him to get his own wound treated. We left the area and that night we found out that the Marine had died. He went into shock. He actually scared himself to death. He died from nothing but shock.

"Several big operations took place on the base while I was there. I was fortunate to direct them from the operations center. We used the *New Jersey* on several of those operations. A junior lieutenant from Gulf Company was involved in one of the operations. It was Chesty Puller's son. I was in the fire mission control center, and they were out on an operation. They were to make a sweep through the village and he stepped on a 105 round that had been triggered as an anti-personnel mine. He sustained major injuries. He had both legs and several fingers on both hands blown off. I was monitoring the net when Lt. Puller got hit. Maj. Wright stuck one hand in each stump and squeezed off the artery in Puller's legs so that he would not bleed to death.

"There was a Maj. Horn who was 180 degrees the other way. I will never forget one night we got hit by rockets. We had a tower there, and we had a railing going up to the tower. The railing was made out of the bedding that was used on the airstrip. The engineers used strips of this to make the railing. When we received mortars that night, I got on the ground and stayed till it was over. We only got about six rockets. Our motor pool got hit. I ran down to see if anyone got hit, then I ran back up toward the tower. I remember Maj. Horn ran up the tower, and I wanted to see what he wanted me to do. Maj. Horn had cut his hand on the rail. He put himself in for the Purple Heart. I thought there was something wrong with that. What he did was stupid to begin with, then to put himself in for a Purple Heart was ridiculous.

"All Maj. Horn could think about was sending the first sergeant out of country to Thailand. He would have him catch a flight once a week to get skin flicks. Maj. Horn was obsessed with sex. I will never forget one day I was supposed to go wake him up, and I caught him masturbating. He never did know that I was there. As soon as I saw what was occurring, I made a quiet exit. I had no respect for him at all.

"We had one interesting pastime in the Da Nang area. It was common to watch the freedom bird come in each night to pick up troops returning to the States. Everyone knew which one was the freedom bird because the tail of the plane was gold. We would all go and wait for the bird to come in. The shorter we got, the more we did it.

"Because of the two weeks of training I had at Camp Pendleton, I got assigned to the executive officer of the first armored Amphibious Company—18 guns and three batteries. To my knowledge there is only one unit per division. I didn't even know they existed. The table of organization included a major with an amphibious MOS [military occupational specialty] a captain with an artillery MOS who was an executive officer, and the platoon commanders who were all amphibious MOSs.

"The lifestyle in that unit was just the opposite of that at Khe Sanh. In Da Nang itself we were with a tank battalion. It was hard to digest the difference in styles. The first night was a rubdown and a steam bath. I went to the White Elephant Officer's Club. The officers were in their dress white uniforms. Something wasn't fair about this. I can recall being told that we would get one or two sodas a day. When we were at Khe Sanh if we got one or two sodas a month, we felt fortunate. It seemed that our rations were being used by the people in the back. I think there was a difference in the way people had to serve in Vietnam. I always felt that I cheated the service that last six months because life was so good.

"We were stationed right on the hilltop where the ammunition dump was for the first Marine Division. The NVA and Viet Cong had tried everything they could for years to set that ammo dump off. Whoever engineered the building of the dump had done an excellent job because they couldn't get to it. They constantly tried to hit it with rockets and mortars. One little old Vietnamese man innocently caught the ammo dump on fire. That was the biggest loss that they incurred during the Vietnam War. We were at least 2,000 meters from the dump itself, and the explosions were throwing 500-pound bombs that far. The concussion waves were so strong that we could see them in the air. When the waves would hit a metal building, they would explode it. Things finally go so bad that they evacuated us 2,000 meters out until it burned out.

"The last incident that I had was when I was shipping out. I got my orders to go to the airstrip and check in. We were to have a good meal, get a good night's sleep, report in the next morning, and wait for our flight. I checked in. We had a good meal, a movie, cleaned up, slept well, and got up the next morning. We were in this large metal building where they were working everyone's orders. All of a sudden there was shrapnel coming through the roof. The thought that went through my mind, and I am sure everyone else's, was that after 13 months it cannot end this way. Everybody was trying to find a table or something to get under to protect themselves. What had happened was that another ammo dump had caught on fire and shells were impacting and throwing the shrapnel across the area where we were. To add insult to injury, after we did get our orders, we went over to the airstrip about 12 o'clock and we waited until about 6 o'clock that evening because our freedom bird had mechanical problems in Okinawa. When it came in, I thought back.

"I could remember when I first came to Da Nang and I had my clean utilities on and watched these Marines that were leaving. They were worn out, tired, and they had aged a lot. They looked very old to me when I came into the country. When I got back on the aircraft, I realized that I was one of those aged persons. I always thought that I would think that now it's your turn, but I had a great deal of sympathy for those new recruits coming in.

"Surprisingly everyone was real quiet on the aircraft. You could almost hear a pin drop on the aircraft. We taxied down the airstrip and as the plane gained altitude, no one said anything, but everyone was staring out the window. I don't know what everyone else was sensing, but I kept fearing that some VC or NVA was going to fire a 50-caliber round and hit the plane. Even when we were over the South China Sea I just wanted the aircraft to get farther away from Vietnam. I looked around and to my surprise everyone was giving Vietnam the finger.

"Then we went to Okinawa. I wanted to get home quickly. But things were winding down in Nam, and there were very few officers coming into country. They needed someone to check in the equipment of each Marine who was going from Okinawa back to the States. Since I was a junior officer on the plane, myself and two other officers were assigned the job. We had to check in the 782 gear. I never saw the reasoning behind it, but we had to take the Marines that were in country and check what meager 782 gear they had left. If they didn't have a Marine officer sign off on the gear, even though they had lost it in combat, they had to pay for it out of their own pockets. After one day of seeing what was going on, I signed off on everybody's gear. A captain noticed what I was doing and commented on it. I wasn't disrespectful about it, but I let him know that I wasn't a real happy person being in Okinawa myself and that I wanted to go home. We were on the next flight.

"We landed at El Toro, California and got the red carpet treatment. The Marine Corps band welcoming ceremony was outstanding. They took care of the accommodations to get us to Los Angeles International. We purchased our tickets and went our separate ways.

"My wife and I were transferred to Camp Lejeune, North Carolina. We had our first child while I was stationed there. The service took care of the medical expenses for us. I had thought about a career in the service. The thing that turned me off was the demonstrations that were going on in Washington, D.C. Every weekend at Camp Lejeune we would go on what we called the hardening of the vehicles. Every Wednesday we would get word that there was going to be a big demonstration in Washington, D.C. So we would have to get a battalion of six-bys with hardened screens over the windows and all kinds of gear put together. We had to put the battalion on alert. No one could leave the battalion area. We would wait all night long to go to Washington to be spit at or called names. At that time there was a lot of racial tension going on. One white Marine was hung. The racial tension coupled with the demonstrations changed my mind. There is something wrong when you have to defend your country and then take that kind of verbal abuse. It was too much for me, and I decided that I wanted out. So I took my out.

"I came back to Cape Girardeau. I always had tremendous family support. I don't think that those of us from southeast Missouri and southern Illinois saw the kind of abuse that the veterans suffered. I guess the thing that bothers me about Vietnam is that I never felt that I did what I could have done in Vietnam. I never sensed, like some people, that we lost, because I saw too many heroic things happen. I saw too many times that, when it came down to it, we kicked their ass. We had it together. The policies, such as you can't fire in the village because it's not a free fire zone, don't expand the war, we will just wear them down, didn't work. They were better at that than we were. It upsets me when I hear we lost the war. We as a country lost the war, but we kicked ass when we wanted to."

Ray Fulkerson sat silently for a moment. He pulled the sleeves of his sweatshirt up slightly off his wrists. Then he reached into an envelope and pulled out a copy of a magazine story and handed it to me. His face was solemn, "I made a comment earlier on about Mike Dewlen and getting our life insurance policies together. He was killed in Vietnam. He was in Khe Sanh on a hilltop, too."

The story, from *Reader's Digest,* was entitled "To Our Fallen Son." It was written by Al Dewlen, Mike's father, and published in March 1969. Dewlen tells the story of the traumatic experience of receiving the news about his son being killed in action, and of the memories that rushed through his mind of Mike's childhood.

Dewlen explains the agony of the endless days of waiting for the return of his son's body, and the funeral ceremony as Mike had requested. Then, in what Dewlen refers to as "the final report card," he explains the circumstances of his son's final stand against an overwhelming enemy. Mike and 70 other Marines, along with the support of six 105 recoilless rifles, were isolated in a sea of grass on a hill near the Laotian border. They were attacked during the night by a battalion of NVA. Hailed by grenades and mortar fire, the NVA penetrated the lines. Mike ran from the command center, down the slope, and rallied his men. With five other Marines, they jumped directly into the line of fire, and fought savagely for over 30 minutes. During the hand-to-hand combat, Mike was cut down by a burst

Ray and Sondra Fulkerson

of fire from an AK-47. The other four Marines were killed also. However, their efforts delayed the enemy long enough for the 105s to get on line and repeal the attack. Mike was posthumously decorated for his heroism.

"I didn't know it until around Christmas when I got a letter from my wife," explained Ray. "She said, 'Isn't it terrible about Mike?' but she didn't elaborate on it. She said that she talked with his wife and that she was doing okay. Two weeks later I received a letter that had been mailed a month before telling me that he had been killed. Mike was an only child."

I handed the story back to Ray. He stuffed the photocopy back into the envelope. "Today I still have problems with unexpected loud noises. I find my finger flexing a few inches before I gain control. I never have been to the Vietnam Wall, but I have been to the Moving Wall and have participated in the programs at that wall. Everyone has to treat it differently. They all have been exposed to different things and think differently, but I did mine out of respect for those who died."

About a month after I interviewed Ray, I received a letter from his wife. She sent a photo that I had requested, a copy of the story from *Reader's Digest*, and a note. Ray had located Mike's father and had given him a call. They talked for a long time and had a wonderful conversation. "I should have done that twenty years ago," Ray said later.

NINE

Capt. Paul Ebaugh, Jr.

Hometown: Cape Girardeau, Mo.; Company Commander; Kilo Company, Third Battalion, Fifth Marines; An Hoa, Vietnam; Tour of Duty, December 1968–December 1969.

> *When the Moving Wall came in here and the media needed someone to interview, they picked a bunch of guys with long beards, old dirty combat boots, camouflage utilities, and a thousand pins sticking all over them. Some had on T-shirts that read, "Jane Fonda's a traitor bitch." That is how Vietnam veterans are portrayed or the way the media wants to portray them. Wherever that wall goes, these guys follow it. They are always on television. They don't represent me or you or most of the other Vietnam veterans. They don't represent anybody but a bunch of losers.*
>
> PAUL EBAUGH, JR.
> March 13, 1993

I slammed the car door and walked briskly toward the front door of Paul Ebaugh's home on Ricardo Driver in Cape Girardeau. I reached up to knock and the door flew open. A huge man dressed in a T-shirt and shorts grinned and said, "Come on in."

I stepped inside and was met by a frisky cocker spaniel pup. "Come on, stop that," the man said as he picked up the pup and took him to another room. Shortly he returned and again smiled widely displaying a mouth full of white sparkling teeth, "Paul Ebaugh, glad to meet you."

"Harry Spiller, glad to meet you too."

"Guess I am dressed comfortable, huh?" he said in a chuckling voice.

"Sure," I replied as I thought of the zero temperature outside.

We walked into the basement of Paul's home and into a den. I took

Capt. Paul Ebaugh, Jr.

a seat on the couch. Directly in front of me was a large window for viewing a sea of trees covering the hills at the back of his home. I watched as the wind whipped the bare limbs of the trees.

Paul left the room and shortly returned with a box of papers and photos. "Thought you might be interested in taking a look at some of these," he said as he plopped down in the chair across from me. He sat for a moment, adjusted his glasses, then began to tell his story.

"I have a strictly middle-class background. I went to school in Cape, attended Cape Central, played in a lot of sports, and got a football scholarship to Southeast Missouri. I did well in football and set a few records in track. I was considered a goody two-shoes. I didn't smoke or drink in high school or college. I always like to think of myself as someone who went against the grain. All the guys in college were finding ways to get out of going into the service so they would not have to go to Vietnam. The more I heard that, the more I decided I wasn't going to do that.

"In 1966, things were getting hot in Vietnam and I went to see the recruiter in Cape. I joined the PLC [Platoon Leader's Class] program. Ray Fulkerson and I went through the program together. We were the only two guys from Southeast Missouri State University. We went ten weeks in the summer and then finished our senior year. In 1967, we went to OCS.

"By the time we were completing basic school, officers in Vietnam were rapidly getting wiped out. We all knew we would be getting orders for Nam as soon as we completed the training. To my surprise when the orders came out, ten other guys and I got orders to Camp Lejeune. I couldn't believe it. I went to Third Battalion, Eighth Marines to go on a Med cruise. I was a platoon commander and given a platoon of about 60 Vietnam veterans as a platoon. They had Purple Hearts, Silver Stars, Bronze Stars. Here I was with my Shirley Highway Ribbon. That's the National Defense Medal. We named it that in OCS. The ribbon is red with the yellow strip in the middle. The Shirley Highway is the highway that runs from Quantico to Washington, D.C. Washington, D.C. is where all the girls are. After 30 days, we earned the ribbon. We liked to think that after the 30 days all we did was travel Shirley Highway to D.C. to find the girls.

"Anyway, I had my Shirley Highway Ribbon and a bunch of Vietnam vets who were real impressed. We got to the Med and started maneuvers. I was supposed to get these guys to assault these beaches and hills while hollering, 'Bang.' It was a real tough experience for a brand new lieutenant.

"When we got back from the Med cruise, a group of us who were real close alphabetically got together and called the monitor in Washington. We found out that we were all going to Vietnam and should be there by December 1. By then the casualty reports were coming in and we knew that they were seriously killing lieutenants. We were real scared. Sure enough I was in Vietnam by December 1.

A 1969 photograph taken west of An Hoa. To the left are Bill Riggs and Paul Ebaugh, Jr. The other two men are unidentified.

1992 photograph of Bill Riggs (left) and Paul Ebaugh, Jr.

"When I reported to my company, Bill Riggs was the company commander. The first thing he said to me was, 'What is your date of rank? You may be the company commander.' We were both first lieutenants. There were a couple of months separating our dates of rank. Bill remained company commander, and I was the executive officer/second platoon commander. We never had enough officers, we never had enough sergeants, and we never had enough men.

"The very first thing they did was make me the pay officer. It was just at the end of operation Mead River. The operation was a meat grinder for our company. I went to Da Nang to the hospital to pay the guys from our outfit and that's when I got my first wake-up all. All these kids had their legs shot off. There were just bunches and bunches of them that were in bad shape. I reported back, and I was immediately sent out to my platoon. There was me and 11 guys in my platoon. It was about 30 minutes before dark. I was introduced to the platoon sergeant, and I asked to take a quick look at the lines before dark.

"We had two fighting holes and a listening post. That's all we had. We were part of a battalion perimeter, and it was about the size of a company perimeter because we were so short of men. I went back to the platoon command post which was a platoon sergeant, myself, a radioman, and a corpsman. We had two guys in each hole and three guys in a observation post.

"As soon as it got dark, not more than an hour later, I heard the machine gun hammering. I jumped up and I couldn't find my .45. I was scrambling all over the place. Finally I got out there. One of the guys on the machine gun had a starlight scope and he had seen some movement. He had started looking around the area and somehow he got turned around and got off on his direction. He saw some movement and opened up on his own LP. He killed two of his best buddies. That was my first experience with a fire fight in Nam.

"Later that night we got back to the CP which was a poncho held up by a couple of sticks and we were lying under them. At this point, I had only been introduced to my platoon sergeant and shaken his hand. We were lying there whispering to each other.

'Where you from?' he whispered.

'I'm from Missouri,' I said.

'Aw, is that right? What part of Missouri?'

'Southeast Missouri,' I answered.

'Where at in Southeast Missouri?' he whispered.

'A little town called Cape Girardeau,' I whispered back.

'Where in Cape Girardeau?' he asked.

'I live on Allendale Street,' I said.

'I live on Good Hope Street. We're only five blocks from each other.'

"I couldn't believe it. On February 22, 1969, he got killed. He was my platoon sergeant and one of the finest guys that I have ever known. He helped me and saved me an awful lot of times. He had three Purple Hearts and could have gone home, but he didn't. He was a career Marine. You won't find him listed around here as local because he moved to St. Louis right before he went into the Marine Corps. He went to junior high and a couple of years of high school here and was actually from Cape. To my discredit when I came back, I could never find it in my heart to go see his mother. Something that I have always regretted that I never had the courage to do. I did write a letter about him to the editor of the paper."

The letter was published in the *Southeast Missourian* on May 29, 1969. In part, this was what Paul wrote:

MARINE CORPS LIEUTENANT FROM CAPE GIRARDEAU TELLS OF VIETNAM DUTY WITH SGT. ERVIN EMRICK

A Marine Corps officer from Cape Girardeau, in a letter to *The Missourian* today, told of serving with Sgt. Ervin J. Emrick, Jr. in Vietnam before the sergeant, also of Cape Girardeau, was killed in action May 11.

"Sgt. Emrick was the finest Marine I have ever known," First Lt. Paul L. Ebaugh, Jr., wrote.

Lt. Ebaugh, son of Mr. and Mrs. Paul L. Ebaugh, 2550 Allendale, is executive officer and a platoon leader in the company in which Sgt. Emrick served.

The lieutenant, who had nothing but praise for Sgt. Emrick, said he first met the sergeant on last Dec. 5 near the An Hoa combat base when Lt. Ebaugh joined the platoon.

"During the next three months, I was to spend every minute of every day with my platoon and Sgt. Emrick was to be with me each of those minutes. From the time I met him he began to teach me all he had learned.

"As he taught me, I learned that it was not only for me, but out of a deep concern for the people we would both lead. As time passed he became a platoon commander in another platoon in the company. He stayed with his platoon longer than he had to and passed up opportunities to come to the rear. He was wounded, made staff sergeant and still refused to leave his people."

Lt. Ebaugh briefly described the action in which the platoon sergeant lost his life.

"Two days ago, Sgt. Emrick was killed by an NVA rifleman as he was retrieving his dead and wounded from a hopelessly exposed rice paddy where they had been ambushed seconds before.

"Sgt. Emrick was the finest Marine I have ever known. And he was a friend. He was an individual who, through his own actions and deeds, gained the complete and total respect and confidence of those of us who knew him."

Capt. Paul Ebaugh, Jr. 115

Sgt. Emrick, 29 years old, had been in the Marine Corps more than ten years and was on his third tour of duty in Vietnam when he was killed.

He is the son of Mrs. Thelma Sides, 1520 Good Hope.

"On the first operation I was on, we were making sweeps and going through the villages. The kids were friendly as hell. Just at the edge of one of the villages we stopped and sat down. There were kids everywhere. Papasans and and mamasans were everywhere.

"I sat down and put my head back to rest on the ground. As I leaned back, my hand went clear through the ground. It was a booby trap—a grenade.

"They had dug a hole, stuck the grenade in the side of the hole, run a string across the top, put a piece of cardboard across the top, and covered it with dirt. So when you stepped on it you would go down through the cardboard, step on the string, and the grenade would blow your leg off.

"It had been raining quite a bit when I went through it and the cardboard was not structural. My hand was not as big as my foot so instead of hitting the string my hand went right through the cardboard and missed the string. I had enough sense not to move. The platoon sergeant ran over. The cardboard had folded up, and you could see the grenade. All that was holding the pin in the grenade was the string. The pin was just barely hanging. I got my hand out and looked up. There were no papasans, no mamasans, and no kids.

"It's interesting. Even when I was in the Combined Action Program, I got access to all kinds of intelligence. I was stationed at the DIOCC (District Intelligence Operations Coordinations Center) which was an Army intelligence sort of thing. We were running schools all around the area for Marines telling them of the terrorist training that children were learning in order to kill Marines. 'They are not going to come over to you and hand you a grenade. They are going to blow both themselves and you up,' we told them. In spite of that, you could not keep them from giving, taking care of, hugging, and squeezing the children. You just couldn't do it. The image of the killers, rapists, and murderers that the media profiled of troops, and especially young Marines, just isn't true.

"I was in the infantry for six months and in the field for eleven months and I didn't see any of that stuff. We burnt some villages down, but they were villages where people were doing bad things to us. We would burn places where their rice or weapons were stashed. I never saw any of those acts done to those people like Oliver Stone portrayed in his movies. Those movies enraged me more than anything because I thought they were a composite of all the very worst things that may have happened over there.

"We spent about two or three months on Operation Tailer Common in which we went way out toward the Laotian border. We were leapfrogging with all the fire bases. And at some point out there we got a big influx of second lieutenants. That meant we now had platoon leaders and executive officers for all the companies. Then orders came from the battalion that all executive officers were to go to the rear. So that was what I did. It made me angry because they were going to send us to the rear and all the troops were going out into the bush. It was right at the end of the operation when they sent us in. After a few days, the company followed us in. It was demeaning for officers who didn't get to go on the operation.

"A few days passed and they were going to send my company on a small operation south of Da Nang in the area of Gonhoi Island. I couldn't go because of the orders from the battalion. That night we got overrun. I never got close enough to any of them to have hand-to-hand combat, but I got closer to them than I ever wanted to get. Five pallets of 105 rounds went up. I was standing by an amtrac. The guy in the amtrac had his head and shoulder out of the amtrac, and the explosion decapitated him. It also blew off my radioman's arm. It was a hell of a night. We killed a bunch of them, and they killed a bunch of us. The next morning the company came back in from Gonhoi Island with their tails between their legs. We had been in a fight all night, and they hadn't fired a shot. I didn't feel so bad about staying behind after that.

"There were bad officers just like there were bad troops. The one thing that the troops wanted to know was if you were interested in them. If you were interested in taking care of them, they would take good care of you. When you get there, they are very stand-offish. They talk about the officer that was there before. How great the guy was, and now you're going to replace him—that kind of attitude. At some point in time, they figure you're not there to get a medal or notoriety. All they want to know is that you're going to get them their chow and that you're not going to throw them into a fire fight where they are all going to get killed just so you can prove some point. When they have decided that you're on their side, which I think 90 percent of the officers are, they are going to be with you.

"At some point my troops decided that I cared about them. I found that out the day I went out to take a shit and they sent two guys with me. Up until then they didn't care whether I got killed or not. That was just a fact of life.

"There were some guys who got fragged. They weren't just officers, some were sergeants. You can't tell where a grenade came from. At night, you have the probes going on. It would be real easy to lob a grenade. The first sergeant in our company got fragged in his bunk back at battalion at An Hoa the week before I got there. He was killed. Those things happen.

"The troops used to get these Swinger Polaroid cameras sent to them all the time. They were the little cameras that you could buy for $19.95. These Marines were so young. They would load themselves up with weapons and then get some charcoal or ballpoint pens and pencil in mustaches. Then take pictures to send home. Here they were in the bush. I mean seriously in the bush — in the middle of the shit — and they were dressing themselves up to look more macho. That's how young they were and how childlike some of them were.

"It's hard to tell some of this stuff because it loses its impact if you haven't been there. To read about something that someone said doesn't lend the same weight that it has in your heart. For instance, it was Christmas Eve. We were a long way out, and we were losing a few people continuously. We didn't have any contact with the main units out there. You have this vision of combat in Vietnam as one being in constant fights. But most of the time it is fast. A hit on a patrol and they are gone. At any rate on Christmas Eve, I got down in this hole with four other guys. We got together, and we whispered "Silent Night." To this day I still can't talk about it or sing it without thinking about them. The guys in that hole never made it. That's hard for someone who wasn't there to know what that was like.

"About ten years ago there was a tornado in Marion, Illinois. There were ten people killed. I was at a dinner party that night with a bunch of people, and none of them had been to Vietnam. These people were talking about how horrible that experience was for the people that lived around those who were killed. How violent that was and how the people involved in it would never be the same knowing their neighbors were killed. How difficult that was going to be for them to have to carry that around for the rest of their lives.

"Yet, those 18- and 19-year-old kids were not given the same benefit. They sat there in their ambush positions so scared they were shitting on themselves. They went through all that trauma. They came back to the States, and they were treated as if what they did was nothing. They were treated as if they should just walk away from that experience and leave it behind. I could never understand that.

"I am extremely offended at the way American troops are portrayed in the United States both by Hollywood and the media. When the Moving Wall came to Cape Girardeau, Ray Fulkerson and myself were both involved in the ceremony. A couple other guys that are now attorneys were involved. They gave a speech. There are a zillon guys that went to Vietnam. I work for a construction outfit, and you do whatever you do. But, when the Moving Wall came in here and the media needed someone to interview, they picked a bunch of guys with long beards, old dirty combat boots, camouflage utilities, a thousand pins sticking all over them. Some had on T-shirts that read, 'Jane Fonda's a traitor bitch.' That is how Vietnam veterans are portrayed or the way the media wants to portray them. Wherever that wall goes, these guys follow it. They are always on television. They don't represent me or you or most of the other Vietnam veterans. They don't represent anybody but a bunch of losers.

"There was a lot of talk about drugs being done over there. I think there was in the rear. But in the field, there was strict discipline about doing drugs and about sleep. The troops were very good about enforcing it themselves. I never had one single incident where guys were using dope.

"The most frustrating thing to deal with was the booby traps. We were continuously having guys get their legs blown off. There were a lot of casualties from these booby traps, but you never saw the enemy.

"When these first kids got killed, I made the same mistake that a lot of other lieutenants made. I wrote personal letters to the parents. That was a terrible mistake. When you write letters to them, you then get letters back from the parents. They are not satisfied with what you give them. They want more than you can give them."

Paul received this letter from a mother in Kentucky:

Louisa, KY
Feb. 24, 1969

Dear Sir,

During times such as we are going through, after losing our son in Vietnam, it was reassuring to hear from one who knew, or who at least spent some time with Larry. I may be asking something of a near impossibility, but if you were to know of someone who knew Larry personally, I would love to have them write to me. It is comforting in no small measure to hear from someone who could tell us about Larry. It is difficult for us to assure ourselves concerning the death of our son and we know that it is difficult for those who were there to speak of it but to know of someone who was near Larry and just to write to us and let us know is more assurance. I realize that this war is terrible and that you boys are going through a lot for us, but losing a son in the war is a loss that can never be repaid, but only to know that he did not die needlessly.

Feel free to write me any time as I appreciate any letters that would tell me anything of my son.

"After about six or seven letters, I quit writing them. It still burns a hole in my gut. There are times still today that I cry about it and hurt inside. These guys would be with their children right now or with their wives.

"I had originally decided that I was going to extend my tour for a couple of months. I was the company commander, and I really enjoyed it. Of all the things I have done in my life, that had to be the best job there is. I was going to extend, but I was replaced by a captain that came in. I didn't extend. My parents thought I was going to be home in January because I told them I was extending. I got out of Nam as I was originally supposed to and arrived in Okinawa on December 23. There was one bird left going back to the States, and I wasn't on it. I wanted to come home for Christmas, but I knew I wasn't going to make it. I went downtown that night and got drunk. I was feeling low. I was in a bar, and I ran across a Sgt. Thompson who had been my platoon sergeant in the Med. We were drinking, and I asked him what he did. He said he was the flight manifest officer for all the commercial flights going in and out of Okinawa. I told him how I wanted to go home and all that. He said, 'Don't worry about it. I will get you on a flight.' I thought, yeah I have heard that shit before. About three in the morning, I went back to the Bachelor Officer Quarters and crashed. About four in the morning some enlisted guy came to the room and said, 'You're on the next flight out. You'd better get your shit together and get down to flight operations.' I couldn't believe it. I never turned in any of the gear that I had brought back from Nam. I just grabbed my gear and hauled ass. They flew me to El Toro. It was Christmas Eve. I caught a flight from there and flew into St. Louis. Mom and Dad still didn't know I was coming. At St. Louis there was no flight. I couldn't catch a bus home so I got a cab to take me to I-270 and I-55 and hitchhiked the rest of the way home. It was just getting dark when I pulled into the driveway. It must have been ten degrees outside and my Mom was out back barbecuing. That's how I got home.

"It's hard to talk about then without it being in the context of now. I can't think of the troops that were in my company as anything but kids. Most of them were younger than my daughter, and I still have to talk to her about hanging the towel up in the bathroom. She is more mature than most of them. Yet they were good troops. The concept of these guys is that they were politically astute, but they weren't. They had no real concept of politics. Their discussions were about sports and sex. They didn't talk about what was going on in the Senate or what the Kennedys were doing. I didn't either. Now when the books and the movies come out of there, you have a very sophisticated youngster that understood the political atmosphere at the time. That just wasn't true. They weren't happy to be in the situation they were in. They were scared to death and so was I. They were good troops. They kept their sense of humor. They were courageous.

"I was treated extremely well when I got out. My experience was excellent. I came back here, and Southeast Missouri made a spot for me as a graduate assistant in coaching. After a year, I decided that I didn't want to do that so I ended up in Memphis working for the Chrysler Corporation. I met my wife, Jeanne Lemser, and went crazy over her. We got married six months later. Then we moved back to Cape. We had two children,

Megan and Kara. Kara is in the nursing program at Southeast Missouri, and Megan is a senior at Central. Now I garden a little. I build a few things. I learned to fly. I played a little tennis. I go to church and believe in God. I love my family just like most of the other vets that went to Vietnam. I would like to think that most of us built on that experience rather than had it tear us down. I got on with it, and all the other vets I know got on with it."

TEN

Capt. William H. Walker

Hometown: Cape Girardeau, Mo.; Helicopter Pilot; Da Nang, Vietnam; Tour of Duty, September 1966–November 3, 1966.

Well, turn my damn foot around so it is pointing up.
WILLIAM WALKER
November 3, 1966

Bill met me at the front door dressed in his white and gold Marine Corps sweatshirt. The 50-year-old ex–Marine extended his hand. "Bill Walker," he said with a wide grin.

"Harry Spiller," I said, returning the smile.

We walked into the living room of Bill's home and right off one thing was obvious. This ex–Marine with nine years of service, one tour of duty in Vietnam with hundreds of combat hours as a helicopter pilot, a Purple Heart, and a disability retirement some 22 years ago is living proof of "Once a Marine Always a Marine."

Bill turned on the stereo sitting in the corner of the room. Speakers placed in various parts of the room began to softly echo the notes of the Marine Corps hymn.

He looked at me with a big smile, "Ever hear that before?"

"Sure have," I said.

Bill and I walked to the kitchen table where he had a display of photos, flight logs, and military records. We took a seat and sipped coffee for a couple of minutes. Then Bill began to tell me of his experiences.

"In high school I had a second alternate appointment to the naval academy from Lyndon Johnson. He and Olin Teague were senators at the time. When that didn't work out, I went to Sam Houston. I lived in a dormitory for nine months and found that I didn't belong in college. So I enlisted in the summer of 1961.

William Walker, Pensacola, Florida, 1963.

"I planned to try for the Marine Aviation Cadet Program. I had always dreamed of being a flyer, but that didn't work out either. When I went to boot camp, I expressed early on that I was interested in the aviation program. I was informed that there would be no opportunity for testing during boot camp. I wrote to my Dad and told him that I would have to wait until I got to the fleet to take the tests.

"We had to hike five miles to get to the rifle range at Camp Matthews. My boot pinched my leg during the forced march and within 48 hours I had blood poisoning. They shipped me to the hospital, threw me in bed, and shot me full of penicillin. The very next morning a colonel came to see me. I had no idea what he wanted to see me for. He told me that the next day I was going to take the test for the two-year-college GED and the officer qualification test.

I took the tests with a 103-degree fever. I passed everything except one section of the GED which kept me from getting the two-year-college equivalency. So I didn't qualify for the program.

"Shortly after that I was at battalion headquarters, and this sergeant put me against the wall and wanted to know who I thought I was and how did I have pull with Lyndon Johnson. I had no idea what he was talking about, but I found out later that someone from Johnson's office had made an inquiry as to why I didn't make the program. It was assumed that I had influence, but I didn't.

"The military had just gotten away from the 'P' stamp. It was stamped on your record in big red letters to indicate political influence. It was like sudden death then. I caught hell for a while, but nothing like it would have happened a few years before. I dropped the idea of the Marine Aviation Cadet Program at that point.

"My first sergeant was with Hotel Company, Second Battalion, First Marines as an infantryman. In that unit I was in a platoon that had a terrible platoon commander, but had an excellent platoon sergeant. We rotated to Okinawa. Part of the time we were the float or ready battalion. In late 1962 or early 1963 one of the float battalions went ashore in Vietnam, but was withdrawn after about a week. My first squad leader was a young freckle-faced corporal named David Sommers. Who would have ever guessed that he would retire as Sergeant Major of the Marine Corps.

"My unit went on maneuvers in Thailand. Nothing was ever mentioned about Vietnam. Just prior to our rotation back to the States, the United States almost committed to go to Vietnam. For a month we were on alert and at one point we had everything on six-by trucks and were in formation all day. At one point the aircraft were turning at Kadena Air Base. That died and nothing ever happened.

"About that time, I transferred to battalion headquarters as the legal clerk. We came back to the States and I was headed downhill on my three-year enlistment. By then, I was planning to get out and go back to school. One day I was in the office and the air liaison officer from the 3 shop walked in and said, 'Hey, Walker I hear you want to be a pilot.' I said, 'Well, sir, that was my plan in the beginning, but things fell apart.' 'Why don't you try again?' he said. I did and decided to apply for every enlisted commissioning program I could. I spent a month of my spare time typing applications. The only hang-up at that point would have been the battalion adjutant. He had kept me from being promoted twice. Finally, he had gotten himself into enough trouble that all the company commanders and executive officers in the battalion went to the CO of the battalion on my behalf.

"Thirty days later I was recording a court-martial. I had just opened the rec room we were using for court and turned on the television. It was the day of President Kennedy's funeral. Suddenly, a corporal came in from the headquarters building and told me to go over and see Sgt. Harold. I wondered what I had done now. The caisson had just started to roll on Kennedy's funeral. I walked into headquarters and Sgt. Harold just said, 'Go pack your bags. You have to be in Pensacola in 48 hours.' I had orders to the Marine Aviation Cadet Program. The interesting thing was that there were at least six officers in the battalion that had applied for aviation, some as much as six months earlier. I was a corporal and had gotten the appointment in a month. It upset some people.

"I went to Pensacola just before Thanksgiving in 1963. Due to the fact that I had less than a year on my enlistment, I should have extended for 18 months to finish the program. It didn't dawn on me until I was comissioned, but I never signed an extension.

"I messed up a knee once while I was in pre-flight and thought I was going to get kicked out, but I didn't. I finished pre-flight and went on to VT-1 for primary fixed-wing training. Everyone goes through fixed-wing first. I had a little trouble. My academics were strong, all of my flight training was strong, but I had probably the worst case of checkitis that you could ever see. I would go out on a check ride and I couldn't do anything. A check ride is a test at the end of a stage. You go through all the academics and all the flight instruction that goes along with it. Your final test is to go out on a check ride and perform everything you have learned. I would just blow the check rides. I actually received a recommendation for no further training once. At that point one of the company XOs had caught up with me from the old battalion. He and I began running the perimeter of Saufley Field every day. I was going back to being a plain old Marine. I got my head straight and moved on.

"In VT-2 I was cadet battalion commander. Things went fine. I then went to VT-5 for carrier qualification and VT-6 for advanced instruments. The training to this point as compared to a civilian's would qualify you as a commercial pilot.

"At that time about 99 percent of the Marines were going through the prop pipeline to helicopters. I went props and learned to fly choppers. I'll never forget the first time I flew a chopper. You learn all of the procedures and new techniques from the books. Then you go out on a first ride. You fly out to a training site with the instructor flying and explaining as you go. The instructor is talking you through everything. He lets you touch all the controls. The rudder pedals at both feet control the direction to point the chopper through the tail rotor. The stick between your legs, which you control with your right hand, pushes your nose down, up, and rolls to the left and the right. The collective, to your left, is pulled up for increasing the pitch on the main rotator blades and pushed down to decrease the pitch. If you increase the pitch, it lifts the aircraft. The throttle is a twist-grip handle on the collective. You twist to increase power. When you push a rudder pedal in a helicopter, it changes the pitch on the tail rotor. Increasing the pitch on either rotor requires more power. So when you raise or lower the collective or push a rudder pedal, a corresponding change in power is required. Keep in mind that you are trying to maintain constant RPM on the engine and main rotor, and every control movement changes the pitch on one of the rotors. This means that your left hand is constantly adjusting the throttle to compensate for every control movement.

"Anyway, remembering how to fly a fixed-wing doesn't completely prepare you for what is about to happen on this first flight. The instructor puts the chopper in a hover at the site in front of a large pole. He lines up on it. He says, 'Put your feet on the rudders.' So you do. 'Just push the rudder and turn either direction.' So you do 'Nice control, everything works just fine. Now take the stick. Move it—left, right, forward, back. Not bad, you pretty well stayed in the right place.'

"Of course, he is handling all the other controls. 'Now take the collective. Now remember you've got to control that RPM.' So you take the collective. 'Not too bad, a little rough. Now get back on the rudders. Get on the collective with me. Get on the stick with me. All right, you've got the rudders. Keep us pointed at the pole. You've got the stick, keep us pointed at the pole and keep us over this spot.' Hey, this is not half bad. 'Now take the collective and KEEP US SOMEWHERE IN THIS FIELD!'

"It is just about that bad. That's when you find out just how uncoordinated you are.

"I met my first wife Betsy Parker while I was in pre-flight and we were going to get married on the day of graduation. I was under contract not to get married until I was commissioned. I passed my final check ride and I was waiting for the papers from Headquarters Marine Corps for my commission. There was a mix-up and I was verbally commissioned. After graduation and getting married I began to think back over the past 18 months and realized that I had not extended my enlistment. I could have walked out, but I didn't.

"I received orders transferring me to California after about 30 days. There was nothing going on so I took 30 days' leave. We stopped in Texas and visited for a few days. Then we went on to Santa Ana and called a few of my classmates. They said, 'Don't check in.' I asked why and they said, 'We can't tell you. Don't check in.'

"They were telling me not to check in because everyone who was checking in was just being assigned generally to MAG 36. MAG 36 was in the process of going aboard ship and going to Vietnam.

"I checked in a week later and was assigned to HMM 165, a newly commissioned squadron. It was commissioned prior to the time I checked in. It was taking all new pilots. We had no aircraft. We would be flying the CH 46.

HMM 164 had the few 46s that there were on the West Coast at that point. HMM 164 was the first squadron to move to Vietnam as a CH 46 squadron. Up until that point everybody else was flying H 34s.

"We spent just about a year getting the aircraft in, putting the squadron together, training everybody in the aircraft and trying to get the supply lines straight so that we could get the spare parts we needed. In that squadron I started off as the legal officer. I spent a lot of time in the Los Angeles courts trying to keep some of our enlisted members from going to jail. After a while, I managed to get into the maintenance department. That was the year of the Watts riots.

"In September 1966, HMM 165 moved as a squadron to Vietnam. We went to Chu Lai. We flew our gear ashore in Da Nang and trucked everything south to Chu Lai.

"October 8 was the first actual mission that I flew in Vietnam. The maintenance officer and I were detached to Dong Ha for a week. I did that week and went back down and flew missions from just inside II Corps on the southern end of I Corps to the DMZ all the way to the Laotian border.

"The day after I returned from Dong Ha I went out on an insurgence for the first time. We were the last of a six-plane flight going into the zone. The landing zone was supposed to be cold. We swung out and then came in so that we would be in line with the jungle line. Just as we rolled level I heard this loud crack. That was all I heard. A couple of planes ahead of us said they thought they were taking fire but they weren't able to verify it. We went ahead and landed, discharged the troops, and then pulled back out. I told the crew chief to start looking to see if we had any damage. I was watching the instruments and there wasn't anything showing. We got on the ground and the crew chief said he couldn't find anything. I told the line chief to have someone go over the plane because I was convinced we were hit. The crew chief told me I had spent too much time at the DMZ and that I was hearing things. I said, 'That bullet went close enough. I heard the crack. Have them check it.'

"A couple of mechanics went over it. They checked everything and they couldn't find anything. So they sent the crew chief back out to clean it up and get ready for the next mission. When the crew chief lifted the seats up to get the mud out, lo and behold there was the spent round under one of the seats. They came and got me and said, 'Here's the bullet. Now how did it get into the plane?' I got back in the seat and went over the flight and when and where I heard the crack. I checked behind me in the hydraulic closet—nothing. We went back to where the bullet was found and the round had come through the outer wall of the plane at just enough angle to penetrate, strike a rib, and fall behind the seats.

"My first trip to the DMZ was a resupply of water to a platoon that was about halfway across the DMZ. There was a clearing in the trees. They told us there was nothing going on and that they would pop a red smoke when they saw us. We were already leery of this red smoke–white smoke stuff because as soon as it was over the radio, Charlie could pop a smoke just as easily. I was flying the plane. They popped a smoke and we started into the zone. Because of the height of the trees we came in very steep to the right over the edge of the trees. Just as I got the treetops there was a hell of an explosion. I had the collective up under my armpit and the co-pilot pulled on his and yelled, 'I've got the plane.' I said, 'No, I've got the plane.' We were getting the hell out of there. Once we decided we weren't blown apart, we called down and asked what in the hell was going on down there. 'Nothing,' they replied. 'We are just blowing mines out of the road.'

"During the first week on the DMZ we were coming back from a resupply close to the same area. They said they had Charlie wounded and alive. They were afraid if they didn't get him out quick he would bleed to death. We landed in the zone. The wounded Charlie was just off to the right. The guy that had him was standing with his foot in Charlie's chest and a rifle in his face. I looked and said, 'He's got no legs.' They dragged him to the chopper and threw him on the deck just like a sack of potatoes. After we were airborne, I looked back to see how things were going. Here is this young Marine still standing there with his foot in Charlie's chest and the gun in his face. The guy's legs were gone. He was going to bleed to death before we got him back to base. They hadn't even put tourniquets on his legs. That was my first insight into how you could get once you have been in war for a while.

"By the end of the month I went back to Dong Ha on another detachment. I stayed there for about a week and then went back to Chu Lai. When I walked into the line shack, the 3 officer said that VMO 6 was looking for pilots. He knew I wanted to be in attack aircraft. I asked him about transition to a Huey. He told me that I would strictly be a safety pilot for their aircraft because they were short of pilots and there was no time to train me in the Huey. I told him that was all right and that I would take it to get into a gun ship.

"The next day I flew to Da Nang and flew medevac chase out of Da Nang. The next morning I was assigned to a pilot named John and we went from Da Nang to Phu Bai. We worked all day flying cover. We returned and hadn't eaten all day. They were serving those real red hot dogs. I couldn't eat. We had some milk and bread, that was about it.

"We had been flying medevac chase. We went back out to their bird to make sure it was topped off. We got called back in the air to go to an area north of Hue Phu Bai that we referred to as the "street without joy." It was along Highway 1 going up the beach. A coffee plantation. It looked basically like a normal evacuation, except that it was ARVNs [Army of the Republic of South Vietnam] that were wounded. There were two or three of them. The H 34 went into the zone and was getting shot at pretty heavy. The guy on the radio reported that they couldn't get them out from under cover to get to the plane. So we got the 34 back in the air and told them to get away from the zone and that we would go in and see if we could provide some cover so they could get them out. We figured most of the fire was coming from an old coffee barn and a line along the highway. We rolled in on a run north to south and ran the guns along there.

"John and I were talking as we finished the run and I said we should drop some rockets in the barn and run them out of there. He agreed with me. We pulled out and made a squirrel cage type pattern coming in for the next pass. He told me to go ahead and switch us over to rockets.

"We turned to the right and we heard a loud womp. I sat there a minute and I thought I'd been shot. The gunner right behind my head was firing the whole time. Just as that big womp sounded his guns stopped. I thought that son-of-a-bitch shot me. The next thing I thought was he couldn't have shot me because he couldn't get the gun that far around. So then I thought, I'm not shot, but I'd better check. I looked down and there was blood going all over the place. I reached for my leg and it just went in two directions. The huey had a button in the floor for the intercom mike and I reached over with my right foot and hit the mike. 'John, I've been hit,' I said very calmly. He looked at me and by then there was blood standing in the bubble of the chopper. He got excited and I could feel the G's as he pulled the plane up.

"John started saying 'Don't worry. Don't worry. We will get you out of here. We will get you out of here.' 'I'm going to bleed to death real quick here if I don't do something,' I said. I finally got him to shut up and I got on the mike again. 'Where is the first aid kit?' I asked. I knew it should have been on the bulkhead right behind me. When I turned and looked, the two crewmen had gotten so excited they had unplugged their helmets and I couldn't even talk to them. The first aid kit wasn't there. Finally I got the gunner and pulled him down. 'Where are the god damn gunpins?' I asked. Gunpins are rods with long flags on them. He got them and I tied my leg off.

"By then John had called the medevac plane. He told them that he was not going to stay and cover, he had to get me somewhere. They decided they needed to find a clearing so that the medevac crew could pick me up. When we landed I threw the door open and jumped out. I knew that my leg wouldn't hold me. So I held on to the chopper on one leg with one leg dangling and the stretcher bearers from the 34 just sat there. They were waiting for me to run to the chopper. I finally got them to come over. We got in that old 34 and got airborne.

"We headed for Hue Phu Bai. Once I heard the rpm settle down, I knew that we were in a steady cruise and I sat up on the stretcher. I reached back and got my survival knife and started to cut my flight suit. The corpsman grabbed me and said, 'No, sir.' I told him I just wanted to see how bad it was. He grabbed me again and said, 'No, sir. Don't do that.' He pushed me back down on the stretcher. He started fumbling with something and while he was I sat back up and started to cut my flight suit again. What he was doing was getting some morphine. This time he popped me with morphine. 'No, sir, lie down.' The last thing I remember saying was, 'Well, turn my damn foot around so it is pointing up.'

"I got to ER in Phu Bai. They put me on the table and cut my flight suit off and my boots off. I was arguing with them about cutting my boots off. I had spent a lot of money putting zippers in my boots and I didn't want them to cut them off. I sat straight up and said, 'Okay, you can cut my flight suit off, but don't cut my boots off and I am keeping my damn .38.' They cut my boots off and took my .38 and gave me a spinal. From that point I don't remember much of anything. They moved me to Da Nang so they could fly me out. Up to that point I had not felt any pain, but when I got to Da Nang I started feeling it. I was hurting. I can remember waking up with a lot of troops in the dispensary. Most of them appeared to have been there for a day or two. When I would wake up, they would try to cheer me up. They flew me to the Philippines and I spent the next day in the hospital at Clark. I was coming around then. I shaved and cleaned up, but I was still in a lot of pain and didn't really know the extent of the damage.

"I learned that the round hit about two inches above my left ankle and went up my leg. It had gone through enough mass that it had shattered the bone from there to my knee.

"I was flown to Japan and they did an exploratory. When they saw how bad it was they said they were not going to do anything there but were going to get me stable. They pinned my leg in a cast so it wouldn't move. They kept me for about 30 days to make sure that I wasn't going to hemorrhage or get an infection. They were especially concerned about the hemorrhage because just before I got there they had lost a patient in transit to the United States. The plane had just gotten to the point of no return when a Marine had started to hemorrhage and they didn't have enough blood. He bled to death.

"While I was in the hospital in Japan, there was a young Army lieutenant in the bed next to me. They had been on a search and destroy mission. He was on an Armored Personnel Carrier. They were moving down a jungle road. Things had quieted down. He got up and sat on the side of the hatch with his feet hanging down inside. Charlie hit his APC with a recoilless. The explosion took his heel off.

"I remember him going to surgery. First his attitude was, 'I am going to lose that foot. That's what they told me in country so I am going to lose it.' By the time he got to Japan, he was getting some feeling in his toes and could move them so he was beginning to think he would be able to keep the foot. During his exploratory surgery though, they found that he had lost his heel and some major blood vessels and nerves. When they brought him back down they gave him his options: We can patch it up and leave it but you will never be able to walk on it. We can cut it off below the ankle, put a prosthesis on it, and you will be playing tennis in a month. Hell of a choice.

"I laid there every day for a week trying to get him to think of the positive side. He was alive. He finally came through all right. They took his foot and he came back to the States and as I understand it did very well.

"There was this old Marine gunny that came in. He felt like hell coming into the hospital with all of the wounded. He had kidney stones. All they would do is pump fluids through him so he could pass the stones. He was in a lot of pain from time to time, and we gave him hell.

"Another Marine artillery officer had gone on a mission that someone else had been assigned to. The officer that was assigned the mission had a chance to go on R&R so this guy took the mission for him. They were making a pass through a valley and he wanted to make another pass. He thought that he may have spotted something. They made a turn and came back. They knew where the village was so they came around and made a pass over the village. They got hit. The round came through the cockpit, through his left femur, through his right nut, and stopped against his right femur. His left leg was broken, he had a hole through his right nut, and he was really worried. Afraid he would never have kids. The nurses were all trying to cheer him up. On his birthday, the nurses went out and brought pints of oysters in for his party.

"If your attitude is right, a lot of this is funny and would be at the time if you weren't so scared.

"I got back to Pensacola just before Christmas. They checked me out and decided that they were not going to do any surgery until after the first of the year. The cast that I was pinned in was okay. My parents came over and I got out of the hospital for two days.

"After that I was pinned in another cast and sent home. I could do just as well at home as I could at the hospital so I stayed home. I would report in every week and they would change my cast every month. My leg wasn't healing. It couldn't stay stable in the cast. The bone wouldn't grow back together. My doctor didn't want to do anything but put me in a cast. After the third or fourth cast, I grabbed him and said, 'I have done my homework and during World War II the Germans put troops back on the line in 60 days. They pinned the bone together. Put a damn pin in my leg.' He argued that he didn't have enough solid bone below the knee and he was afraid that if he put a pin in it, it would split the bone out. He finally agreed to put one in. I went back in the hospital, got some muscle back on my leg, and he operated and put the pin in. By the next cast change there was callus forming. It was going to heal. The only thing was the round had severed the deep peroneal artery and nerve and I wouldn't be able to lift the inside of my foot. I didn't know what that would mean until later.

"A new doctor came in as chief of orthopedics and he started seeing me as an outpatient. I became pretty good friends with him. I told him one day that I had to get back to flying. I had been sitting on my ass for a year. He pulled the cast off. I got a special crew up and flew for the first time since I was wounded on May 28, 1968. I convinced the doctor that I could qualify for category one flight status. He knew I couldn't run at that point. He set up my board. The chairman was a retired Navy captain who just happened to be a Naval aviator as well as a flight surgeon. When I went to the board I was still using my cane to get around. I left it under the bench in the passageway, went in, and got my category one flight status.

"I went to VT 4 and told the commanding officer that I wanted to fly his jets. He looked at me standing there with a cane in my hand. And said, 'What kind of a pilot are you?'

"I said, 'What do you mean, good, bad, or indifferent?'

"He said, 'Yes.'

"'A damn good one,' I replied.

"'Do you think you can fly the jets?' he asked.

"'Get me in the cockpit and I'll show you.'

"A couple of days later I was transferred to VT 4. I can remember the crew chief pushing me up the side of the plane because I couldn't climb. I passed.

"After that I fought air to air gunnery in the squadron until about April 1970.

"As the end of 1969 approached, I realized that Vietnam was going to end. I was a reserve officer and was wounded just before I could augment. I couldn't augment while I was in the hospital. I had good fitness reports and was doing a good job, but I couldn't run. I knew I couldn't augment under the present circumstances. I knew that the Corps would reduce their manpower dramatically. I knew they would retire me. So I decided to get out. I retired with 30 percent disability.

"When I first got out I went to work for Lamar Advertising in Pensacola. Three years later I got my real estate license. I worked for a realtor in Florida.

"Information pouring out to the public largely through the media sometimes can be a disservice to veterans—all veterans whether they be Vietnam veterans or others. Start with PTSD [post-traumatic stress disorder]. In my own case I don't think I have ever suffered from it, but my wife caught on to it through the media. She claimed that I was suffering from it to the point that my friends would call, concerned—she had convinced them that I was crazy. I told them that I was fine, and when my friends sat and talked with me, they would realize her side didn't make any sense. But, how many people, because of the media transferring that information to spouses or family members, have said, 'Well, he is acting odd so it must be PTSD.' How many people were totally misdiagnosed or labeled by people who had no idea what they were talking about in the first place? And, how many were diagnosed by professionals who didn't know what they were doing? It is a lot like other things. When the wave starts and something sounds good, everyone grabs it and takes off with it. I think a lot of people just suffered from being associated with Vietnam. If you aren't acting the way people think you should, then you must be suffering from whatever the most recent popular malady is.

"Agent Orange is another point. I was a crop duster. Agent Orange is a chemical that is known in industry as containing 2,4,5,-T. 2,4,5,-T was used in this country for years before it was ever used in Vietnam. It was used to kill broadleaf hardwoods in pastures and crops. Perhaps in the rates that it was being used in Vietnam a direct exposure without being cleaned off could have had some effect. But that reaction should have been more immediate. You have too many crop dusters who have handled that particular chemical for too many years without any problem for it to have had the effect claimed in Vietnam.

"I was divorced. My rapport was good with my wife's family and I lived with my brother-in-law. I went to work as a general laborer for a while. I decided that if I was ever going to go to school now was the time to do it. I enrolled at Louisiana Tech and majored in aviation because I had a lot of experience that would translate into courses. I knew I could finish in less than four years. I completed a bachelor's in aviation.

"I bought a plane and began crop dusting. My wife and I got back together for a short time and went to Texas. While I was in school for my bachelor's, most of my friends were getting their MBAS. I decided I was going back to school to get an MBA.

"I went the next fall to enroll at Louisiana Tech. I completed my master's and was talked into staying for a doctorate. I went to the University of South Alabama. Then I went to work at Southeast Missouri State University in 1986."

Today Bill is an associate professor in finance, teaching classes in investments, portfolio management, and futures. He was coordinator of the MBA program and has been chairperson and member of numerous university, college, and department committees. He was chair of the Cape Girardeau Chamber of Commerce Air Transportation Committee for two years and is a member of the Cape Girardeau Municipal Airport Board. He is the founding commandant of the D.S. Cole Detachment of the Marine Corps League.

Bill met Deanna Middleton from Cobden, Illinois, after moving to Cape Girardeau and they were married in 1987. Deanna teaches at Jackson Junior High School in Jackson, Missouri.

Bill has two children. David, 25, is a police officer for the Creola (Alabama) Police Department. Kimberly, 21, is a student at Pensacola Community College.

Bill stood and motioned for me to follow him. We walked into the living room where he stopped and pointed to a photo on the wall. "That's me and David," he said proudly.

Two separate photos displayed Bill and David in their dress blue uniforms. We both stood quietly looking at the photos. Then I turned and asked, "Is there anything else you would like to say?"

Bill's face tightened. "For a long time I felt guilty about the retirement. I can't explain that. Hell, I can walk. Most people who know me today and don't know about the damage to the leg, will say they never noticed a limp or anything else. If I get out on the dance floor too long I have to sit for a while, and I pay the price the next day for doing anything strenuous on my feet. But I can stay up with the best of 'um."

PART V
Crossing Paths

ELEVEN
Sgt. Donald Buatte

Hometown: Bloomsdale, Mo.; Recon-Sniper; Third Recon Battalion, Third Marine Division; Dong Ha, Vietnam; January 1966–December 1967; First Recon Battalion; Quang Tri, Vietnam; April 1968–July 1968.

> *On the way home I guess I had this scary look in my eyes and everybody wanted to stay away from me. Everybody was staring and watching me. This guy came up to me in St. Louis and said, "Thank you." I thought damn, maybe it was worth it after all. The only other person that ever thanked me was Mr. Shelley, the father of one of the girls that I dated.*
>
> DONALD BUATTE
August 1, 1992

I pulled up in front of the Dew Drop In at the edge of Bloomsdale, Missouri. Facing me was a large building with old curved and warped weather-beaten boards. I stepped from the car and looked at my watch. I was 15 minutes early. I was supposed to meet Don Buatte at 8:00 A.M. I stepped up on the porch of the old tavern and walked toward the door. The boards squeaked with each footstep. I opened the door and to my surprise the bar was full of men. Some were at the bar drinking either coffee or beer. A couple of old men were sitting at a booth fanning the flies to keep them off of an open box of donuts. I looked around and no one seemed to have noticed that I had walked into the tavern. I walked to the back of the room and went inside the men's room. Shortly, I walked back out and I was face-to-face with a stockily built man about six feet tall. "You Harry Spiller?" he asked.

"I sure am. You must be Don Buatte," I replied.

"Yeah, I will buy you a cup of coffee," he insisted.

We drank our coffee and reminisced for a few minutes before we left the tavern. I followed him out of the parking lot heading south on Highway 61. He was driving a pick-up and about a quarter of a mile down the highway we pulled into the driveway of his home. I just passed his place coming up here, I thought.

As we walked toward the house his son Vance was coming up from the pond with a stringer of catfish. He looked up, grinned, and waved. We went into the house and Don poured us a cup of coffee.

Don handed me a copy of his military papers, saying, "I thought you might want to see these before we get started." I began to read the list of operations that Don had participated in while he was in Vietnam: Operations Kansas, Montgomery, Mobile, Washington, Colorado, Morgan, Sutter, Sierra, Lancaster, Kentucky, Osceola, Saline, Neosho, Napoleon, Osceola II, Lancaster II, Scotland II, Charleston, and Rice. A total of 19 operations in two tours of Nam.

While I was reading I kept thinking about our meeting. Why did he have me meet him at the Dew Drop In? I passed right by his place, which was easy to find. Don had appeared from nowhere. Why? It wasn't until he told his story that I realized that Don had developed a mistrust for people as a result of the war.

"I grew up on a small farm just north of Bloomsdale. We had one of those gravel roads with the grass growing in the middle that led to our farm. There were seven of us. Four older girls and three younger boys. I was second oldest of the boys. I went to grade school here in Bloomsdale, I hated it. I went to high school and loved it. I played a lot of sports and was a pretty good baseball player. I thought I was good enough to play special baseball. I played baseball in high school and played for the old Zel baseball team. That was a bi-state league and some of the old guys were semi-pro. Some of them got paid pretty well. We used to play over in Illinois, Cape Girardeau, Sikeston, New Madrid. We even played teams out of St. Louis. I was about 15 years old. I wasn't even old enough to drive. I tried to play ball with those big boys and I could hang with them pretty well, but since there were no colleges and nobody was jumping at the door I thought I would go into the Marine Corps. I thought I was still good enough. I thought I had enough time to go into the Marines, stay three years, and still play baseball. But that didn't work out.

"I signed up when I was 17 and started active duty July 2, 1965. I went to boot camp at San Diego, came home on leave in November, and then I went to Okinawa, also known as the northern training area, in December 1965. Everybody stopped there for a month before going down to Vietnam. The Corps was checking everyone's records looking for rifle experts. They

Don Buatte (far right) waits with fellow Marines to be airlifted to the field.

wanted snipers. I didn't want to be a sniper. I sure didn't want to sit up in a tree shooting at people. Then I got to thinking about it and I asked the sarge what the snipers would be doing. He said that they sit back in an area well-protected till they are needed. I thought that didn't sound too bad and it would get me another month here at Okinawa so I went to Sniper School. There were about 30 of us that went to the school, but they didn't tell us we were going to go to Recon School, too.

"I went to Vietnam in January 1966. I was prepared for war after all that training. We got off the ship with a rifle issued to us and four or five rounds of ammunition. Some war. The platoon that I was assigned to hadn't gotten there yet and I was put on mess duty. We had a mess tent right out by the China Sea. It was a secure area and we didn't even carry weapons.

"After two weeks of that I received orders to A Company First Recon Battalion at Chu Lai. It was the most screwed up platoon I ever saw. Everybody was confused. We had a second lieutenant that couldn't read a map. He didn't know anything. A lot of the patrols would get out there in the mountains around Chu Lai and lose radio contact. Another patrol would be sent out to get in contact with them so they could relay radio traffic. The first patrol we went out on we were supposed to find a patrol that had lost radio contact. We got lost, didn't know where we were at. We ended up getting back all right.

Don Buatte (left) on patrol outside Quang Tri.

"The first time I got shot at we were shooting at one another. We went out to make radio contact. There were 18 people. That was too many people, but they sent us out with that many. They split us up and sent a squad of four or five people up this hill to see if they could make radio contact with the patrol. Later we went back to hook up with them and they thought we were the enemy. They opened up on us with a machine gun and a couple of rifles. There was some yelling back and forth and it was all stopped. I thought, this sure is going to be a long tour.

"After about three patrols of getting lost, the older NCOs told the lieutenant to forget a whole lot of what he had been taught in OCS and pay attention to them. After that things shaped up pretty well. The NCOs made sure everyone knew how to read a map, use a radio, and call in artillery. When we started we were probably one of the worst patrols in recon, but a year later we were probably one of the best.

"We were surrounded seven different times. The gooks like to show you three different sides when they surrounded you. They wanted you to try escaping by taking the fourth side. Of course, they would have an ambush waiting on you. So we would just stay right there and not move.

"I found out later that's what the general wanted them to do. He was sending us out there to find the enemy, stick around until the enemy came to us, then he would send the infantry in to rescue us. The infantry would say, 'Yeah, you are always getting into trouble and we have to come out and save your asses.' But it was all by design. That was one of Gen. Walt's strategies. We were just bait.

"I never could figure out why we had to do all that running in Okinawa. Three miles in the morning, up to seven miles in the afternoon. Well, about three months later I found out. We were on a patrol up by Chu Lai. There was a lot of jungle there. On the last day we were supposed to get picked up in the evening. There were about 14 of us. We had to go up this mountain to a clearing so the choppers could pick us up. We took our time. We never walked trails, but this time we had to because the jungle was so thick. It took us all day to get up there. We got about 200 meters from the clearing. We looked down the hill and at the bottom there were Viet Cong everywhere. They were a long way off, but we were never going to make it to the choppers. They had seen us and they were moving around like a bunch of busy ants. We had to go back through the jungle. We made that whole day's travel plus another whole day's travel in less than three hours. You talk about running. The gooks were right behind us. The choppers had gotten there and they knew we were in trouble. There were about four of them after us. They were catching up. The last man in our column would throw a red smoke grenade. We would call the choppers on the radio and say, 'See the red smoke?' They would say, 'Yeah.' We would tell them we weren't there anymore. The gooks were throwing red smoke, too. If we threw one, they would throw one to confuse things. The gun ships kept them off our back long enough for us to get into a clearing, and to let us get out of there. I sure was glad we did all that running in Okinawa.

"On another patrol we went into Laos. They wanted us to capture a prisoner. To do this you split up your patrol and watch the trail all morning.

V : Crossing Paths

Don Buatte on patrol outside Quang Tri.

Then you send half your patrol down by the trail and the other half is up on a hill watching the trail. They can see the whole thing. They can tell you who is coming along. One Viet Cong, two Viet Cong. So they would call and say you got one Viet Cong coming down the trail, get ready to jump him.

"We were by the Ho Chi Minh Trail for three days watching all these people moving south. There were groups of them, but not all of them were soldiers. There would be women and children carrying supplies with one soldier. They would be carrying them on their backs or by bicycle. There was one trail going east and west and just a few of the Vietnamese were taking that trail. We went down there. I was supposed to go on the other side of the trail. Me and one other guy were supposed to jump this one VC. They gave us the word that there was one coming up the trail. I went across the trail and got ready to jump him. The other guy was in the bushes across from me. He stuck his head out and said I should come back. No, I thought. I had finally psyched myself into it and we were going to do it now. I'll beat that sucker to death if I have to, I thought, but we are going to do it now. 'Come on back,' said the other guy. 'Damnit, there are more of them than they thought.' I ran back across the trail. We slid down in the rice paddy about ten yards from the trail. I counted 40 sets of shoes that went by. If I had jumped that guy I would have had 39 right behind him.

"I was down at Chu Lai. I went on R&R in Malaysia, and had come back to Da Nang. I knew my brother was in the area somewhere and I asked around until I found out where his outfit was located. I found out that once I got to the area where he was located I would have to spend the night because it was a secured area. I told the other guys I was going to find my brother, and that if I was not there in the morning to go on down to Chu Lai without me.

"I found him just as they closed the roads down for the night. We sat and drank beer until about two o'clock in the morning. I had to catch a ride back to the airbase the next morning. I made it back in time. But it wouldn't have made a difference. I was going to go see him.

"I finished my tour and went back to Camp Pendleton. I was there for most of 1966, but I started getting into trouble. I had three office hours in three days. I thought they had too many stupid rules. I was a sergeant, too.

"I wanted to go back to Vietnam. I kept reading the papers and I knew or thought that the Vietnamese were going to make a big push in 1968. I figured we would kick their ass and that would end the war. I wanted to be there for that. I thought that I would get one of the easy jobs in the rear area because I had been over before and I figured they would give me a break.

"So I volunteered to go back. Right after that I got a call for a tryout with the California Angels. I played with the minor league players at UCLA for a couple of weekends. They told me that they couldn't contract with me because I was already under a contract. I could have cancelled the orders, but I thought I'd go over and get that tour over with, then come back next July and try out again.

"I went over in December 1967. They put me right back doing the same thing I was doing before except that they sent me to Dong Ha with Third Recon. They had hard-back tents. I went to the sergeants' quarters. I looked up at the roof and asked, 'You guys get hit with artillery much up here?' 'Ah, not too bad,' they said. I looked up at all those holes in the roof and said, 'I think you guys are full of shit.' They laughed and said, 'You're right.'

"They would hit us with artillery every day. They would start hitting us in the morning, then about the time we would be getting used to it they would change it. Most of the time no one got hurt, it was more harassment than anything.

"The second time I was over there I noticed right away that the officers from captain through major were a lot different. The first time I was down there we had a better grade of officer. The weaker grade was in 1967 and 1968. They just weren't very good at all. So I figured when I went back to the States that if the baseball didn't work out, I would go back in the Corps and try OCS.

Don Buatte in front of the headquarters building at Dong Ha.

"We had this lieutenant. He was real gung ho. He wanted to go out on every patrol. I went out on a patrol as the patrol leader. 'Cloudy Sky' was our call sign. The gooks were getting pretty smart by then. They would have teams looking for recon because recon was doing a lot of damage to them. So we would have teams looking for them and they would have teams looking for us. It was a big cat and mouse game. They would listen in on our radio traffic and they had equipment that they could hone in on us and pinpoint our location. They would get on our radio frequency and say, 'You're going to die, Cloudy Sky. Tonight is going to be your night.' They were trying to get us to get on the radio and call so they could pinpoint our location. A couple of times they were calling for Cloudy Sky. It was early in the morning. I knew we would get picked up in a short time, but I started to talk to them just before we caught the choppers. 'When you come tonight make sure you bring your sister.' As we flew off in the distance two or three artillery rounds hit where we had been picked up.

"Every morning we would get a report about what was going on around the area. Everything was getting pretty hairy around the Tet offensive. I thought, this is all right. It is exactly the way I had it figured out. The VC are going to attack, get their ass kicked, and all we have to do is go out there and stomp on them, and the war will be over. So they did. They hit Da Nang, Phu Bai, Saigon, and all the other areas. Every morning we would go to a briefing and the VC were getting their asses kicked. I kept waiting for orders for us to move out and go find them. I thought was were going to make a big offensive, but it never came. That's when I realized that President Johnson had stabbed us in the back. We could have won the war right then, but it was all political. I have hated the man ever since. He didn't have the guts to go after them. I went on a three-day drunk. I lost all faith in the military, the government. They weren't going to let us win it. I got over that and I said the hell with it. From then on when I went out on a patrol all I cared about was getting the people back safe. We were supposed to find the enemy, but we never looked. The hell with it.

"I decided to go home and see if I could play baseball. I really didn't want to do that either. The whole thing was kind of a letdown for about a year. When I got home I called the scout from the California Angels. He had told me to call when I got back. I had decided I was either going to get a ticket to San Francisco or to St. Louis. I called him up and he said the best thing to do would be to go back to the Midwest because all of their tryouts were over. This was in July 1968.

"On the way home I guess you've got this scared look in your eye and everybody wants to stay away from you. Everybody is staring and watching you. This guy came up to me in St. Louis and said, 'Thank you.' I thought damn, may be it was worth it after all. The only other person that ever thanked me was Mr. Shelley, the father of one of the girls that I dated.

"There wasn't much around here. So there didn't seem to be much going on against the war. There were some hard feelings around here but that was all. My younger brother had it rough though. He was going to college down at Cape and they were having a lot of demonstrations against the war. It was hard to have two brothers in Nam and be a part of that too. I just stayed out in the country. Of course, I had a reputation of being a bad ass. People would say you'd better give this guy a little room. I didn't mind that because if someone wanted to give me a hard time they would think twice before doing it.

"I was 21 when I got out. I got married to Rose Lee six months after I was discharged. I went to work at River Cement. I didn't think I would last six weeks, but 25 years later I am still working for them. Having a family made a difference. It ended my roaming days. I had a responsibility then. The important thing was to get the kids raised.

Rose Lee explained how she and Don had dated during high school but had broken up and were not going together when Don went into the Marine Corps. "After he got to Vietnam," she explains, "I got a letter from another guy who said Don had given him my name so that the guy would have someone to write to. I found out later that he did that really to get me to write to him. After that we would date when he came home.

"The changes that I saw at that time were changes that you would expect of a guy that had gotten out on his own. He was more mature. His mother told me that when he first got home it was hard for Don to sit still. He even had trouble sitting down and having a meal. It took him a while to get back into that. He didn't say much about Vietnam and never said that he had just gotten back from Vietnam. As a matter of fact, he avoided talking about it.

"I guess the Vietnam War affected me in a lot of ways," said Don, "but the most is the trust. I don't trust the government, I don't trust organizations. I trust some people when I get a read on them. Anything that has to do with a bunch of people making the decisions I don't trust. Maybe that isn't the war. Maybe it is because I am getting old.

"The Persian Gulf War showed that there were a lot of mistakes made back then. Not being behind your troops. What's hard to do is fight and not have the people behind you when you're over there. You need more of a reason than just because the President says go fight. When you're sleeping in the mud and you wake up every morning with leeches in your mouth and you're doing all that dirty stuff, you're not doing it for nothing. You've got to have a reason. People went against us and took the reason away from us. I think they learned that in the Gulf War. Schwarzkopf put it right. He said we made a lot of mistakes and when you see the mistakes, you don't walk away from it, you make changes."

It wasn't until years later that Rose Lee began to realize the effects of the war on Don. "The Third Recon Battalion contacted Don and we had our first reunion at Hilton Head Island in South Carolina. They had some meetings and had the wives meet with guys from the Veterans Center out of Savannah, Georgia. They told the different behaviors that the Vietnam vets experienced. The mistrust of people. They told us that vets had the complete lack of trust for authority. Not letting their feelings out. I would say to myself, "That's why he was acting that way."

"When Don's mother died he went off into the woods by himself and when he came back he was okay. He did the same thing when his dad died.

"Now you discuss things. Twenty-five years ago you didn't discuss things. I can remember talking to a friend who was married with three children. Her husband was in Vietnam and she told me that she ignored certain conversations with people back then to save the embarrassment of them finding out her husband was serving in Vietnam.

"We both were unsure about the reunion when we went down, but it was good for us both."

Don has begun to open up more and talk about Vietnam. He knows that the war is going to be controversial for a long time. He wants his grandchildren to know what he did and what he experienced so he is now writing down a few stories. This is one:

Sgt. Donald Buatte

Don and Rose Lee Buatte at the 1991 Third Recon Battalion reunion.

It looked like a pretty good place to spend the night. The canopy wasn't thick and the ground cover around the trees was open. It resembled the hardwood forest of the Missouri Ozarks more than the jungle of South Vietnam near the Laotian border.

I didn't necessarily like the idea of bivouacking on the side of the hill instead of the hillcrest. All through military history the advantage of being on top for defensive purposes has been crucial. But Lt. Jones knows what he's doing—I've got confidence in him.

Below us is a 20 foot bluff that covers our whole southside and wraps around to the westside where the bluff fades to a steep hill. It is impossible to climb without making noise. The eastside is fairly steep, but on the same grade that we're on. So if there's any trouble it'll probably come from the higher ground of the north. That's the side I'm on. Oh well, luck of the draw, I guess.

My name is Donald Buatte. My outfit is the Third Marine Division, Third Recon Battalion, H&S Co., Sniper Platoon attached to Alpha Company, Second Platoon. I've been attached with these guys for six months, since they arrived in South Vietnam in March 1966.

When we first started going on recon patrols six months ago, I thought we had to be the worst disoriented group to ever run a recon patrol in South Vietnam. But things are different now. After Lt. Jones stopped doing things exactly the way he was taught in OCS and everybody realized the best way to survive over here is to be the best recon Marine you can be, things started shaping up.

They say the most dangerous thing over here is a second lieutenant with a map and compass. Shit, they're right! But Lt. Jones is one of the best map readers around now. He worked at it. Now everybody knows how to read that map. We worked at a lot of other things, too.

V : Crossing Paths

How did I ever get in this outfit? I broke the cardinal rule of the military—Don't volunteer for shit because they never tell you exactly what you're getting into.

When I was on Okinawa for three months of training, all the men qualified expert on the rifle ranger were asked if they would like to go to Sniper School. And, after asking a few questions about snipers in Vietnam, I decided what the hell, six more weeks of Okinawa would be pretty nice. Besides, this cat wasn't shooting out of trees.

They didn't tell us that we had to go to Recon School also. The Marine Corps got me that time. Live and learn, dumb ass!

I plan on getting four or five hours of sleep tonight, between two one-hour guard shifts. This is our third day on patrol. The choppers are supposed to pick us up tomorrow. We haven't seen much. Although we did call 175mm artillery on a North Vietnamese patrol early today. Other than that, things are pretty quiet.

God, I hope we don't have to call any artillery support because the only support we've got is those 175s and we're at their maximum range of 22 miles. At that range their accuracy isn't worth a damn.

After my first watch I fell asleep. My night's sleep was cut short. All hell broke loose about 0200 hours. The enemy opened fire on us from the south, below the bluff. God, I've never seen so many different colored tracers in my life—blue, green, and two or three shades of red.

Shit! All the rounds are going over our heads. The damn gooks are shooting at the hillcrest. They're trying to find us. They think we're on top of the hill instead of on the side. They want us to fire back to give away our position. God, I can't believe nobody fired back. Thirteen people on this patrol and everyone held their cool—or everyone was too scared to fire back. The shooting stopped. They're going to find out we're not up there, then they're going to search the hillside for us. Shit, what time is it? 0215 hours. Damn, three hours till daylight. I'd better put my watch in my pocket so they don't see the luminous dials in the dark.

I put my cartridge belt on and grab my M-1 with the scope as quietly as possible. I grab my pack and move up closer to some big rocks I've been sleeping behind. On one hand this place provides good cover from up above, on the other hand, with the brush behind the rocks, I can't see anything coming down the hill. Hell, as dark as it is, I can't see shit anyway. About six to seven feet to my left is a bush that is three to four feet wide and six to seven feet long running up the hill. Beyond the bush another eight to ten feet is Gomer. Gomer's the type of guy that's quiet, but never misses a thing—he always knows what's going on. To my right is thick brush that extends from the rock ten to twelve feet.

There's a rule in recon: Always sleep with your head pointing north [if you can]. That way as soon as you wake up you know where you're at. Gomer and the bush is to the west, the brush is to the right and the bluff and the rest of the patrol is to the south.

What time is it? I get my watch out of my pocket—0245 hours. Put your watch back in your pocket, dumb ass. They might see those dials! Hurry up daylight and get here!

Oh! Oh! I hear some noise from up the hill. It sounds like one to three gooks sneaking down the hill looking for us. Damn, it's quiet, but I can hear them about 50 yards away.

Sgt. Donald Buatte

Shit! The way they're coming they're going to head straight for that bush to the left. They're either going to go to the left or right of the bush. If they see these rocks they'll figure this is a good spot for me to be and maybe throw a grenade.

I only hear one gook coming down the hill now. The other two must have stopped.

I grab my pack and rifle and move quietly behind the bush. I've already got my cartridge belt on with K-bar taped upside down on my left shoulder strap. I can grab it quietly and be ready in one easy motion.

Holy shit! Now I'm starting to shake. I'm shaking so bad, I'm making noise. What do I do when he comes around that bush? Do I stab him with my knife and have some hand-to-hand combat which is dangerous shit? Or do I shoot him with my M-1 and give our position away?

It doesn't make any difference. If I don't stop shaking the son-of-a-bitch is going to hear me and throw a grenade. Shit! What do I do? Hand-to-hand or shoot him? I can't make up my mind.

I dig two holes in the ground with my fingers about a foot apart, almost ripping off my fingernails. I put my knees in the holes hoping that will keep my knees from knocking. That doesn't help. I'm still shaking enough that he can hear me.

Why am I shaking so much? I'm not a rookie at this shit. You'd think I'd be a hardened veteran by now. I've always kept my cool before. I can't make up my mind what to do when he comes around the bush.

Well, shit! Looks like I'm going to die tonight. I wonder if they give you full home cooked meals in heaven and C-rations in purgatory.

I stopped shaking! I stopped shaking! I'm as cool as Cool Hand Luke. I know exactly what I'm going to do when he comes around this bush.

The bastard's getting closer. He's throwing rocks in Gomer's direction. He knows we're close, but he doesn't know exactly where we are. He's throwing rocks, hoping to hit one of us or our gear. Maybe we'll think it's a grenade and dive for cover — giving our position away. Gomer will hold his cool. He always holds his cool under fire.

The son-of-a-bitch is on the other end of the bush now. He's hiding on one end of the bush and I'm hiding on the other end of the bush. Six to seven feet away.

I hear another sound now. It's the sound of an approaching plane! We've got some support coming! Shit's going to hit the fan any second here! But things are beginning to stack in our favor. I don't know how much support one plane can give us, but it's sure going to make those gooks nervous.

I'll say he's nervous. He's fidgeting on the other side of the bush. He's going back up the hill. God, I'm glad he's not coming around this bush! We might have both died, but he definitely was going to.

The sound from the plane was like that of a plowshare scraping concrete. I've never seen so many tracers coming from a plane in my life. If every fifth round is a tracer, like machine guns, there must be a thousand rounds per second coming from that plane. God, that's beautiful! That must be Puff the Magic Dragon [an H-46 helicopter]. I've heard about him. God, he's beautiful!

I can hear the other two VC moving back up the hill. There must have been four or five of them. They're not worried about being quiet.

I hear a low-sounding thud about 10 to 15 feet beyond the bush. That's right about where that gook should be. Shit! That goddman Gomer is throwing the rocks back at the gook! He's throwing rocks back at the goddamn gook!

Wait a minute. How did that plane know where we were at and that we weren't the enemy? I looked behind me to the south and I saw a strobe light flashing at the top of a tree. Lt. Jones must have climbed that tree and put it up there to let Puff the Magic Dragon know our position. God, that had to take some guts!

Daylight is about a half hour away. I think it's going to be a good morning. I'm going to be alive.

Don continues to work at the concrete plant. Rose Lee retired recently. Their daughter Dana, 23 years old, completed business school and is working locally. Vance, 20, is in his third year at the University of Missouri at Rolla.

Don and Rose Lee are planning to go to the next recon reunion. "The war was wrong," Don said. "But if I had to make a choice I'm glad I went to fight for my country. People don't know all that happened over there. They need to know. I want my grandchildren to know." He smiled, "I'm not done writing yet."

TWELVE
Sgt. Lloyd Schweigert

Hometown: Ozora, Mo.; Third Battalion, Third Marines, Third Marine Division; 0361 Recoilless Rifleman; Chu Lai, Vietnam; Tour of Duty, May 1965–February 1966.

> *You will kill ten of our men, and we will kill one of yours, and in the end it will be you who tire of it.*
> HO CHI MINH
> September 4, 1967

"I was born and raised in Ozora, Missouri. Ozora is a Dutch town. The town had a population of about 60 families, a church, a parish, a country store, and a tavern. It's kind of funny. You could go to the town on Sunday and everyone would be in church. Afterward, everyone would go to the local tavern for beer—just the ways of the people. Anyway, I was the second oldest of three brothers and one sister. I went to Ozora grade school and Ste. Genevieve High School.

"I played football in high school. The football coach was an officer in the reserves. He was a big tough man. He was tough on us. They had all these John Wayne movies. I saw some Marines in the dress blue uniform. That uniform sure was attractive. Then because of my size, 140 pounds five foot five inches, I thought it would be great to be a tough Marine. The recruiter came by and four of us signed up on the buddy program.

"In May, we flew to San Diego for boot camp. We went through eleven weeks of boot camp, the four weeks of Infantry Training Regiment, and home on 30 days' leave.

"I had orders to report to the First Battalion, First Marines, First Marine Division at Camp Pendleton. I was given the MOS 0361 recoilless rifle. They trained us for a few weeks, then we went into lock on, a

The firing of a recoil rifle near Chu Lai. Lloyd Schweigert is on the left.

phase where we were trained for several months to prepare to go to Vietnam.

"In January 1965, we boarded ship and went to Okinawa. For three months I went to Radar School and trained. We were on two shifts. One week we would train all day and the next week we would train all night. Our training included rappelling, jungle training, and beach landings in rubber rafts. We had hand-to-hand combat and judo training. The training was rough. One night they dropped us off three miles out in the ocean. The tide was wrong, and we missed our beach assault by six miles. They had the bear pit where they put two fire teams in a big mud hole full of water. The object was for us to work together to get the other fire team out of the hole. It turned into a big fistfight with a lot of busted noses and lips.

"The training was about over, and we all got orders to go to Mount Fuji for cold weather training. We were issued all the cold weather equipment and boarded ship. We no more than got out into the ocean when we were called back and took all the cold weather equipment back to supply. They issued us mosquito repellent and mosquito nets and put us back aboard ship. We were out for a couple of days and came back again. Then after one day at Camp Swab, we boarded ship again. We sailed for three days. No one told us anything. Then on the third day we were called up on deck in teams of eight and issued live ammunition. It was a real shock. I will never forget a buddy of mine, George Hinson, turned and looked at me and said, 'Hey, these ain't blanks.'

"They took us up on the flight deck put us on choppers and flew us into Chu Lai. We set up a perimeter and dug in. When we landed, we landed with unloaded weapons. After we were on the ground, they let us put our magazines in the weapons. But we were under strict orders not to shoot. If you saw the enemy, you had to report to the next senior man. He would report to the sergeant who would then try to spot the enemy so you could shoot. When we first went on patrols if we got fire, we couldn't return fire.

"For the next couple of weeks we dug in, spreading the perimeter, digging foxholes, and securing the area. We got some sniper fire, but that was about it. We finally got the area secured and the Seabees came in and started laying an airstrip.

"One day we were sitting around eating lunch and this one Marine was messing around with his .45. It was an accident, but it went off. It killed the boy next to me. I was a witness. The boy that he shot was white, and the boy that did the shooting was black. It didn't have anything to do with race, but the prosecutor was trying to get the Marine on murder. The defense was trying to use the only defense they thought they had and that was to prove I was prejudiced against blacks. They were trying to claim I didn't see what I thought I saw. I was 19, and they worked me over pretty good. The guy got off with manslaughter.

"About a month after I was there, we started doing patrols and company sweeps of the area. As time went on, we moved out farther and stayed longer. We also ran into more enemy.

"Gary Tate was from Corpus Christi, Texas. He was attached to the recoilless rifles at Pendleton with us. He was a country boy. We got to be good friends. They split us up. Some went with one platoon and some with the other. Gary was with the other platoon. We started getting incoming, light sniper fire. I didn't even know he got hit. I went out with him and said, 'I will see you later.'

"They had some amtracs, and they were going to run the amtracs up into the area where the VC were and drop the Marines off. They had some Marines inside the amtracs and some sitting on top. They ran up there, and this sniper kept shooting at them. Everyone was lying flat. Being the tough guy that he was, he stood up to get a better look and got shot in the head.

"I didn't know he got killed. We came back to battalion, and I asked, 'Where is Gary?' This guy said, 'Didn't you hear? He got killed.' I said, 'No, you must be mistaken.' He said, 'Yeah, he stood up and he got shot right through the helmet. Come over here.' There had been eight Marines killed that day, and they had them lying by the intelligence tent in body bags. He took me over and unzipped the bag. It was Gary. He only had two weeks left in Vietnam. He was getting out on a hardship. He was the only son in the family. One of these days that will be another place that I will have to visit."

Lloyd's eyes filled with tears as he pushed his muscular frame up from the table and walked to the front door. He stood silently staring out the window. The sunlight reflected against the silver lines in his jet black hair. Moments later he returned, opened a scrapbook and pulled out a clipping from *Stars and Stripes*. "That was our first big operation," he said as he handed me the paper.

I sat back and began to read. On the first major search and destroy mission that Lloyd was involved in, he captured the first VC. As the story is written in *Stars and Stripes*, the Third Battalion, Third Marine regiment was involved in a search and destroy mission that resulted in 11 VC killed and 47 captured. Four company assault forces were heli-lifted into an area five miles south of the Marine airfield near Chu Lai.

Twelve Skyhawk jets from Marine Attack Squadron (VMA) 311 cleared the two landing zones with a 15-minute air strike. Then 29 choppers from Marine Medium Helicopter Squadron landed the Marines while they received cover from huey choppers.

The 850 men from the regiment formed a 4.5-mile skirmish line along the Tra Bong River reaching to the South China Sea.

The first enemy was sighted and captured at 8 A.M. when Lloyd Schweigert, then a lance corporal, found a VC hiding in a cave on top of a sand dune.

A total of 5.5 tons of bombs were dropped on the enemy.

"That's quite an accomplishment!" I said as I finished reading.

"It was nothing compared to what a lot of guys did," he modestly responded.

"Operation Starlight was the one that really hurt us though. It really got tough. We went with 1,200 men, a battalion, and came back with 355.

"The operation was like a dream. Several companies were flown to one end of the peninsula and dropped off to set up as a blocking force. We boarded Mike boats and went down the peninsula to what was called the horseshoe. It was a river that came inland, curved, and came right back out into the ocean. We made a beach landing and immediately took on enemy sniper fire. We assaulted the beach and took only a couple of casualties. We set the beach head up and flushed the snipers. Then we began to move inland. Mike company contacted us and said they had spotted some enemy reenforcements trying to surround us. We started to move up on their flank to support them. They were waiting. They hit us with mortars first. I was blown to the ground three different times. I lost my helmet. I was trying to find cover. There were 18 killed on the first attack and many wounded. Then air strikes came in and the mortars stopped. We called in choppers to evacuate the wounded and dead. They had a hard time getting in because of enemy fire, but we got all but four of the bodies out. We gathered their weapons then dug in for the night.

"The next day it was all different. The enemy had made a big mistake. They moved back toward the ocean. When they did that, we just formed a line across the peninsula. We backed them up into one square mile. We called in air strikes and artillery and flushed them out. Then it was our turn. It all happened so quickly. We didn't find out till later that we had killed over 1,500 VC. It didn't seem real. I mean, when we hit the beach it was like the John Wayne movies, but it was hard to put it in your mind that it was real.

"Then after that they didn't consider us battalion strength anymore. They took the colors back to Okinawa with half the men to regroup. The rest of us were shipped out to different units. I was shipped to the First Battalion, Ninth Marines at Da Nang. All we did was perimeter watch around the base for the rest of my tour.

"I was shocked when I got back home. I mean here we were fighting communist aggression and we didn't have any support at home. I was disappointed with the war. To say that all these men that got killed were a waste is bad. We could have won the war. We did not lose the war. Washington, D.C. might have lost the war, but we did not lose the war. Look at the casualty count. We won the battles. We didn't lose a damn thing. Washington lost the battle. The kill ratio was ten to one.

"The only time I ever had any resentment because of the war was when I was on my way from El Toro to Los Angeles Airport. A bunch of us stopped at a local bar to have a beer. We were all 19. The bartender wouldn't serve us so we started raising hell. The bartender called the police. The officer came up and told us that he was a Korean War veteran, he knew that we had fought for our country, but they would not serve us. He asked us to go on home and not make him have to do something that he didn't want to. We did as he asked.

"I came home for a 30-day leave. I flew into St. Louis Airport, and a friend of mine picked me up and took me home. No one was home at the time. I wanted to see my younger brothers and sisters who were in grade school at the time. I drove up there, and they wouldn't come to me. They didn't know me. I had a hollow look. I weighed 130 pounds and had a real dark complexion. My younger brothers and sisters were scared of me. It took the entire leave before they were really comfortable with me. I spent 30 days at home then went to North Carolina.

"In 1967, I came home and married Margie Nager. I took her back with me. My daughter Gail was born at Camp Lejeune shortly after that. It's astronomical what it costs to have a baby today, but it cost me $8.35 to have Gail.

"Tony, named after my best friend killed in Vietnam, came shortly after that. A couple years later my daughter Julia was born.

The Schweigert family. *Left to right:* Gail, Lloyd, Margie, Julia, and Tony.

"I got out and came back to Ste. Genevieve. My Dad worked for a plumbing outfit, and I got a job with him that paid $2 an hour. I almost starved to death. I worked there for three years then went to the Mississippi River transmission natural gas pipeline in 1971. I jumped from $2 an hour to $5.85 with good benefits. I've been with them ever since.

"I never thought the war bothered me much. But, my wife says it did."

"He got back in 1966, and we got married in 1967," recalls Margie. "It bothered him a lot — especially his sleeping for about a year and a half. For about ten years after he got out, he and all of his buddies that he joined with would get together and have one heck of a time. It would always end up with them in a little group reminiscing over what happened.

"I think the thing that bothered me the most was that they never got any recognition for what they did like they did in the Persian Gulf War. I thought it was very unfair. They were going out and serving their country and doing what they were told to do. In the end, it was like what are we really doing it for when so many of the people in our own country are against it. Was it all a mistake?" Margie said.

"They know they treated the Vietnam veterans wrong. That's why they had such a big welcome home for the troops from the Gulf War," Lloyd blurted out. "They were trying to make it up. You can't make it up. It should have been done at the time. The President can say, 'Well this is going to take Vietnam off our backs.' But it isn't going to do it. It isn't going to take it off the Shuh's back. It isn't going to take it off my back or my family's back."

"The Gulf War was a dress rehearsal. They went over with thousands of troops in Desert Storm. And all they did was go over there and pitch a tent, stay for a while, and then come home as heroes. In Vietnam it was 13 months of blood and guts. I was proud of our soldiers in the Gulf War and proud for America that we showed our power. But to get such a heroic welcome...."

"I'm proud I served my country, and I have no regrets. Don and John Buatte and some of our other buddies try to get together once a year. We have a good time.

"I want to visit Tony's grave. I know all I will do is walk up to it and look, then walk away. But some day I will pay him a visit."

THIRTEEN

Sgt. John Buatte

Hometown: Kaskaskia, Ill.; Combat Engineer; A Company, Seventh Combat Engineers; Chu Lai, Vietnam; Tour of Duty, June 1965–November 1966.

> *He pointed to a mountain and said, "I am only about 50 miles from here if you can get over that mountain." I never knew he was there until he told me. I don't know what Mom and Dad would have thought if they knew we were over there together.*
>
> JOHN BUATTE
September 10, 1992

"I was born in Kaskaskia, Illinois, in 1951. We got flooded out and moved to Kensey, Missouri, which is at the north end of Ste. Genevieve County. I lived on a farm up there until I went into the service. I went to grade school at Bloomsdale and to high school in Ste. Genevieve. I played baseball, basketball, and football. I wasn't no hero, but I wasn't no goat.

"I had two uncles who served in the Navy and one uncle who served in the Army during World War II. My Dad served in the Army in World War II. I didn't want to follow in their footsteps so I decided to join the Marines. In February 1964, the Marine recruiter came to the school and me and three other buddies joined the Marines.

"We left on May 31, 1964, and on June 1 we were in San Diego, California, putting our feet on the yellow footprints. From then on it was one day after another. We finished boot camp and infantry training and I was stationed at Camp Pendleton. I was assigned to a combat engineer battalion.

"In May 1965, our entire unit was placed on lock on. We went to San Diego, boarded ship, and went to Okinawa. We were there for just a short time and then were shipped on down to Chu Lai, Vietnam.

"We landed at night. We were told we were going to get hostile fire.

We were all gung ho but scared half to death. We didn't know what to expect. When we stepped out into the water instead of the water being two feet deep, it was maybe seven feet in places. Holes all over the place. People were stepping off into them, but we all made it to the beach okay. When we hit shore, we had the shore patrol waiting on us. They were just sitting, watching, and waving as we came in.

"The night was pretty hectic. We were all scared and trying to get to a camp, but no one knew where it was. When we did finally get to the camp, we listened to the 155 howitzers banging all night. The rounds were whistling over our heads. We were scared to death. It took a couple of nights for us to settle down.

"The officers didn't know what to expect either. They were as confused as the troops. A few nights after we got there we received some hostile fire in Happy Valley. As soon as it would start getting dark, we would get some fire but nothing serious. It was harassment more than anything.

"As the roads and bridges got built up, we would take more territory. About ten miles south of Da Nang, we took over Hill 52 and began building roads. We caught fire almost every night. Mortars sometimes, but we never got overrun.

"I operated dozers and cranes. We built a lot of bridges and roads. We got called out a lot at night to rebuild bridges that had been damaged or destroyed. We would take the bridge apart after we got our units out so nobody else could get out. We would blow up a bridge, then two days later go out and build it again. We had one bridge that was blown up six times. We built it seven times. The same bridge over the same river.

"We would go out at daylight. We had mine sweepers that would go out ahead of us. We were always picking up something. We always had infantry ahead of us. So I can't say that there were any VC forces that tried to stop us directly.

"When we went out at night to rebuild a bridge, we would always get sniper fire so we would be working with our lights out. You did most of your work by feel.

"We spent the first 12 months without a day off. The guys were silly. They would go get a couple of beers and really start acting crazy. One day this corporal came into the tent and picked up an M-14 and pointed it at me and said, 'Hey, Buatte, what would you do if I pulled the trigger?' I woke up a little and pulled the mosquito net back and sat up. He pulled the bolt back and a round came out. He just froze. He realized how close he was to shooting me. That's what happens to a person when they work 12-hour days with no time off.

"A workday would start at 5:30 in the morning. You would go eat chow, then head for the maintenance shed, get your equipment and go out. You would eat C-rations for two meals. You came back in at dark, ate a hot meal, and took a shower. If you didn't have guard duty, you could get a ration of two cans of warm beer. But most of the time you would come back after pulling a 12- or 16-hour shift and have to pull guard duty all night. Two hours on and two hours off. Then at daylight you had to go back to work all day.

"When we had gone into lockdown at Pendleton, no matter how much time you had left in the Corps you still went to Vietnam. We had guys with two or three months left in the service that were forced to extend their enlistments. Some Marines were ready to be discharged immediately. With the long work hours and the frustration, they would knock a person on his ass for nothing.

"One thing that bugged us a lot was not getting uniforms and boots during the monsoon season. We would see the Vietnamese in Da Nang in brand new uniforms, brand new boots, and here we were just barely making it with what we had. We would have to wait for months to get a new pair of boots. Here they were getting our uniforms, and we couldn't get them.

"We had a motor pool and would have to go beg, borrow, and steal to get parts for a truck. Two miles away the Air Force would have a garage sale, selling parts, and sometimes trucks.

"Another thing that bugged us was the civilian contractors. I never did figure out what they were doing over there other than building fancy living quarters for the dignitaries. They were getting paid $1,000 a month and were living in air-conditioned trailers. We were three miles away living in tents.

"Before we moved out to Hill 22, we had an officer who went to a village to give out toys to the kids. One day the village decided to give him something. A little girl walked up to him and gave him a box. When he opened it up, it was a booby trap. He was killed. We never trusted anyone after that.

"I remember back in August 1966 there was a guy who had two days left in country. He had been making runs back and forth, and I offered to take his run for him. He could get a good night's rest, pack the next day, and leave. He said no, he would do it. Along about his third trip, he was coming through a village and a VC threw a grenade in the truck. He jumped out of the truck about the time the grenade went off. He got shrapnel in his leg and back. The truck went into a village hut and killed a villager. The guy got court-martialed. He was told that he should have stayed with the truck and driven it out of the village. The truck blew up as he jumped. There was no way he could have driven the truck out of the village. When he left, he didn't have use of his legs. The first sergeant got involved in it and finally got the court-martial stopped.

"On Hill 22 I was on a water tower that stood about 50 feet in the air. We had a machine gun mounted on it. Mortars came in one night and blew

John Buatte in Da Nang, 1965.

one leg out from under the tower. The tower went down, and I went down with it. It was like a swimming pool when we hit, but it could have been a lot worse.

"Once we were out at the construction site and had headed back to the base camp. All the roads were secure at 6 P.M. We broke down about 5:30. Everybody else had gone ahead of us. No one sent any help back out to us. So me and another guy slept underneath a crane all night. The next morning we swore we saw a war going on and had nothing to do with it. All we saw were tracers going all night in the distance. We just laid there all night and watched the whole thing. Nobody, good or bad, came and checked us out.

"I found out that our outfit was moving up near the DMZ. I wanted to go and see what it was like up north. So I extended my enlistment. We went up north and built a pony bridge. It took us three months to build it. We worked around the clock. We worked twelve on and eight off and back to work again. We finished the bridge about the middle of September, and it lasted until about the middle of October. The monsoons hit and filled all the rivers and creeks up and pushed all that garbage down the Da Nang River into the South China Sea. The water made a big bow in the bridge. It busted and ended up in the South China Sea with all the garbage, after all that work.

"One day the radio operator from my outfit sent word that my brother Don was in Da Nang. I went to my first sergeant and asked if I could go pick him up. It was one in the afternoon on Saturday. I grabbed a shotgun and took the first sergeant's Jeep to Da Nang. We picked Don up and brought him back to the base. The roads were secured at 6 o'clock so he could leave that night. We spent half the night in our makeshift club. He pointed to a mountain and said, 'I am only about 50 miles from here if you can get over that mountain.' I never knew he was there until he told me. I don't know what Mom and Dad would have thought if they knew we were over there together.

"I must have been naïve or something because we didn't have a drug problem in our outfit at all. We did have a lot of guys who were catching venereal diseases. That was real common.

"The only person that I knew of who had a drug problem was a corporal. He was sent back to Japan because he got hurt. He was there for awhile, and they kept giving him pills. One day they told him he was going back to Vietnam and he couldn't have any more pills. He told us about it when he came back, and that's the only person I ever heard of having the problem.

"I remember when the monsoons came. It was Christmas, and Bob Hope was coming over. The brass didn't want the Jeeps throwing mud up on the people in the show or on the generals who were coming up for the

John Buatte in Da Nang, 1965.

show. So they had us scraping mud off the sides of the road by hand. We were out there day and night scraping mud in the rain to keep the highway clear for them. It was ridiculous. We would throw two scoops off and three would come back in. It was just soup. It was the most ridiculous thing that I had ever seen for a military combat unit to be doing for anybody. I don't care how important they thought they were. They could have done it a lot differently. I never got to see a USO show the entire time I was there.

"During the USO show we had to go up in the mountains to get a load of rock for this road. We watched the Vietnamese break up the rock by hand, then load the rock by hand. We got two truckloads in ten hours. We could have gone up there with jackhammers, drilled holes, shot it out, and had 20 truckloads. But they would do it just to keep the Vietnamese happy. They would pay them by the day to do it. That's what it was all about. Just to keep them happy. They were afraid if we came in there with all that equipment we were going to put them out of work for the rest of their lives.

"I thought that the villages were backwards, a hundred years behind us. They were riding water buffalo, working rice paddies, no shoes, black pajamas, young kids herding cattle out in the fields. It was just backwards. There was no electricity or anything like that.

"I was over there about a year. I went in the service with Lloyd

Schweigert, George Henson, and Bill Freeman. One day I was going from the boondocks back to the water buffalo to pick up some drinking water. Going the opposite way on an ammo truck was George Henson. We didn't get to say hi or bye, we just got to wave at each other and that was as close as we came. About a month later, I was in Da Nang doing the same thing and at the airbase I came across Bill Freeman. He was sitting there with his bags waiting for a plane. We got to talk for about half an hour.

"About two months later I was back getting supplies, and I ran across Lloyd Schweigert waiting on a plane. So while I was over there I got to see my brother and the three guys I went into the service with.

"I came home five months later. We were supposed to land at an Air Force base in San Francisco, but there was a lot of flack with us being over there and they expected problems at the base so we were flown directly into El Toro. My orders were for Camp Pendleton. I went down there for about a month and then came home for 30 days.

"When I came home I noticed that the high school friends that had not been over in Vietnam were indifferent to us. They seemed to be ashamed that they didn't go over. They would just say hello and walk away. I went to a couple of high school games, but none of the high school kids at that time knew us. They didn't know us before we left so they wouldn't know us when we came home. All my old girlfriends were gone.

"I went back to Camp Pendleton for the next three months. I was stationed at a radar site. I was a heavy equipment operator so they had no real use for me. I just kind of floated around while they prepared to go to Vietnam. They were due over in June, and I was getting out in May. When they would go for training, I would always get put on the aggressor's team. Then in May I was discharged.

"It was 1967 when I came home. I started looking for work. I found a job in St. Louis working for Raymond Concrete and Piling which is kind of ironic because that was the same civilian outfit in Vietnam that built all the concrete bunkers where I was stationed.

"I met my wife Shirley Ann Grass six months after I came home, at the Saturday night dance held at the VFW. We were married in 1969. In 1970, I went to work for River Cement in Ste. Genevieve, and I have been there ever since.

"We had three children: Michelle, Carla, and Victor. Then in 1985 my wife died with cancer. I raised my kids by myself. Then my girls went off to college. I met Pat Coeiler in 1990. We got married a year later.

"The war didn't affect me. I took it all in perspective. I figured the people that were raising hell didn't know what it was all about. They were ashamed they didn't go so they had to raise hell about it.

"Me and George Henson had one incident. We had just gotten out of the service. After the dance one Saturday night, we stopped at a restaurant to get a cup of coffee. As soon as I parked, two guys jumped out of their car, one with a chain in his hand, the other with a belt wrapped around his hand. They made a few comments about two heroes coming back and taking their girlfriends away from them. George and I were both 21 and these kids couldn't have been 18. We didn't know who they were. We ignored them and, not knowing what to do, they finally left.

"For the first five years anybody who'd had nothing to do with it had an indifference. The incident at the restaurant was the only one. Other people didn't bring it up, but there was always that indifference.

"When we were in Vietnam we talked about what we were doing. Of course, we didn't know the political side to it. Come to find out that was what it was all about. But we figured if we stopped the communists there, we wouldn't have to worry about them coming across the Mexican border some day. Just a couple years ago they came pretty close. I have always said that if we had kicked their ass over there, we would have never had the problem down in Central America. We wouldn't have had Grenada.

"There were an awful lot of lives lost and a lot of people wounded. And if it was all politics, it was just a waste. But I never regretted going over. I wasn't happy about being stuck in the engineers all the time. But I never regretted it."

As we walked to the car, John proudly boasted about his children. Michelle, 22, was studying at Southwest Missouri State University to be a physical education teacher. Carla was at Southwestern, studying political science, and Victor was still in high school at Ste. Genevieve.

We were standing in the driveway and John glanced at his pick-up. His 160-pound frame was silhouetted against the evening sun. He glared for a moment. Then he turned and said, "I was lucky while I was over there. The war was pretty ho-hum for me."

PART VI
Coming Full Circle

FOURTEEN
Sgt. Carl A. Meyer, Jr.

Hometown: Mounds, Ill.; Infantryman; A Company, First Battalion, Fifth Marines; An Hoa, Vietnam; Tour of Duty, June 1968–March 1969; Two Purple Hearts.

> *When I first got out of the Marines and was old enough to drink, I tried to join the VFW, but they wouldn't let me join. They said that I wasn't in a war because it had not been declared.*
>
> CARL A. MEYER, JR.
> January 7, 1992

"Ever since I was young I always wanted to be a Marine," 43-year-old Carl Meyer explained. "I used to see friends come home on leave and I was impressed with the dress blues."

A grin came over the stocky ex–Marine when he recalled our meetings back in 1968 at the Mark Twain Restaurant in Cairo, an historic river town located at the junction of the Ohio and Mississippi rivers in the southernmost tip of Illinois. A couple of steak dinners and a few signatures later, Carl was an enlistee for the U.S. Marine Corps. He went to boot camp at San Diego, infantry training at Camp Pendleton, then home for a 20-day leave before leaving for Vietnam.

On June 18, 1968, Carl arrived in Phu Bai, Vietnam. He was 18 years old. The young leatherneck was assigned to the Fifth Marines and for a while his unit ran bridge duty, night patrols, and ambushes. He quickly realized that the enemy included not only VC, but monsoon seasons, land leeches, and mosquitoes. Carl was hospitalized for a short period of time for malaria then became a casualty of jungle rot from the wet climate and walking through rice paddies full of human feces. He returned to his unit and a month later they moved to An Hoa.

"That's when we were really getting in the shit—in Arizona territory," Carl explained. His squad participated in many ambushes and patrols in the An Hoa area. Carl moved up the ranks first as fire team leader then replaced the old squad when the squad leader and two other men were wounded. Although a squad consisted of 12 men, Carl's squad was always short of manpower. "The most we had in our squad was nine or ten people," he said. There were "too many people getting hit."

Carl's squad worked along Liberty Bridge in an area called Booby Trap Alley. Saturated with village huts, rice paddies, and jungle, the alley got its name because of the enormous amount of booby traps placed in the area. It was also a free-fire zone. "Anything you saw you shot," Carl explained.

On February 3, 1969, Carl and his platoon were on patrol in Booby Trap Alley. They came upon a well when suddenly an explosion ripped the well apart throwing shrapnel, dirt, and dust in all directions. Carl crashed to the ground, his face in the dirt. He looked up and saw an F-4 fly over. Damn! They dropped one on us! he thought. He struggled to his feet, his face and neck numb. He swiped at his neck and got a hand full of blood. One man was down in front of him. "Corpsman up! Corpsman up!" he screamed.

The corpsman scurried to his location to help.

"Not me, I'm okay," he said. "Help him."

The corpsman quickly moved to the other man and turned him over. His neck and lower jaw bone were gone, and large hunks of meat were thrown from his legs. He was dead. The corpsman moved to another man.

Carl and the other wounded Marine were placed on the helicopter. He was holding an air splint for the other man. The wounded Marine stared at Carl. Carl stared back knowing that the Marine had shielded him from most of the blast. "It's going to be all right. You're going to be fine," Carl said trying to reassure the badly wounded Marine. Carl learned that he died four days later.

Altogether there were three killed and seven wounded from the box mine. The other two Marines were found in a rice paddy 75 meters out. One of the Marines was called the "Old Man." He was 26 years old. His wife had just given birth to a baby two weeks before. He had volunteered for Nam to see what it was like.

Carl was in Da Nang at the hospital for about eight days with superficial shrapnel wounds to his neck, then returned to his unit. Three weeks later on March 8, 1969, Carl was still not assigned back to patrol duty because he was waiting to see if the government was going to send him back to the States. He had lost partial hearing in one ear. Carl was sitting in a tent in the headquarters area when a siren began to blare. He jumped up to put on his cartridge belt when at the same time a mortar blast hit the tent. Carl was knocked to the ground.

This photograph of Carl A. Meyer, Jr., was taken during Infantry Training at Camp Pendleton. He was 18 years old.

He tried to get up, but his legs were numb. He could not feel them. The ground shook beneath him as one mortar round after the other exploded in the headquarters area. Carl began to crawl on his elbows dragging himself toward the safety of a bunker. Out of nowhere two Marines pulled him into a bunker until the mortar attack was over. This time he was sent to the USS *Repose* and 19 days later he was back in the States.

"Looks like you have spread out a little since the last time I saw you," Carl Meyer, Sr., said with a grin.

"You have too," I responded.

I first met Carl in February 1969 when I made the first casualty notification that his son had been wounded. Now 25 years later he recalled the incidents as we sat in the living room next to his wood-burning stove.

He showed me the Purple Heart that Carl had sent him along with a flask containing a piece of copper-colored jagged shrapnel taken from the wound inflicted on his son.

"I remember the first time that you came when he got wounded. I, of course, thought the worst, and I was shook up. But when you came three weeks later I knew it had to be bad. After you left, my ulcers began to bleed and I drove to Tamms to the doctor. They had to put me in the hospital. That was a bad time, but, thank God, we got through it.

"After Carl, Jr., got home I had a lot of problems with him. So many of those boys came home from that war smoking dope. Carl was wild. One day I went to town and Carl drove the car over a curb. I stopped and asked him what was wrong. He stared at me wide-eyed and said nothing. I couldn't smell anything on him, but I knew he was on dope. I finally had him admitted to the hospital in Anna to get straightened out.

"He's made a good man. Done all right for himself. I think the service made a man out of him."

"People just didn't know what had happened to us. They didn't seem to know or care," Carl, Jr., recalled. "When I came home I was hooked on prescription drugs. After I was wounded they sent me to Great Lakes Hospital. Their answer for everything was Valium. If I told them I hurt, they would give me pills and say, 'Take them.' They did that to everybody. There were a lot of guys hooked. When I got home I took anything I could get my hands on. I remember taking the little pink ball out of the capsules and only taking the powder. Then when I would get five or six of them, I would take them all at once to get a real high. What really brought things to a head was when I took some of my grandma's heart medicine. I thought they were uppers, but whatever they were, they almost killed me. I slept for three days. That's when I went to Anna for detoxification. I was off the drugs after that.

"I had trouble with my Dad because of authority. Dad didn't understand. I was 20 years old and he tried to set a time when I could come in at night. Like I was a little kid. I couldn't handle it. Everybody looked at us different. He thought that I was smoking dope and all. I never knew what the stuff looked like until I became a cop.

"When I first got out of the Marines and was old enough to drink, I tried to join the VFW, but they wouldn't let me join. They said that I wasn't in a war because it had not been declared. For a long time people just looked at you differently and treated you differently.

"When I applied for jobs I didn't tell anybody that I was a Vietnam vet. People acted like we were unstable, like we were a bunch of crazy people. I had a boss who was always slipping up behind somebody and goosing them. He did it to me and, before I thought, I turned around and punched him. He wanted to know what was wrong with me. People used to ask me

The Meyer family. *Left to right:* Deborah (daughter), Carl, Deborah (wife), and Carl III.

about the wounds on my arms. I would tell them that I got the scars in a motorcycle accident. Finally I started wearing long sleeve shirts."

A couple of years passed and on January 8, 1971, Carl married 18-year-old Deborah Finley from Charleston, Missouri. Deborah, a petite brunette, grew up in a small southeast Missouri town and had paid little attention to the Vietnam War and its aftermath. Little did she know at the time how this war would affect her life.

Carl worked at Berkheart's in Cairo. In 1972, Deborah gave birth to their daughter, Deborah, and then to Carl III in 1974. Carl was a good provider for his family, but he wouldn't get close to them. Deborah noticed that he seemed to keep his distance. But as she said, "I was only 18 and had only been married to Carl. I thought that's the way it was."

Carl would yell a lot and have temper flare-ups often. He didn't go places with his family and on occasion Deborah would come home and find him sitting in a closet or dark room by himself. Deborah often thought his rages were her fault. She thought she had done something to upset him. When the kids got a little older they would ask their mother why Daddy yelled so much. She would make excuses like Daddy is tired or he had a rough day. Not one time did Carl or Deborah ever discuss the rages. Then Carl began to have nightmares, waking himself and his family with screams. Often Deborah had to change the sheets which were soaked with sweat. Carl drank a lot for pleasure he said, but he knew deep down something was trying to surface that he wanted to suppress.

In 1979, Carl changed jobs. He became a police officer for the Mounds Police Department. Carl liked the work because there was some excitement, but he liked it for another reason. He could work at night. Often Carl would work the second shift and then double over and work midnights. He didn't want to sleep. For some reason he could sleep better during the day. After four years as a police officer, Carl landed a job at the Vienna Correctional Center.

By now Carl had quit drinking, but his indigestion was giving him fits. He took Alka-Seltzer by the box. Then one night in 1989 Carl woke up with heavy chest pains. His left arm was numb. "God, I'm having a heart attack," he thought. He woke his wife up and had her rush him to the VA hospital. They checked Carl over and told him that there was nothing wrong with his heart. He thought the doctor was wrong so he went to a heart specialist. After several days of testing, he was shocked to learn that he had a healthy heart. He was further shocked when he returned to the VA hospital and found that his real prognosis was post–traumatic stress disorder. That's when he started seeing a counselor and taking medication for his anxiety attacks.

Carl found that his drinking for pleasure was really to keep the past from surfacing. The more his past tried to surface, the more he drank.

"I didn't know why I worked the evening shift and then would often carry over and work the midnight shift. But then I found out that I didn't want to sleep. The doctor told me that the reason for this is because in 'Nam everything happened at night and I really didn't want to sleep."

Today Carl's memory of Vietnam is scrambled. He remembers the events at the well in An Hoa, but has difficulty with it. "His last name was Miller. I can't remember his first name. I can still see his eyes staring at me. His throat was gone, he couldn't talk, but he kept looking at me. I was holding an air splint on his left arm. I kept telling him that it was going to be all right. If he hadn't been right in front of me I might have been the one that got hit."

The other names that Carl remembered were Cook, Moore, and Barry. Recently, at a counseling meeting for his post-traumatic stress disorder, he found out that Donald Carl Barry was the full name of the "Old Man" as he was called, who had been thrown into the rice paddy.

There are other events he wasn't proud of. "We were in a free kill zone. You see something, you can shoot. Because we lost Cook, we would call artillery in on kids. I can remember having an M-79. There was a paddy dike about 600 yards out and this old man came out in the field. He was dressed in white. I don't know what he was doing there. The lieutenant asked, 'Can you hit him?' I said, 'Yeah.' He gave the go to shoot. We killed a lot of civilians that way. I'm not proud of what I did, but at the time it felt good. We called it payback for our guys getting killed.

"I killed this gook. We went out to get him and he didn't have a rifle. He was a kid of about 15. This wasn't a free kill zone so there was an investigation. I told the investigators that I saw him crouch and aim, but I had a hard time getting them to believe me. It bothered me because I was questioned."

One problem that Carl remembers is the 90-day wonders. "Dufus Dan was what we called the lieutenant in charge of our platoon. He couldn't read a fucking map for shit. One night our platoon got into a fire fight with another platoon from our company. Shit, we were at it hot and heavy for 15 minutes before we realized what was going on. Dufus had read the map wrong and we weren't even supposed to be there. Luckily nobody got hurt."

"These 90-day wonders did get a lot of men killed though." Once while Dufus Dan was on a patrol in which Carl was covering the rear, the patrol unit started into a village. They all noticed a strange looking piece of bamboo in the pathway. Everyone stepped over the bamboo very carefully. Carl looked at it as he passed by and thought it was a booby trap. The unit searched the village. On their way out everyone stepped over the bamboo again. Dufus Dan walked up to the bamboo and kicked it. It was a bouncing Betty. "Dumb shit got his nuts blown off, but he also got three other men wounded," Carl recalled.

Carl is dealing with PTSD very well. He started with counseling every week. Now it's down to twice a month. "I found that I wasn't alone. I don't blow up as much as I used to. I knew I had a family, but I tried to stay detached—not get close to them. If you get close and let your guard down, the same thing can happen to you as it did to Miller."

The counseling has helped Carl and his family. He is more easygoing than he used to be. He grinned as he told about a recent incident in which he, his wife, and his daughter all left their keys in the house after he locked the door. In the past, Carl would have blown up, but this time they all just laughed about it.

Carl still has physical problems with a stiff leg from his war wounds. On February 3, 1992, exactly 24 years to the day after he was first wounded in Vietnam, Carl reported to the VA hospital. He went from 201 to 168 pounds in six days. Unable to eat and having problems with his liver because of malaria he picked up in 1968, he says the VA won't admit the problem is a result of the malaria.

In spite of his problems, Carl has been promoted to sergeant at the correctional facility where he works. He has taken up taxidermy as a hobby. He proudly displays some of his work in the living room: a gray squirrel, the head of a six-point buck, and a mixed array of wild turkey feathers. His wife spoke with a smile, "I think he would trade me in before he would give up his trophies and gun collection."

Carl's daughter Deborah is married and attending cosmetology college in Marion, Illinois. Deborah resembles her mother and has the same quiet passive nature. Carl III lives at home and is attending Vienna High School. Both of the children know little about Vietnam. It's a faraway place and a war that happened a long time ago. They love their father dearly. The children and their mother are interested in reading more about the war to try and understand Carl better. As our interview ended, I closed my briefcase and stood by the kitchen table. Carl's daughter was sitting on one side of the table and his son sat on the other side. Carl III had this boyish grin — a face of innocence mixed with a mischievous smile. Deborah looked up at me and said not to be fooled by his apparent innocence because, as she says, "He's a mean little shit."

FIFTEEN
Sgt. Carl E. McCory

Hometown: St. Louis, Mo.; Combat Engineer; Lima Company Fourth Battalion, Twelfth Marines; Dong Ha, Vietnam; Tour of Duty, February 1968–September 1969.

> *It was about three o'clock in the morning. Everything was quiet. I was thinking about it all, and I just couldn't stand it anymore. I cut both wrists. Blood was running down my M-16. It was everywhere.*
>
> CARL E. MCCORY
August, 1992

Carl McCory was born in St. Louis, Missouri. Five years later his father bought an 85-acre farm in Hickam, Missouri, located 13 miles outside of Fredericktown. Hickam was a community of about 30 to 40 people scattered over a 30-mile area. He attended school in a one-room schoolhouse with about 20 other students. In 1955, the schools consolidated and Carl attended junior high and high school at Fredericktown.

Carl liked animals. He did a lot of fishing, hunting, and overnight camping. He also watched as three brothers, one by one, left home for the service. One brother joined the Air Force, another the Army, and the last one, the Marines.

When they came back from the service, he listened to them talk of their experiences. The two brothers hated the Army and Air Force, but the third said, "You weren't shit unless you were a Marine." Carl decided that if he ever went into the service it would be the Marines.

"Actually I hadn't really thought about going into the military. I had met Barbara Jennings at Doe Run in 1966, and we were engaged a year before I enlisted. I kept up with what was going on in Vietnam, but I had no thoughts about enlisting. I had been working at a gas station since I was 15 and going to school. I was working there in the evenings six days a week. Back then money was real short and I helped put myself through school. I bought my own clothes and my own car.

"I had made arrangements to meet my Dad on the day that I enlisted. I had found a 305 Yamaha motorcycle in St. Charles, Missouri. He was going to meet me at the loan office. They had already approved the loan, and he was going to sign the papers and get me that motorcycle.

"We had an assembly that day at school. I remember you were there, Harry, in your dress blues. You talked to us about the Marines. Me and Steve Tinsley came down to the first floor after the assembly was over. We went into the bathroom and discussed it. We decided that we were going to go in on the buddy system. We met you down at the counselor's office and signed up.

"Later that day I met my Dad downtown. I told him that I didn't need the money for the motorcycle because I had enlisted in the Marine Corps. He was shocked because I had never said anything about the military."

Barb was devastated. "He told me that the draft was really strong and he didn't want to go into the Army," she explained. "He wanted to be a Marine. He just felt so strongly about it that there wasn't very much that I could say about it. It was already done."

Carl finished school after enlisting on the 120-day program. Then he went to San Diego as a "Hollywood Marine" as they were called. He was in the first squad, and Steve Tinsley was in the fourth. They only saw each other 10 to 15 times at the most.

"The drill instructor meets you at the airport," remembers Carl, "and he is a super nice guy. Then you get on the bus and they close the door. Boy, does he make a transition. With the buses so loaded we lined up and sat in the floor. Your eyes had to be straight ahead. We get to the base, and they run us off the bus. Stand on the yellow prints. It's 3 in the morning. They played fun and games with us until about 4 A.M. They put us in the racks and got us up at 5 A.M.

"We had a staff sergeant who was the platoon commander. He was the nice guy and the other two sergeants were assholes. But we had one other sergeant that far exceeded being an asshole. We called him Barefoot. He was a little guy, but meaner than shit. When we first got to boot camp, Barefoot took this guy who had a mustache and told us he was going to show us how to shave. The guy was about six foot tall. Barefoot made him get on his knees then cut his mustache off. He was beyond asshole.

"He was shorter than everyone else and always in someone's face. If there was anybody that could break you, he was the one. He broke a lot of people. But that was his job. If you couldn't make it in boot camp, they didn't want you in combat."

Carl came home on leave, and as Barb explained, "That's when the trouble started. I was a junior and he was a senior. He decided to join the Marines. When he came home after his first leave, I wasn't sure if we were going to make it or not. He had changed so much. He was 100 percent Marine. Everything was Marines. He would tell me how childish he thought I was. We would get into terrible fights over it. We went through a few leaves like that. And when it was time for him to go back, we would make up. We wanted to get married before he went to Vietnam. My parents were afraid that I would quit school so they would not let me get married."

"After boot camp, infantry training, and leave, I went to Camp Lejeune, North Carolina," Carl continued. "I went to heavy equipment school. My main piece of equipment was a heavy bulldozer, but I was also licensed for road graders.

"I was then assigned to Second Battalion Shore Party. They did cruises in the Mediterranean. We would practice setting up assault beaches and everything. I had been with them for two weeks. One morning at assembly, the gunny came out and said he needed six volunteers for Vietnam. So there were six of us who were all new guys. We raised our hands, and they told us we couldn't volunteer because we were new. They said that they hadn't even gotten the paperwork done for us being transferred into the outfit. At noon we had another assembly and the gunny told us that all six of us got to go to Vietnam. After they checked it out, all the old Marines had been to Vietnam before and some had been two or three times. A short time later I was home for 30 days' leave and then to Camp Pendleton for jungle training and equipped for Vietnam.

"After two weeks of training, I got flown to Okinawa in December 1967. I was assigned to Headquarters 1/13. I was there until January 1968, when we finally got enough troops from the States to make a full battalion.

"They send you over to Vietnam with real good-looking stewardesses. You all fly in. The general conversation is that none of us knew what we were going into other than what we had been told or had seen on TV. Everybody was talking about it. We landed in Da Nang. Everybody had on their brand new jungle utilities. We got off the plane, got into formation, and were marching in step across the runway. A platoon that was returning to the United States passed us. Their utilities were dirty and torn. None of them were walking in step. Most had longer hair. They were yelling, 'Fresh meat. Glad to see you, I'm going home. Have a good time.' I thought, 'What have I got myself into now?'

"I took my orders to flight manifest, and they told me what part of Vietnam I was going to. Then I got assigned a number and I waited for a flight going north. It may have been a helicopter or a C-130. I had to find this out on my own. There was absolutely no one telling me where to go. I stopped anyone with brass and asked them. My number was 98. I spent the entire day there. And when they shut down at night, I was still sitting there. I asked around and there was no place to get anything to eat. I was on my own. I didn't eat that day.

"We found some bunkers near the airstrip that were empty, and we spent the night in them sleeping the best we could. We fought mosquitoes all night. The next morning we got up, and all went back to the manifest. I was still there that evening, but by that time I had latched on to a guy who had come in from Dong Ha and he was going back to the States. He told us about a bus shuttle that would take us to a place called the Da Nang Hilton. We could get a bed and eat, and the bus would take us back out to the airfield the next morning to catch our flight. So the second night I stayed at the Da Nang Hilton. I ended up spending three days there.

"Finally, I got low enough on the roster on the fourth day and got a flight out to Dong Ha. It was like Da Nang except the airstrip was a little smaller. I ended up spending a week there. They had just started the siege of Khe Sanh and they couldn't land anything. Every time they started to land, Charlie would mortar the airfield. Planes dropped food by parachutes. A Marine from a dog team was near the airfield. He had come from Khe Sanh and was trying to catch a flight back up. He said that he had been there for eight months. He said that you stayed red the entire time that you were there. When it was dry, there was nothing but red dust — when it rained, red mud. He gave me some C-rations to eat because again there was no place to eat.

"He also told me to get rid of any girlfriends that I might have back home. 'They will find someone else,' he said. I wrote and told Barb I wanted to break it off."

Barb recalls getting the letter. "Right after he went to Vietnam I got the letter where he wanted to break it off. I was very headstrong so I packed up all his stuff and took it to his mother. If he wants to break up, fine. We both tried to get back together through the mail. But we didn't find that out until 1981."

"After about a week, I caught a C-123 to Khe Sanh," Carl explained. "Just about the time we got there a guy in the back of the plane told us that we were getting ready to land. He said, 'When we do, Charlie is going to have a reception for you. When we get to the end of the runway, we are going to drop the bay door. Run and get into the first hole you can find. Don't worry about your gear. I will throw it off. Just get in a hole. The plane landed and sure enough the mortar rounds were coming in. I jumped into the first hole I could find. I looked down the runway at the plane and as the plane was taking off the guy was throwing sea bags off the runway. When things let up, we would take turns running out and getting one or two sea bags and dragging them back.

"Khe Sanh was small, half a mile wide and about a mile and a half long. They had a perimeter guard during the day that they called the 'bird watch.' We went to them and asked how we got to our outfit. One Marine told us to go up the road about a half mile and look for the tent with the big hole in it. 'The first sergeant got killed there last night. A mortar round came through the side of the tent. You can't miss it.' We all gathered our gear. He told us not to go up there two at a time, but to spread out at least 20 or 30 feet apart. If Charlie saw more than two together, he would start chucking mortars in. We started up the road, and I guess we got too close together because it wasn't long before Charlie started chucking mortars in right behind us. So we took off running, found headquarters, and got into a bunker. Once you got into a bunker you were all right."

"We were assigned line duty at the airstrip because every night Charlie would try to take it. It was a nightly thing. Sappers did get in there. They had a ridge built. Behind the ridge they had built bunkers. The bunkers were covered with dirt. We were on the opposite side of the ridge. Behind the ridge was where they lived.

"Every 50 or 100 feet they had a Vietnam shitter which was nothing but a 50-gallon drum cut in half with a lid on it. That's where we went to the bathroom. One morning we heard an explosion. A guy went down and lifted one of the lids up and it exploded. It was booby trapped with a grenade. After that, battalion headquarters put out orders for everyone to look for booby traps. We found a booby trap on every one of the 155 howitzers in the artillery battery. Three more shitters were booby trapped. Sappers had gotten by our perimeter, set the booby traps, and gotten back out without us seeing them. Fortunately for the company, but not for the Marine that was killed, the booby trap went off. Because shortly after that Charlie started a mortar attack. Normally, the artillery battery would have immediately started firing. They would have all been wiped out.

"I was there for about a month. Things were hot and the C-130s couldn't land any longer. They were too slow. And most of them were hit before they could get out of the area. The only thing that was coming and going were choppers and that is what I left on. I went to Kilo Fourth Battalion, Twelfth Marines at Camp Carroll. Camp Carroll was about 40 miles north of Dong Ha on Route 6.

"Well, they dropped us off, and I had no one to tell me where 4/12 was located. A guy I went through boot camp with came by in a truck loaded with power. I yelled at him and asked how I could find 4/12. He said, 'That's where I am headed. Go in this direction, heading north. Look for this emblem,' which he pointed to on the side of the truck. He told me to go to the ammo dump and catch a truck. I went to the main ammo dump. There were three more 4/12 trucks. I told them I had orders for Kilo 4/12. They said to climb on up. I sat on top of 155 howitzer rounds all the way.

"When we first took off, there was nothing but grass on both sides of us. Then there were rice paddies. The further north we went, the closer the jungle came in on us until there was nothing left but a one-lane road. When we came down off a little hill, they hollered back to hang on because when we hit the bottom of the hill, we were going through Aw Shaw Valley. This is where we drew all of the sniper fire. Aw Shaw Valley separated Camp Carroll, Khe Sanh, and Dong Ha. If they could take the valley, they would own everything north. There was a constant battle going on to take control of the valley.

"Anyway, they put their foot to the floor board and hauled ass through the valley. They had to slow down at the bridge where Kilo First Battalion, Ninth Marines, known as the Walking Dead, had a checkpoint. When we pulled up, it stunk. It was the most awful smell. I have never smelled anything that stunk so bad. When we went over the bridge, there was some freshly turned dirt. There was an arm sticking out here, a leg there, a head, body parts. When I got to Camp Carroll, I found out that about three days before the NVA had made an attack on the base. When it was over, the Marines dug a big hole and pushed the NVA bodies into it. They covered it over as best they could. To them, death was nothing. Nothing ceremonial. To them it was the enemy—no big deal. We all had to do a three-month stretch in this area before we rotated out.

"There was no heavy equipment so I was a fill-in. If a man rotated home, I took his place until he had a replacement. The 155 team was short-handed, and I was assigned to gun maintenance. One of the guys rotated home and I took over being the power monkey. I fused the rounds. Then I would go to the line. I never worked heavy equipment. Then we abandoned Camp Carroll, after the government said we didn't need it anymore.

"I was transferred back to headquarters First Battalion, Thirteenth Marines but they were no longer at Khe Sanh. Now they were at Da Nang. They had given up Khe Sanh. The 1/13 was attached to the Twenty-sixth Marines. They decided they were going to sweep from Da Nang up through Hue Phu Bai and clean that all up. We went to Hill 10 outside of Da Nang until the generals decided what they were going to do. They massed the biggest convoy of Army and Marines moving together. We got right outside of Hue. The Twenty-sixth Marines went back in and the Battle of Hue was on. The battle consisted of two weeks of house-to-house fighting. We were there for another two months.

"After about nine months in country, I got into it with a first sergeant for disobeying an order. I had been on perimeter all night and had come in. The colonel decided that we could have four hours' sleep then get up and do our daily duties. He came in after I had gone to bed and told me to get up and distribute the mail. I didn't do it and got office hours. Right after that I put in for a transfer back to Kilo 4/12. I had my fill of headquarters. The captain refused to let me go because he said I was so good at what I did. But after about six months, the captain approved my transfer and I went back to 4/12.

"We were located at Alfa Charlie One which was right on the DMZ. I was assigned as an ammo tech. I was responsible for moving all the ammo into the area and securing it at the base.

"We were there for about a month, and they decided to move us to what was known as the 'Rock Pile.' That was located about ten miles north of where Camp Carroll had been located. Intelligence had decided that the NVA were coming through that area opening up a supply group. They wanted us to stop them. They flew powder into LZ Stud which was about ten miles from where we were located. That's where I ran convoy up there to pick up powder.

"I went out on some listening posts while I was there, which I don't ever want to do again. It was too damn scary. You string your com wire out about 50 to 100 yards outside the perimeter. You're out there listening for movement. All you have is that com wire for communications. You're there with a 45 that's all. If anything happens like they get behind you and cut you off, there ain't no cavalry coming after you. You are just expendable. It's just too damn scary.

"I was in a number of fire fights while I was over there, and one of the things that always pissed me off was how the brass lied to us. They were always giving us these big numbers of VC casualties. You killed 300 or 400 VC. We would get hit, but we never found over 20 or 30 bodies. They never told the truth. They wanted us to believe we were winning the war. You're out there seeing your friends die and they are lying to you. They tell you all the fabulous things. You're young enough in some cases or drugged up enough in other cases that you don't care.

"People you come in contact with come and go. When you get hit, you run and jump in your hole. You're in there with people you don't even know. And you see guys getting hit, corpsmen patching them up the best they can, and you just don't make friends. It's a pointless issue. Those people are going to rotate back to the States. And if they don't, they are going to die. You made acquaintances. You didn't know their name and they didn't know yours. You may go together and get drunk down at the club. But I didn't want to know their names, and they didn't want to know mine. Maybe tomorrow you'd be gone. It was too painful to try to keep track of all that. Most people went by a nickname. Not their real name.

"A couple of times I attempted suicide. I cut my wrist real good. I was at the Rock Pile. It was late at night and I guess I had been in country for about 15 months. I just couldn't take it anymore. I couldn't take the killing. I couldn't take watching acquaintances die. I was totally disillusioned. By

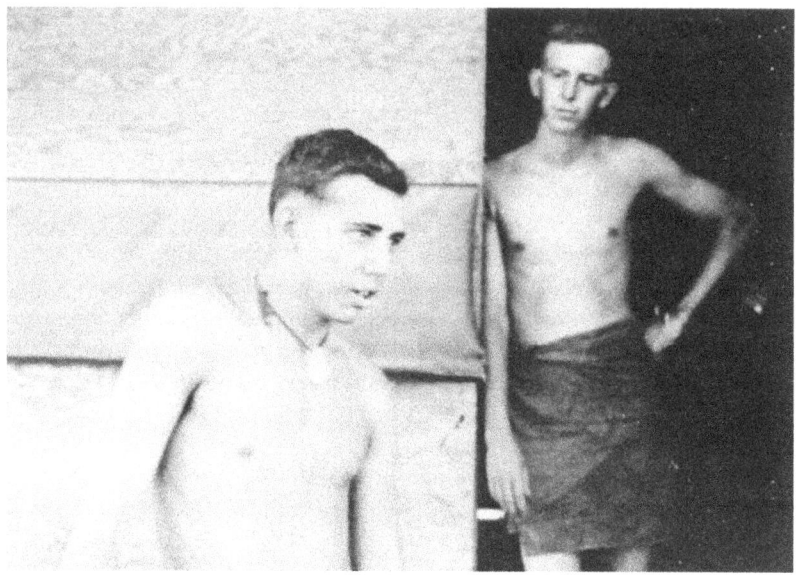

Carl McCory ready for a shower. Dong Ha, 1968.

then I knew we were being lied to. If we wanted to get the war over with, we could have started south and went to the DMZ. There were enough of us there that we could have taken South Vietnam over.

"But, instead every time you threw a grenade or fired a rifle you'd better have a body. Because if you didn't, they would prosecute you. Sometimes we would be out on line and come under fire. You would call back to your outpost and tell them you were under fire. 'Stand by, watch them, and we will get a hold of company.' Company says, 'Stand by. We will call regiment. Regiment would call back and say, 'That's great. Observe. Do not fire under any circumstances.'

"You stayed in a bunker and they didn't move. Charlie knew where the bunkers were. I just couldn't take it any more. The first time I attempted suicide I was on inner perimeter patrol. There were two of us. One goes one way and one the other. I pulled that duty all night long. There was nothing going on, and I had too much time to think. It was about three o'clock in the morning. Everything was quiet. I was thinking about it all, and I just couldn't stand it any more. I cut both wrists. Blood was running down my M-16. It was everywhere.

"The funny thing was that I went and checked in like I was supposed to. When I walked in, they called a corpsman. He stitched me up and gave me some tranquilizers for a day or two. They asked me why I did it, and I said that I got depressed. That was good enough for them and for me, too. I thought that I was okay.

"A couple of months later I tried it again. The drugs they had me on helped me come out of it at first. I felt really stable. But I couldn't stay awake to pull my shift. So I quit taking the medication and little by little I fell back into a deep depression. I cut my wrists again. They did the same thing for me the second time.

"At the very end I had put in for R&R in Australia. I had it approved. I was within a week of going. I got orders to go to Lima Company 4/12 because they needed a heavy equipment operator. We were located at Dong Ha North. I was with them for a month. Fifteen of us went back to Okinawa ahead of the company. We had to get Camp Swab ready for the companies to come in. I spent a couple of weeks with them and then got my orders back to the States.

"I came back to Fredericktown for 30 days. Most of the same families were there. People treated you like you were just gone for a while. Nobody talked about the war. It was as if you had been to summer camp or something. I got married to my first wife in 1970 and then went to Camp Lejeune. I was with Second Marines Division Engineer outfit. I was discharged in May 1970.

"We came home and stayed with my folks for a couple of weeks. My wife was an LPN and she got a job at Farmington. So we bought a trailer and moved to Farmington. I drove back and forth from Farmington to Fredericktown and worked at my old job at the gas station. No one would hire me as a heavy equipment operator because I wasn't civilian trained even though I could work the equipment."

Carl and Barb crossed paths again. "When he came back from Vietnam, my firstborn was about 18 months," Barb explains. "My husband and Carl's first wife were good friends so the four of us got together. It wasn't long before Carl and I realized that we still cared for each other so we decided that it was best if we stopped seeing each other now that we were both married. So we broke that off.

"He didn't seem like the person I knew before. He drank all the time, he was real white, had long hair and looked like a hippie. He was just really different," Barb recalls.

In 1971, Carl landed a job at the state hospital. He worked there for 13 months and then he went to LPN school for one year. After that he worked for the state hospital for ten years.

"When I came back to the States, I didn't get any help and I had a complete nervous breakdown in 1973. The doctor said that I had post-traumatic stress disorder. I found out that they were treating a lot of people from this area for the problem.

"They always preach at the state hospital that there is no shame in seeing a psychiatrist. But I kept fighting it. The depression got so bad that I finally drank a bottle of iodine. I took a bunch of potent mediation and just for a kicker threw in some drugs. I was separated from my wife at the time, and I stayed in what they called the 'Hartwell House,' a sleeping room on the second floor of the hospital. For three days and three nights, I was between hallucination and reality. I would come back, and I would be in the hospital someplace. I was walking down the hall. I asked this guy in a trench coat and a black hat for a light for my cigarette. I couldn't see his face. I came to reality, and I was talking to a fire extinguisher on the wall, and I didn't have a cigarette. I turned around and went back to my room and locked myself in. I had a black light and posters. I talked to the chairs and furniture in the room. I can remember wanting to get to my .38 which was in the closet. I could never stay in reality long enough to get to it. It was in the closet loaded. But every time I got up and started moving around I was hallucinating again.

"When I would come around, I would always be in some other part of the building, and I wouldn't know how I got there. I would always go back to my room because I was safe and I locked myself in. I would lie down and close my eyes and the next thing I knew I was talking to people. There was a chair directly across from my bed. It kept turning into people. About the third day, I could make that chair turn into whomever I wanted to. When I got done talking to them, I could make it go away.

"The fourth day I wasn't hallucinating any longer. I went to get a drink of water and my hands shook so bad I couldn't hold the glass. I called my wife and she came down, picked me up, and took me to my family in Fredericktown. They took me to the family doctor. He talked to me for a few minutes and put me on a medication and wrote me out a slip to get off work for a week. I went to my folks and stayed for about four days popping pills and sleeping. Every four hours my mother would wake me up and pop a pill down me.

"After that I started seeing a psychiatrist. He got into the why's and what for's. He explained that I was suffering from war depression. He kept me on medication for about six months. I got back together with my first wife, and we conceived a boy. About six or seven months later, I was feeling great. I thought I was cured. The doc kept reducing the medication until I finally quit taking it. The marriage wasn't working. I was a wild child. You name it, and I was into it. Partying, running around on my wife, taking any drug that was available—most of which I learned to do while I was in Vietnam.

"You see, the second week after I got to Vietnam an acquaintance was elected to find out if I was cool. So he gave me a joint. Certain guys did drugs, but it was a prosecutable offense if you were caught. You could do up to six months or a year in Port Smith. So when the new guys came in they all drew lots and one person had to go and approach the new guys about drugs. What was your stand on it? Would you do drugs? Would you turn someone in? So one person was at risk. I took the joint. It was a joint rolled in paper and soaked in opium. I went down by the showers all by myself and smoked it. I had a hell of a time getting back. I did every drug they had at one time or another. We did shifts of 12 hours on and 12 hours off. Your 12 hours on you were straight. Your 12 hours off you did everything. Just to forget where you were at and forget what was going on. One half of the company was straight, the other half was totally wiped out. You got to where you lived for your 12 hours off. When I got Stateside, I just continued with the drugs. I stuck with the hallucinogens. I didn't mess with the heroin or cocaine. In Nam it didn't matter because you didn't know if you were going to be alive from one minute to the next, but in the States it was different. I didn't take the heavier drugs because in my mind the less dangerous drugs were okay. I didn't see myself as having a drug problem. I could control myself and what I took.

"I left my first wife, and I met my second wife. We had a child. The thing to do is to get married. So I divorced my first wife and married my second wife. That lasted for about three months. Then I was seeing another woman who lived in a little white house down from the trailer where I had been living with my second wife. I used to go over to my girlfriend's house after work and party. She told me about a girl who had three kids and who lived right in front of her. No way did I associate Barb with this gal my girlfriend was talking about. The last time I knew anything about Barb she had one kid.

"I ran into her at a little grocery store in Doe Run. Barb told me that she was divorced and living by herself. Then she told me where she lived. By then I wasn't seeing anyone. I made a date with her."

"He still had some problems. He was having nightmares and night sweats. He wouldn't talk about Vietnam at all. He was drinking, taking medication, and smoking pot," Barb recalls.

"In both of my marriages I was on drugs for depression," Carl said. "When I got off, I would have suicidal thoughts. I had a lot of nightmares. It was a recurring thing over and over.

"After I divorced my second wife in 1980, I decided that I was going to get off the medication. I wasn't going to spend the rest of my life taking medication. I blamed my second wife for a lot of my problems so I got rid of her first then quit taking the medication. I still took street drugs for recreational purposes.

"The state hospital closed down so my job as an LPN was being phased out. I didn't like the RN that I was working for so I told Barb that I was packing up and moving to South Carolina. I wanted to get out of Missouri and away from the ex-wives. I told Barb that she could come with me or stay, but I was leaving. So she packed up and went with me.

"From June 1982 I worked at Roper Hospital (South Carolina) as an

LPN. It is a bigger hospital than Barnes. We were down there for five years. I was still taking recreational drugs, stimulants and pot. I was tapering off. I began to cough and choke and I was diagnosed with a touch of emphysema. So I had to get off pot. I would do sedatives. Maybe on a weekend I would take some acid. I drank heavily. About the only time I was sober was when I was at work.

"After I divorced my second wife, I thought I had a pretty good handle on my life, especially Vietnam. Then one day I rented a tape called *The Deer Hunter*. I lasted for about 30 minutes. It was too real. It was too much. I had to leave the room. I shook violently. Barb came in and held on to me. After about a fifth of vodka, I was okay. Then the movie *Platoon* came out. I couldn't watch anything associated with Vietnam. It would stir things up in my head.

"I finally tapered off to weekend drinking. Then I gave up my recreational drugs. I have been off of them for about eight years. I don't have the head problems that I used to have.

"I came back to Farmington and applied for work as a nurse at Farmington State Penitentiary. I went for four interviews and got turned down four times. A friend of mine told me to go in as a correctional officer and then do a lateral transfer after I had the job. I went to work over at Potosi in 1988. I liked the job, and I needed to get away from nursing. I had been a nurse for 17 years, and I had six ulcers. I couldn't leave my patients at work. I brought them home with me. Since I have been a correctional officer, I have not had any stomach problems.

"I look back and realize that when I was 20 years old, I was radical, very disillusioned, and hellbent on getting back what I had lost—my youth. Not just me but all of us.

"My mother made a very profound statement. She said, 'I sent my son to Vietnam and I got back a stranger.' It changes you—the shit you see and the things you have to do.

"You go over a kid, and you come back feeling like you're a hundred years old. During the time period you're gone, the rest of your friends are dating, partying, and going to the show. You're over there killing and watching people die. Watching people you know die.

"When you first go over there, you're doing things that you believe in. Then after you are there for a while, you begin to realize you are being lied to. They won't let you do your job. It's like putting a guy in the boxing ring and tying both hands behind him, then telling him to win the best he can. You just become totally disillusioned. You don't grow up like a normal person does. You go from a young person with all your life ahead to an old man, in a matter of eight or nine months. Your growing process is escalated beyond belief.

"When I came back and was running around on my wives, I was trying

Carl McCory, 1990.

to get my youth back. I had lost all of that. I went to fight for the United States and to win the war. We didn't win the war, and we were lied to. When we came home, it was like we had just moved out of state for a while. It was no big thing. Everyone should have been sent to a psychiatrist when they got back, not just sent back into society. Because society changed while we were gone, and we changed. I probably would have done everything that I did when I got back except take on a wife. I took on a wife and at the same time ran around like I was 18 years old. I was doing all those things and trying to keep them balanced. I just couldn't.

"I have always been in uniform. I came back and went to work at the gas station, and we had a uniform. I went to work at the state hospital, and

190   VI : Coming Full Circle

Carl McCory during a reunion with his son William (right), 19, whom he had not seen in 16 years. McCory's son Daniel, 14, is in the middle.

we had a uniform. I became a nurse and had a uniform. I became a correctional officer, which means still wearing a uniform and being in a paramilitary organization. I like it. I feel comfortable with it. I probably should have stayed in, but at the time I hated everything.

"Barb and I have been together for five years. We moved back here and have been together ever since. We are grandparents now. We have two grandbabies. For a long time we couldn't seem to click. Even though we wanted to be together, we didn't seem to be able to get things together. Either we were at odds with the kids or each other. But, for the first time, things seem like they are on the right path. I could go out and be a low-life son-of-a-bitch with anyone. But I couldn't do it to Barb. She was the one I broke up with when I went to Vietnam. I broke up with her because all the guys that I talked to who had done a tour in Vietnam told me not to leave anyone behind. They would forget you or run off with someone else. Or you may not come back. It's better to break it off before you go. So 15 years down the road, we ran into each other. I just could not be bad to her. We made a date and have been married ever since.

"William Shan is my first child. He is nineteen. When my first wife and I divorced in 1977, he was three years old. She married a guy in the Air Force, and she took him clear across to Washington State. I hadn't seen him until December 1991. He called me up out of the clear blue from Texas where they live. He talked with Barb first and said that he would call back. I was working at the time. He called back that night, and we talked for three hours. I hadn't seen him for the whole time. I would hear through the grapevine that my first wife had been back to Perryville to see her parents. But I would find out after she was gone. I was never allowed to see him or make contact.

"He is going to college down at Southeast Missouri State University, and he is talking about coming up and spending the summer with me. We don't write, but he calls and we talk on the phone all the time. He is telling me what he is doing and what is going on and I am telling him the same. We are getting to know each other.

"Daniel, my second son, is 14. We have had contact ever since the divorce. I have had him for most summers. I see him all the time.

"Barb can tell you that sometimes it still is rough, but nothing like it used to be. As I get older, things seem to be easier. I don't have nightmares now."

Carl walked me to my car. I looked back toward the house at Barbara. She had a content look on her face—one that expressed a relief that Carl had come full circle with his Vietnam experience. Maybe it was the openness he expressed in telling his experience to his former recruiter who crossed paths with him at a high school career day 23 years ago, or maybe it was that he told anyone.

I turned and looked at him. His lips thinned as a wide smile crossed his face, "You sure looked sharp in them blues."

"Yeah. I guess so."

"It's good to see you after all these years. Maybe we can get together again?"

"Maybe we can. I would like that."

I backed out of the driveway and waved at both of them as I pulled away. A thought crossed me mind. What if he had been absent that day?

SIXTEEN
Cpl. Gordon W. Huckstep

Hometown: Cape Girardeau Mo.; First Forced Reconnaissance; Da Nang, Vietnam; Tour of Duty, February 1969–January 1970.

> *As far as I am concerned, the people of the United States are entitled to know everything that they possibly can with regard to any involvement of the United States abroad. There are no combat troops in Laos. Our involvement in Laos is solely due to the request of Souvanna Phouma, the neutralist prime minister, who was set up there in Laos, as a result of the Laos negotiations and accords that were arranged during the Kennedy Administration. We are also, as I have publicly indicated and as you know, interdicting the Ho Chi Minh Trail as it runs through Laos. Beyond that I don't think the public interest would be served by any further discussion.*
> RICHARD NIXON
> December 8, 1969
> News Conference

"I joined the Marine Corps because of the John Wayne movies," Gordon Huckstep said in a chuckling voice. Gordon, a 43-year-old businessman, was born and raised in Cape Girardeau and attended Cape Central High School. In April 1968, he enlisted for two years. He left for boot camp at San Diego, California, on July 1, 1968. After boot camp, infantry training, and a 20-day leave, Gordon returned to Camp Pendleton with orders to Vietnam.

On January 28, 1969, the 18-year-old Marine boarded a commercial airline. Fourteen hours later the plane landed at Da Nang Air Base in Vietnam. Gordon stepped off the plane and the 110-degree temperature brushed against his face. "It was like walking into an oven," Gordon explained.

Beads of sweat rolled from his forehead as he stood in line for his orders. An hour later he received his assignment to the First Force Reconnaissance Company located at An Hoa.

"When I first went to Vietnam, we had about eight or nine men in our unit. A man by the name of Chuck Courtney from Youngstown, Ohio, took me under his wing. All new guys had to have somebody to take them under their wing until they knew what was going on. Luckily, I was with one of the old teams. They had worked together a lot. Maj. Simmons was going to insert us from a CHS-40 helicopter in an old fire support base. We would get on this helicopter in an old fire support base. We would get on this helicopter and Courtney would tell me don't worry. We haven't seen a fire fight in months. It will be a piece of cake. We were hovering over this old fire support base and we saw one gook rise out of this bunker and start firing at the helicopter. There were windows down the side of the helicopter and all the old timers jumped up sticking their rifles through the windows and firing. They were yelling, 'You fucking gooks!' I thought it was neat. It was just like I had seen in the movies. The helicopter lifted and took us back to our base camp. That night we had a party and laughed about the incident that day.

"The next day we went back and the helicopter was hovering. Two gooks came out of the bunkers and started shooting. This time I got to shoot through the windows. We lifted off and went back to the base with no one hurt. We partied that night.

"The third day the major sent us to the same spot. My adrenaline was pumped up. I was excited. Just as we hovered over the old fire site a tarp flew up. This time there were more than two gooks and they had a 50-caliber machine gun. They started shooting down the helicopter. They killed the pilot and the door gunner.

"There was a guy sitting beside me and I can remember looking up and seeing his arm get hit. Actually, it was only a nick, but I thought that it was a lot worse. He said, 'Put a battle dressing on it.' I got it and I was shaking so bad I couldn't get the battle dressing opened. Pretty soon he took it away from me, opened it with his teeth and slapped the bandage on the wound. 'Now, can you tie a knot?' he asked.

"The gooks had hit the hydraulics and the chopper landed on its side, hitting against a sand bar at the bottom of the hill. Every man on the chopper was wounded except me and a man named Leo Lambert. Both of us had been in country two weeks. Courtney was screaming and he was trying to pull his pants down. He had been hit between the legs with shrapnel and he thought that his balls had been blown off. When we hit all of us were thrown to the front of the chopper except Courtney. I looked back and Courtney was sitting on this seat with his pants down and his balls in his hand jiggling them and laughing, 'I still got them! I still got them!'

First Force Recon Unit, 1968. Gordon Huckstep is in the center of the back row.

"That was my first experience in Vietnam and I found out that it wasn't like the movies."

Gordon ran point most of the time for a kill team of nine men. According to Gordon, the commanding officer of his unit, Maj. Simmons, knew little about the proper deployment of the recon units. "We spent several months sporadically running patrols and ambushes. Our mission was to run long-range patrols and gather intelligence which we weren't doing, but then in May, Maj. Bond took over and ran the unit properly."

Three months after Gordon arrived in Vietnam he was wounded. "All I remember is that I was walking down a trail and this gook threw a hand grenade at me. I was running backup that time, instead of point. I was lucky because the point man took the total blast. I got hit by a couple pieces of shrapnel in the chest and stomach, but it wasn't a big deal. The other guy was evacuated to Japan."

In September, the Marine Corps awarded Gordon the Silver Star for bravery. "In my eyes, it happened a lot differently than the way it was written up. I had a lieutenant who was good with words. That's why I got it. As far as I was concerned I was just doing what everybody else did. I didn't deserve it. We had been sent out in the bush on a recon. We had been out

Cpl. Gordon W. Huckstep

for about a day. We were coming down a mountainside and we could hear Vietnamese chatter. The lieutenant and I broke away from the team. That's a no-no for a recon team to split up, but we went down about a hundred yards closer to where we heard the chattering. We got down near a trail. We never could see them, but we could hear a lot of gooks talking. The lieutenant and I opened fire and then ran back up the hill to the rest of our unit. We had evidently fired into an NVA base camp because we received a tremendous amount of fire as we ran up the hill. We returned fire for about five minutes and then ran through the jungle for what seemed like hours." This in part is what the lieutenant wrote about Gordon's heroic actions:

> On September 18, 1969, Lance Corporal Huckstep was point man for an eight-man reconnaissance patrol which was operating in enemy territory southeast of Da Nang when he alertly observed 13 hostile soldiers occupying an ambush site and, reacting instantly, opened fire on the surprised unit. After only one round, his rifle became inoperable and Lance Corporal Huckstep, boldly remaining dangerously exposed to the intense counterfire, quickly corrected the malfunction. Delivering a heavy volume of suppressive fire on the enemy emplacement, he killed one soldier, enabled the team to gain fire superiority, and was instrumental in routing the remaining men. While still under sporadic fire from the retreating North Vietnamese soldiers, he fearlessly assisted in covering the team's deployment to an alternate location and, en route, detected the sounds of another group of hostile soldiers approaching from a different direction. With complete disregard for his own safety, Lance Corporal Huckstep immediately ran toward the advancing men and initiated a lone assault against seven enemy soldiers, forcing them to withdraw hastily. Attempting to gain a vantage point, the Marines were maneuvering toward a small knoll when they observed five more hostile soldiers descending its slope and Lance Corporal Huckstep, in a daring display of valor, again commenced an aggressive attack and caused the enemy to retreat. Attaining their objective, the Marines established themselves in defensive fighting positions and Lance Corporal Huckstep, repeatedly exposing himself to North Vietnamese fire, boldly moved about the fire-swept terrain to check the defensive perimeter and shout directions and encouragement to his companions.

"I saw the only USO performer killed in Vietnam. When we had a USO show, the enlisted men got a regular performance of singing and acting. At the officer's tent a lot of times the women would take their tops off while they were performing. Enlisted men would sneak down to the officer's tent to take a peek. There was a lot of resentment between the enlisted men and officers over privileges like that. On July 20, a group called 'Sweethearts on Parade' was touring Vietnam and came by to give our unit a performance. We were about four rows back from the stage and my platoon sergeant, Sgt. James W. Killian, was drunk. Our recon unit was equipped with .22 caliber semi-automatic weapons and Sgt. Killian had carried his weapon to the show. We didn't know he had it. He had decided that he was going to kill the former commanding officer Maj. Roger E. Simmons. It was about 9:15 in the evening and Cathy Wayne had just finished her performance. Sgt. Killian fired at the same time Cathy was taking a bow and she bowed right into the Sarge's fire. She gripped the microphone and fell silently to the floor. The courts found Sgt. Killian guilty of murder. The Marine Corps dishonorably discharged him and gave him a 20-year prison sentence."

Toward the end of his tour there was a lot of movement of NVA troops from one area to another. One day Gordon's team was on an intelligence mission to gather information. "I'll never forget it. We spotted a defector with the VC. We were supposed to get the intelligence and return without contact, but without a word every single man on patrol released the safety on their guns. If we had shot, we would have all been dead because there were only nine of us and about 300 VC. Luckily, we didn't.

"The deserter was Bobby Garwood, a staff driver for the Third Marine Division at Da Nang. Garwood went to pick up an officer from a reconnaissance company near Marble Mountain at China Beach. The Viet Cong captured him. Garwood was 19 years old and had 12 days left on his tour. Fourteen years later Garwood returned to the United States after he supposedly managed to get a message to a neutral country. The message ended up in the hands of a BBC television network. As a result, North Vietnam released Garwood and the Marine Corps dropped charges and Garwood was set free. In the book, *Kiss the Boys Goodbye* by Monika Jensen-Stevenson and William Stevenson, the argument is made that Garwood was actually a prisoner of war. He was released because the message ended up in the hands of the media and because of the repercussions against Vietnam. The U.S. government treated him as a deserter to cover up the fact that they had abandoned prisoners of war.

"We had pictures of him on Route Charlie Ridge and he didn't look like any prisoner of war to me. He worked and carried guns with the rest of the NVA and was free to move wherever he wanted. He was a traitor to our country. It doesn't matter whether it was the Vietnam War or not. He comes back here and is just set free. It's a bunch of bullshit."

Gordon returned to the Marine base at El Toro in January 1970 for discharge. "While waiting on the paper chase to be completed, me and several of my buddies partied up and down the coast of California. A lot of times, we partied with hippies and Vietnam was never mentioned. Vietnam didn't bother me much at the time because I was too young. All I knew was that my country needed me. When your country needs you, you've got to go. That's all there is to it."

It wasn't until years later that some of the experiences in Vietnam began to bother Gordon. One night he was watching a telecast in which President Nixon stated that there were no troops in Laos nor had there been any killed or captured. Gordon knew that was a lie. He and a recon team went into Laos on an intelligence mission in November 1969. They were given specific coordinates to follow. "Someone must have known that there was a camp there because we came across a prisoner of war camp at the exact coordinates we were given. There were two prisoners in cages at the campsite, but they wouldn't let us get them out. When we got back, we told command that we wanted to get the prisoners. We argued that one of the teams had already been in Laos so they knew we had been there. It did no good. We had a general that debriefed us one at a time. He asked us what we saw. Then he told us that we had seen nothing, that we had not been in Laos, and that we were never to talk about it to anyone. That's the one incident that has bothered me over the years about Vietnam.

"My only hard adjustment was the environment change when I got home. You're accustomed to the environment that is around you. I was in fire fights. At night you were on edge in Nam. Then one week later you're back home in the good old USA. I had real troubles that first month — everybody just lying around and stuff.

"In April 1970, my friend had a birthday party. He bought a lot of beer and we partied all night. We were drunk. I had a pistol in the car and we were riding around shooting at rabbits. The next morning we were parked along the road. A boy got out of his car and went up to my friend's car that was parked in front of me. He cut one of the tires. He walked up to my car and told me he was going to cut my tires. I said, 'No, you're not.' He reached down to cut them. I reached in the glove compartment and pulled out my pistol. I pulled the trigger and held the hammer back so that all I had to do was drop the hammer for the gun to go off. I was going to shoot him. If he cut my tire, I was really going to shoot him. Luckily, he didn't. That's when I started thinking about it. I really sat and thought and thought. I decided that I wouldn't think anything about Vietnam. I was going to put it out of my mind. It worked for me."

Gordon went to work at the family business, Huckstep's Body Shop, located on Kings Highway in Cape. The business was started by his grandfather, Albert Huckstep, in 1936. His father Gene took over the business in 1947 and retired in 1979. And as Gordon said with a big grin, "Here I am." He worked as a special deputy sheriff for Cape County for a couple of years, but he just did it for the enjoyment. "I couldn't do it as a regular job because I couldn't see arresting somebody for something that I had already done."

About six months after Gordon returned home he married Carmen Anderson of Cape. They had three children Tara, Holly, and Zackary. Tara was killed in a car accident in 1989 — just two weeks after she got her

198   VI : Coming Full Circle

The Huckstep family. *Left to right:* Zachary, Carmen, Holly, Gordon, and Tara, on her knees with the dog.

driver's license. She was 16 years old. Holly is 16 years old and is a sophomore at Jackson High School. Zachary is eight years old and attends St. Paul School in Jackson. He is in the third grade.

Today Gordon and his family live in a ranch-style home in the country just outside Cape. Next to the house is a large pond. On the other side is his parent's home. Gordon runs the body shop with his wife and other family members. He also enjoys fishing.

Gordon doesn't think much about the war anymore. He said that after I had contacted him, he did look up a phone number in Youngstown, Ohio, for Chuck Courtney. He also had a copy of the book *Inside Force Recon* by Michael Lee Lanning and Ray William Stubbe. The cover photograph is of a force recon team. Gordon is the third on the left with his 6'3", 220-pound frame towering over Chuck Courtney, who is standing beside him. As I looked at the picture, I realized that I had seen the picture in the bookstores before, but had paid little attention. It seemed so funny. I had often looked at a picture in my scrapbook of myself and Gordon shaking hands in the recruiting office where he enlisted. I had often wondered what had happened to him. He was right in front of me all this time.

In Gordon's opinion the Vietnam War wasn't a good war. "It was run by politicians. Wars should be run by generals. Like the Persian Gulf War was run. I was proud of those boys. They did a good job. We didn't have any business in Vietnam. A country as big as ours in a little country like that. I never did understand why we should be there. There was a lot of money made, I understand. But we didn't make any of it. I will say this though . . ." Gordon said as he choked up, his eyes filling with tears. He looked down at his desk and sat quietly for a moment. ". . . we have the greatest country in the world. No matter what happened in Vietnam, I still love my country."

SEVENTEEN
Sgt. Ronald A. Lowes

Hometown: Jackson, Mo.; Photographer; First and Third Marine Division; Tour of Duty, October 1966–April 1967.

Jerry, I didn't forget you.

RON LOWES
April 23, 1989

Ron and I walked into the kitchen of his modern ranch-style home. He introduced me to his wife Marilyn. Just as we started to sit down for a chat a young blonde, blue-eyed girl popped into the room from the hallway. Her teeth glistened as she smiled. She fidgeted nervously waiting for her Dad to introduce her. "Oh, this is Jill. She's my 12-year-old."

"Hi," she said giggling, then disappeared quickly.

I sat down and made sure that my tape recorder was working properly before I began the interview. Just as I noticed the centerpiece on the table, Ron grinned and said, "I brought it back with me." His helmet cover sat in the middle of the table. The green and brown camouflage had faded some. The cover had a faded line around the lower part where the helmet liner had been folded up under his steel pot. The front of the liner had USMC–Photographer in black letters. On the upper left was the slogan: "I may be dumb but I ain't no lifer." The combat operations that Ron had participated in while in Vietnam were written on the helmet: Gulf, Dover III, Sutter, Roachrider, Sierra, Stone, Early, Humbolt, Union I, Union II, Hickory I, Hickory II, and Buffalo.

We both sat silently looking at the helmet cover for a moment then Ron began to tell his story.

"I went into the Marine Corps for a whole lot of crazy reasons back then. My Dad had fought in the Philippines and Okinawa and he received two Bronze Stars and one Silver Star. He wasn't one to spout off about what he did in the war, as a matter of fact, he was anti-war. But he had the tradition. His three other brothers had served in World War II. One of them served with Patton. I grew up with that.

"I just got out of college and had a lot of rough edges. The family thought I was crazy, but like I said, I had a lot of rough edges. I thought I was John Wayne, but I found out that I was more like Wayne Newton. I didn't have any regrets going in. I didn't have any regrets serving. And I don't have any regrets now. It was one of the turning points in my life. Vietnam didn't have anything to do with it. The Marine Corps helped me grow up.

"I had no idea what I was going to get into in Vietnam. I thought we were unprepared. For instance, the tactical operations weapon was going to be a pistol. I had fired a pistol before — a .45. I would say the majority of the boys that came over there were given a pistol and had never fired it. They didn't know how to clean it.

"It was a little bit strange. I know my Dad had told the story about going to Europe. They went by ship convoy. On one side they had to worry about the Germans and on the other side they had to worry about the Japanese. Hell, we flew to Vietnam in a 707. I can remember watching a movie called *The Black Box*. It was shown about three times while we were flying over. It was a terrible English comedy.

"We dropped down at Midway. I was a history buff and I was kinda disappointed because there was nothing there. We flew to Okinawa. I was sure then that I was going to get greased in Vietnam. But instead I won a bunch of money on a slot machine. Then we flew in 'Nam.

"I had visions of jumping off a plane with blazing guns. We flew in and they came to a stop and opened the doors. It was hot as hell. We sat there and sat there. Everyone was sweating. Finally they got us off the plane. We were all standing in a group and they gave us our assignments. 'You go to Chu Lai. You go to Phu Bai,' they would say. 'Go catch a flight.'

"We didn't have any weapons at all. Nothing. I caught a flight down to Chu Lai. I got off the plane and somebody said, 'Well, you go up on the hill over there and report in at that tent on the hill.

"So I went up and got introduced to first division photo lab. I met everybody I needed to meet. I was issued a pistol. Another guy who got there when I did was issued a pistol. He had never used one before so he got the Marine Corps guidebook and learned how to take it apart and clean it. He had never fired one.

"I spent a few days meeting people that I needed to meet. I could go to the club or do anything else I wanted those first few days. We were told back in the States that when we got there to stick with a Gunny Jones. He knew his shit and he would teach us what we needed to know. I found out

Ronald Lowes

when I got there that he had never been to the field. I met Sgt. Mike Warden who was a short timer. He had been out there in the shit and he helped the guys coming in. He taught us what we needed to know — tying your shit down so it didn't rattle, get black paint and paint everything that is silver black — the little things that keep people alive. He was super. He made sure that everybody coming in did the little things.

"The job that was laid out was to document all activities of the Fleet Marine Force West Pac. That means a lot of things. I didn't realize what it meant until I got involved with recon and found out how far into Indian country we were going to go. It meant anything from sitting in the lab taking a photo of a light-headed brigadier general and making him look like he had a tan, to humping with recon.

"The photographers were out there all the time documenting. We operated separately from other units just like the artillery or any other units would do. We were always short-handed. We had a lot of casualties. Four KIAS while I was there.

"Early on in my tour I got to go down to Quang Ngai on a piddly sweep. Actually, I was going to watch NBC do a documentary called "The Face of War." They had followed a Marine platoon around the several months. Everybody had left the area and went north, but this platoon. We went to film the crew that was filming the documentary. We were sitting on a little hilltop the first night and got semi-overrun. Not a single Marine got hit, but they hit the wire and everything broke loose. We set the claymores. Guys were jumping in the holes. Guys were firing at anything that moved. It was how stupid the war was. We had a water trailer sitting right in the middle of the hill. Wire all around it and the gooks threw a satchel charge right in the middle of it. They lost about eight or nine gooks on the wire. The water trailer blew straight up in the air and came crashing down. Their objective was the water trailer. That was my first vision of how crazy the war was.

"There were good people and bad people. Not that they were bad, but they didn't seem to know what to do. Their commanders didn't make them do what needed to be done. So it became quite evident early on who you wanted to go with and who you didn't want to go with in the field. For example, when the Twenty-Sixth Marines first came over, they were like the ARVN. They were loud and everything clanked. They were shooting their mouths off. You couldn't tell them anything. They thought we were the old guys and didn't know anything. We were like a bunch of old men that were trying to get home. But we knew some things you did and some things that you didn't do. They were just bad and they paid for that. They had a lot of casualties.

"If you went on patrols you went with Charlie 1–5. They would find the shit and you don't want to find the shit but there's a reason for this. Buck Darling was the company commander of 1–5 and had built a reputation for himself. He made a lot of contact, got the job done, and had a low casualty rate. He was one of the better company commanders. He was very much in charge. He was not your friend, but he got the job done. I spent a lot of time with Charlie Company First Battalion, Fifth Marines and you might say I got broken in by them. I learned more about what it meant to be a combat Marine by just keeping my eyes open and watching them. They were very professional.

"From my standpoint, shit started to hit the fan about Christmas of 1966. When the Christmas truce was called, we were moving down

Booby trap in First Corp area (photo by Ron Lowes).

Highway 1. I thought, man, we got it made. This is a holiday. Then we saw these flashes way across the rice paddies and these green tracers started sliding across the road. I remember saying, 'Hell, this isn't fair. They're not supposed to be doing this. I'm going to get killed during the Christmas truce.' Anyway we got to this big hillside. The Marine Corps flew Christmas dinner in to us. Everything was wet. But we had turkey, mashed potatoes, the works. Another guy and I exchanged gifts. I gave him my pocketknife and he gave me his. We switched back later, but we wanted to be in the Christmas spirit.

"For the rest of the year through the following November activity never let up. We moved from Chu Lai up to Da Nang and set up a photo center. We were low on people. Always low on people. We had various teams that were going out with units and staying out there and occasionally rotating in and bringing film.

"One of the things that would cause a problem was a lot of teams were getting good stuff and a lot of reviews. We would get word from Washington, 'You are getting some great stuff! Keep it up.' So the commander would make the units that were getting the good stuff stay in the field. It went over and over that way. I know one time that we had been out for weeks. We had nothing going on. It was a dead spell. The monsoons hadn't quite started. We came back and found out they were having a big barbecue. Steaks, beer, everything at China Beach and we came looking terrible. We were dirty as shit. The commander said, 'What the fuck are you doing here? Get your ass back out there.' We had just gotten back and done our captions and had heard about the party. We did get a chance to eat. And I got my chance with one of the pogues [slang for Marines who stay in the rear]. His name was John T. Loyd. He was married.

"'You're really sucking up to McCoy's ass so you can stay in the back, aren't you?' I asked.

"'Uh, but I'm married and I'm coming back,' he responded.

"'So it gives you some kind of special points,' I said.

"'If I got to lie, I'll do anything I got to do to stay in the rear,' he said.

"I hit that son-of-a-bitch just as hard as I could. McCoy called me in for hitting one of his favorite sons and I told him exactly what John T. had said. The incident was dropped.

"A few days later I was back with Charlie 1–5, and we got hit. We called for more help and they were sending in a couple of platoons on 34s. I had shot a lot of film and I had run out. We kept in radio contact with the rear and I asked for more film. McCoy sent John T. The 34s came in, some 46s came in to unload a bunch of C-rations. We popped a smoke and the choppers landed. John T. came struggling off carrying all this extra shit. He was a little ways from us. We were waving at him, but he didn't see us. He was running and falling down. All I could think of was that John T. Loyd was going to see the shit. John T. was standing there and some rounds popped off. You could hear them go by zinging. I yelled and told him to get down. 'What's, what's going on?' 'They're fucking shooting at you, John. They are trying to kill you.' He looked at me real strange and then threw up.

"Part of our job was to provide support to ARC lights. ARC light was a B-52 which would strike in South Vietnam and Laos. In Laos, the way it was explained to us, they would strike where the Ho Chi Minh Trail went through Laos. The Ho Chi Minh Trail wasn't just a trail, but many, many trails coming out of North Vietnam. The job was one of the most stupid that the Corps put Marines at risk for. The photographers were sent into Laos to take pictures of the damage when they could have taken the same pictures from the air. I mean the air photos could pick up a leaf off the ground if they wanted to. But the First Division photo team was given the task over a period of several months to go over these ARC lights. We had this guy named Keith Hall on the first ARC light operation. He came back and lived with me and my wife for a while. He was a shit bird but a good kid. He would say, 'Ron Lowes, you saved my life. I will do anything. I owe you my life.'

"Keith was 18, a short guy, a shit bird. Most of us were older guys in the photo team. I was 23 and the others were in their twenties. He would follow us around like a pup. During the first ARC light operation, the recon people almost killed Keith. We used 70mm cameras. They had to be loaded up in the darkroom. We had several loaded and Keith got the first draw to go out and take the photos. They dropped them in at dusk. They got up early the next morning and he took the photos. He got back here and there was no fucking film in the camera. I thought that the recon guys were going to kill him.

"We got a bad name for ourselves. They started calling us a bunch of pogues. Anyway, we had this Gunny Jones in charge of the photo center. He didn't show us anything; he didn't teach us anything. He slept on lace sheets, a lace pillow, and made sure he didn't go to the field. He had this big barrel right beside his tent and one day we came in from patrol. We had been out for a week. We were a mess and Hall smelled like shit.

"He kept saying, 'What am I going to do? What am I going to do about these clothes?'

"I told him to take them off and put them in the barrel, put some water and soap in the barrel, and get some bleach too. Then stir them. There he was standing by Gunny Jones' tent in his boots and hat, naked as a jaybird, stirring these clothes. Here comes Gunny Jones. He went ballistic. We caught a lot of shit from that.

"The ARC lights didn't happen very often and usually we didn't find much. The command center usually had something in mind that they were looking for. It was kind of spooky. We usually got down there right at dawn or at dusk. I found some body parts. I remember taking a picture of two feet that were in the sand that had been sheared off. I found some big craters.

"I was in the first division up until April. I was promoted to corporal around that time and then I was transferred to the Third Division in

Da Nang. I got assigned to a ready team. That was a team that if anything got really hot they were sent in to rescue the unit. My first rescue mission was on a village south of Da Nang. There was a company set up there. We got on 46s and flew out to the position and circled. They kept flying and flying in circles. It was darker than hell. I was leading the team. We set down. The back wheels of the chopper landed on top of a rice paddy dike and the front wheels were hovering out in mid-air. Everybody started jumping out of the chopper and landing up to there ass in the water. No one could see or move because the paddy was so muddy. And it was pitch black out. Everyone was pissed off and yelling at each other. We were actually jumping off the chopper and landing on top of each other. Green tracers were everywhere. What in the fuck am I doing out here? I thought. It is dark and I can't take any pictures. Things finally calmed down. For the next ten days we walked in the sun, but never saw a thing. Nothing.

"In late April, things were bad up north and it was a matter of either volunteering to go up north or be ordered to go anyway. So I went voluntarily. It was a world of difference between the area where before we were looking at going into the Aw Shaw Valley maybe or along the coast sweeping. Instead we were talking about Dong Ha, Con Thien, the Rock Pile, and Khe Sanh where it was just beginning to get hot. There was no doubt that we were going to be very busy. I really remember Con Thien. Con Thien sits out in the open. There are mountains to the west where the VC can shoot out of and then to the north is the DMZ. I was with a team right away. ABC news was shooting. Operation Buffalo was going on. The First Battalion, Ninth Marines, known as the Walking Dead, was really taking some hard knocks. They were bringing bodies back out on tanks. *Time* magazine got shots of the bodies being brought back out. I went up there to catch the Second Battalion, Fourth Marines and damn near got killed by our own aircraft right off the bat. The concussion of one explosion blew me out of my hole. That's how close they got.

"We got in on Buffalo. I shot a lot of film there. There were so many bodies that they were wiring their hands together to keep them from flopping. Then they were piling them up in tents. We finished our photos and found a place to dig in for the night. The next morning when we got up, I found out that we had dug in right by the fuel dump. I caught the shit for that. God damn, it was pitch dark out there. I didn't know we were by a fuel dump. Guess I was the fearless leader, huh?

"I went to Khe Sanh. One of my buddies had been on in the 861 north and 861 south and he told me what kind of screwed up deal that was. We weren't generals, but we still had a brain between our ears and anyone who had been in the Marine Corps long enough could see what was happening. When I flew into this place, I couldn't believe it. You had this low plateau.

Marine unit under fire outside Phu Bai (photo by Ron Lowes).

You got hills all around this plateau. The Marines had taken Hill 861 north and south. I went on some patrols. It was really eerie. Nothing ever happened. But it was eerie because you knew something was out there, you just never saw it. A lot of guys talked about it. We went up to Hill 861 north after the North Vietnamese tried to take it. M-16 rifles were new. They were replacing the M-14s at the tie. I had heard about rounds jamming in the barrels of the M-16s. A buddy of mine took some photographs of dead Marines trying to push the jammed rounds out of the barrels of their rifles. They were killed by VC while trying to unjam their rifles. The photos and negatives disappeared and were never seen again. We never found out what happened to them.

"We were on a search-and-destroy mission and we were taking some captions. We had a village we were burning. Nothing in the village. It was empty. Burning it, that's all. John Hart from the program "Discovery Today" was working for NBC news at the time. He came up to a paddy dike in front of the village and asked us to move out of the way. We cleared out, and John Hart lay down against the paddy dike, his cameramen in a position so they could film him and the burning village. He said, 'We just came under fire.' He stopped and then said to pop off a few rounds, and started rolling the cameras. That son-of-a-bitch. He is on 'Discovery.'

"I had about a month to go and had brought the whole team back in to the photo center. The top sent me for some guard duty and some other

Marine base at Phu Bai (photo by Ron Lowes).

light duty because I was a short timer and he didn't want me to have to go back out in the bush.

"Cpl. William T. Perkins was my replacement. He was a good kid. Clean cut. He was not foul-mouthed like the rest of us. He had problems with his parents and with his girlfriend when he went in the Corps.

"Anyway, the plan was that my team would go back into the field and Perkins would be in charge. Perkins did not know any fear. He would jump out under fire and take photos. He did things that you just don't do. They went back to the field and in just a short time he was killed in action. The sergeant went up to identify the body. The patrol had gotten into a heavy fire fight and Perkins dove on a grenade saving the other Marines around him. He was recommended for the Congressional Medal of Honor.

"The last night I was in Vietnam I was dressed in white shorts and a white T-shirt. I had given all my green shit away and bought all new clothes. I was laid-back and ready to celebrate. Suddenly there was a rock attack. We headed for the bunkers and all of us were in the mud and shit. I was dirty from one end to the other. The other guys laughed their asses off about that.

"The next day I was getting ready to go home. I was down at air freight. The top showed up and told me that he wanted to see me before I left. I couldn't get a flight out right away so we went down to the club and got a couple of beers. He took the stripes off and we had a father-son talk. He was getting out in three months and was going to retire. He told me that he

VI : Coming Full Circle

Marine wounded after a battle (photo by Ron Lowes).

Medevac during Marine operation (photo by Ron Lowes).

could have gotten me home a couple of weeks ago, but he wanted me to escort Perkins' body back home. I hugged him when I left. He is the only Marine I ever hugged.

"I came back from there feeling like I had done the best I could. No hero. Just the best I could. I didn't do anything that I was ashamed of. I just tried to be as professional as I could. Nobody wants to be in a war, but if you're going to be in a war, the Marine Corps is the way to go. They never lied to me. They treated everybody alike—like a bunch of assholes.

"I got off the plane in Cape. The Ozark Airlines was still running then. I got off the plane and I walked into the terminal. I saw a girl that I went to high school with.

"'Ron Lowes, where you been?' she said.

"'Uh, here and there,' I responded.

"'I didn't know you were in the Army.'

"The last night I was in 'Nam I was sitting in a white T-shirt and shorts and three days later I was in Flo's Cab riding down the street in Jackson, Missouri. It was a quick change. I guess what you call culture shock. Mom and Dad were gone when I called them. Flo pulled up in front of the house and helped me get my bags out of the car, and here comes Dad out the door with tears in his eyes. We went in the house and all sat around and cried like babies for a while. There was a big welcome sign that they had put up in the living room. It was like no transition at all. We were over there, then home. Hell, I went to Vietnam in a 707 and came home in Flo's Cab."

Ron's mother Juanite recalls the day. "We knew he was coming home, but we didn't know just when. I put out the red rugs that I had used in the back so he could come in on a red carpet. I had a big sign made 'Welcome Home' and had it sitting on the kitchen table for him. I was really tickled to see him. It sure was a relief to have him home.

"I remember one time my husband Albert and I were watching television and McNamara was on a visit to Vietnam. Ron was shooting some scenes for McNamara and he came on TV. As soon as I saw his arm, I knew that it was him. I almost had a heart attack and his Daddy did too. We were so surprised. It was an awful worry while he was there. We kept track of all the news on TV. He had changed an awful lot. He was so restless. Things were too calm. He didn't know what he wanted to do. He worked at Sears for a while and didn't like that. He wasn't satisfied here at home and he had been before.

"I got married to Marilyn about six months after I got home," Ron said. "Then who showed up? Believe it or not—Keith Hall, the shitbird.

"'You saved my life,' Hall would say.

"All I did was pull him down," Ron explained. "He had some rounds kick up in front of him and I reached up and pulled him down. Here I was married and I still had the shit bird hanging around. He stayed for about a month, then left.

"I taught world history at St. Vincent in Perryville and was a football coach there. I taught for about five years and got an offer with NPS Manufacturers in Perryville. I have been there ever since.

"You know the thing that irritates the hell out of me is that I didn't care about marching up Pennsylvania Avenue or in any ticker-tape parade. I didn't care about any of that. But when I first got home every jackass Hollywood producer was portraying every Vietnam vet as some war-crazy, child-killing maniac. And there were thousands upon thousands upon thousands of Marines, Army, Air Force, and Navy personnel who just came back and got on with their lives. So many movies portrayed us just like we were some kind of criminals. It still irritates me today. There are still some things that I won't watch on TV. I came home thinking the war was lost on the streets of America and in the halls of Congress not on the battlefields in 'Nam. I can't think of an action that we lost. We have had to live with that. It is difficult for me to say that we lost the war. But we did.

"I never had what you call flashbacks until I watched a movie called *Apacalypse Now*. I had some then, but not right after. I had a dream every night for about 18 months. It started about six months after I got married. I would be in some heavy growth sitting next to a tree with an M-16 which I never carried in 'Nam, I carried a pistol. Coming up this hill to my right are some troops. I can't determine if they are ARVN or NVA. I am hesitating and hesitating then all at once I have been shot and I am holding my chest saying I was too late, I was too late, I should have fired. I had 18 months of that dream.

"He has gotten easier to live with over the years," Marilyn said. "He used to have dreams and flashbacks. He could never watch the movies. I remember one Fourth of July we were having a barbecue and some firecrackers went off. Ron went running across the yard looking for cover. Later we had a laugh about it. He isn't jumpy like that anymore."

Ron and his family continued with their lives as years passed by. Vietnam seemed to be in the distant past. Then in 1989 the Moving Wall came to Cape Girardeau, Missouri. Ron went to the wall the night before the official opening. He didn't know what he would feel or how he would handle it. But he knew he had to go. He walked past the rows of names and knew he would need help finding where they were listed. He stayed until the next morning and some kind ladies helped him out. Because some of the names were the same, they wanted to know the Marine's name and state. Ron found himself spilling the names out faster than they asked him. Each time Ron found a name, he choked up. The grief that had been boarded up for so long let go. He mourned their loss. He realized that he had come to bury them, though they had long ago been committed to the soil.

He visited the Wall every day and had a friend deliver a single rose to the Wall. The card read: "Jerry, I didn't forget you." Jerry C. Bennett was a second lieutenant in the Marine Corps. He was killed in action in 1967 during a rocket attack on Marine positions near Con Thien I Corps near the DMZ. He was from Oklahoma. He had a pretty young blonde fiancée. She wrote him every day. His Mom would write him and in each letter he got a special note from his Dad. He was 23 years old when he died.

Joe Aragon was on the Wall, too. Joe was a full-blooded Apache Indian from the desert badlands west of Tucson. He was called Chief. He hated that name. He hated to get wet too. He hated the monsoon. He was a combat photographer. People in Force Recon said he was the best they had ever seen in the bush. He was fearless. He died during a fire fight with elements of the 325th North Vietnamese Regiment, while attached to the First Battalion, Ninth Marines, Charlie Company.

Alan Gelb grew up in a tough Jewish neighborhood in Brooklyn, New York. He was a little guy. He was always cocky. When he made sergeant, he was insufferable. They called him Sergeant Rock behind his back. He wasn't one of the most favorite people, but he was professional. He died on his second tour. While crossing a monsoon-swollen stream, he was hit by sniper fire. Losing his grip on the throw line, he drowned. He was 28 years old.

Ron had one last name to find, William T. Perkins, which is listed on panel 27E #97. Ron remembered that Bill came to Vietnam two weeks before it was time for Ron to rotate home. He remembered that he was from Englewood, California. He was a tall kid with curly hair and a baby face. Perkins had just made corporal and was to take over Ron's four-man photo team. Ron remembered telling him to get with Charlie Company because they were good and they would take care of him.

Ron remembered the talks he had with Bill. "When the shit hits the fan, stay away from the area where the command post is set up. Stay away from the radios." Bill died in September 1967. He dove on a grenade, a grenade thrown in the command post area during hand-to-hand combat with North Vietnamese regulars. He was awarded the Congressional Medal of Honor.

Ron's day-to-day visit to the Wall brought him full circle with his experiences in Vietnam. He realized that they would be a part of his life until his death. They were the friends and loved ones lost in the war. They were all brave and gave the supreme sacrifice.

The Wall helped Ron deal with the losses. His last day at the Wall he walked away, turned and looked back. He would go on now, but with a lasting thought of the war. "It is right that we should honor their names. They were the best of us. They shall always be a part of us. There is no glory in war. That is best known by those who must fight. There is honor! Honor by having the privilege of serving with these brave souls. Now, may they rest in peace."

Appendix

This combat casualty list includes persons in Harry Spiller's 11-county recruiting area who died as a result of either a hostile or non-hostile occurrence in the Southeast Asian combat area (1957–89). For those who died while missing or captured, the date of casualty is the date died or declared dead, not the date declared missing or captured.

Legend: "Home" does not necessarily refer to the place of birth, residence of the next of kin, place of longest residence, or other common uses of the term "hometown." "Home" is identified by the serviceman or woman upon the last entrance into the military service.

DOD — Date of Death   POD — Place of Death
H — Hostile   NH — Non-Hostile

These records were obtained from the National Archives and Records Administration Office in Washington, D.C.

Age 18 – 3 deaths	Age 22 – 5 deaths	Age 31 – 1 death
Age 19 – 14 deaths	Age 23 – 7 deaths	Age 33 – 3 deaths
Age 20 – 23 deaths	Age 24 – 2 deaths	Age 35 – 1 death
Age 21 – 11 deaths	Age 28 – 1 death	Age 41 – 1 death
Total Deaths = 72	Average Age = 21.7	

Illinois

Pulaski County

Name	Rank/Service		Home	DOD	Age	POD	Type of Casualty
McCall, Phillip Glen	PFC	Marines	Grand Chain	22Aug69	20	S.VN	H – Killed
Neely, William Merritt	PFC	Marines	Olmsted	21Apr68	19	S.VN	H – Killed
Neill, Joe Melvin	PFC	Army	Mounds City	22Feb68	18	S.VN	H – Killed
Shoemaker, Ronald Eugene	Sgt	Army	Mounds City	15Sep67	20	S.VN	H – Killed

Alexander County

Name	Rank/Service		Home	DOD	Age	POD	Type of Casualty
Beeler, Russell Richard	PFC	Marines	Cairo	02Mar70	19	S.VN	H – Killed
Cross, Bennie Lee	Sgt	Army	Cairo	07Mar67	23	S.VN	H – Killed
Guerin, Walter Thomas	Sgt	Marines	Cairo	07Feb66	23	S.VN	H – Killed
Johnson, Marshall D.	SSgt	Army	Cairo	30May68	21	S.VN	H – Killed
Jones, Richard William	PFC	Army	Cairo	17Oct67	19	S.VN	H – Killed
Profilet, Robert C.	Capt	Air Force	Cairo	02Oct68	28	Thai	NH – Died—other
Terry, John Francis, Jr.	PVT	Marines	Cairo	22Oct67	18	S.VN	H – Killed

Missouri

Mississippi County

Name	Rank/Service		Home	DOD	Age	POD	Type of Casualty
Carlyle, Donald Richard	PFC	Army	E. Prairie	24Jan69	20	S.VN	H – Killed
Clay, Charles Edward	Sgt	Army	E. Prairie	26Feb69	31	S.VN	H – Died—wounds
Davis, Don Eddie	PFC	Marines	Charleston	18Jul67	21	S.VN	NH – Died—other

Name	Rank/Service	Home	DOD	Age	POD	Type of Casualty
Henderson, Rufus Q.	SP4 Army	Charleston	20Mar68	21	S.VN	H – Killed
Higgerson, Tommy Doyle	SP4 Army	E. Prairie	01Mar67	21	S.VN	H – Killed
Naile, Thomas Glen	PFC Army	Charleston	28Oct67	23	S.VN	NH – Died – missing
Plummer, John David	WO Army	Charleston	19Aug69	20	S.VN	H – Killed

Scott County

Name	Rank/Service	Home	DOD	Age	POD	Type of Casualty
Blattel, David Lee	CWO Army	Scott City	05May68	22	S.VN	H – Killed
Boardman, Michael Kenneth	LCpl Marines	Sikeston	19Jul67	19	S.VN	H – Killed
Burks, Virgil, Jr.	PFC Army	Sikeston	25Apr69	22	S.VN	NH – Died – other
Burnett, Curters Joseph	Pvt Army	Sikeston	21Nov70	19	S.VN	H – Killed
Dobbs, Ronald Gene	Cpl Marines	Chaffee	02May68	21	S.VN	H – Killed
Hill, Alan, Jr.	PFC Marines	Sikeston	27May70	20	S.VN	H – Died – wounds
Hyde, Wayne	Pvt Marines	Sikeston	04Jun66	21	S.VN	H – Killed
Karnes, Leslie Leroy	SFC Army	Sikeston	16Feb71	23	S.VN	H – Killed
Marshall, Larry Hunter	SSgt Army	Illmo	04Feb71	33	S.VN	H – Died – wounds
Mullen, Clifford Truman	CET3 Navy	Benton	03Jan69	21	S.VN	NH – Died – other
Pennington, Thomas Jack	PFC Marines	Scott City	27Jan68	19	S.VN	H – Killed
Russell, Clarence Dean	SP4 Army	Sikeston	23Feb69	20	S.VN	H – Killed
Slayton, Ronald Dennis	SP4 Army	Sikeston	15Jan69	23	S.VN	H – Killed
Templeton, Clarence Wayne	Cpl Army	Sikeston	15Apr70	20	S.VN	H – Killed
Thompson, James Edward	PFC Army	Benton	31Dec67	21	S.VN	H – Died – missing
Woolf, Dwight D.	SP5 Army	Oran	04Aug67	20	S.VN	NH – Died – other
Wyatt, James Edward	SSgt Army	Sikeston	09Mar68	23	S.VN	H – Killed

Cape Girardeau County

Name	Rank/Service	Home	DOD	Age	POD	Type of Casualty
Benton, Carroll Joe	Sgt Army	Cape Girardeau	12Jun71	20	S.VN	H – Killed
Brock, Terrance Lee	SP4 Army	Cape Girardeau	04Jan69	22	S.VN	NH – Died – other

Name	Rank/Service		Home	DOD	Age	POD	Type of Casualty
Burford, John Shelby	Maj	Army	Cape Girardeau	30Aug67	33	S.VN	H – Killed
Busch, Elwin Harry	Capt	AirF	Cape Girardeau	09Jun67	35	S.VN	H – Died – missing
Finley, Charles Richard	PFC	Marines	Cape Girardeau	11Apr68	19	S.VN	NH – Died – other
Gregory, Robert Raymond	LtC	Air Force	Cape Girardeau	19Nov73	41	N.VN	H – Died – captured
Hogan, Billy Jack, Jr.	Sgt	Air Force	Cape Girardeau	29Nov70	21	S.VN	NH – Died – missing
McFall, Robert Dale	Sgt	Army	Cape Girardeau	10Mar70	20	S.VN	H – Killed
Middleton, Richard Wayne	PFC	Marines	Jackson	25Apr69	20	Thai	NH – Died – other
Peel, Steven Blake	SP4	Army	Cape Girardeau	07Aug69	21	S.VN	H – Killed
Schemel, Gary Leroy	PFC	Marines	Cape Girardeau	26Sep65	19	S.VN	H – Killed
Taylor, Robert Lee, Jr.	Cpl	Army	Cape Girardeau	08Mar68	20	S.VN	H – Killed
Tharp, Earl Watson, Jr.	SP5	Army	Cape Girardeau	26Jun70	20	S.VN	H – Died – wounds

Madison County

Name	Rank/Service		Home	DOD	Age	POD	Type of Casualty
Combs, Clifford Dale	PFC	Marines	Marquand	25Feb69	19	S.VN	H – Killed
Francis, Lindell	PFC	Marines	Fredericktown	09Mar69	19	S.VN	NH – Died – other
Mills, Lawrence Steven	PFC	Marines	Marquand	11Apr69	18	S.VN	NH – Died – other
Young, Jimmy Ray	Cpl	Army	Fredericktown	08Jun68	20	S.VN	H – Killed

Bollinger County

Name	Rank/Service		Home	DOD	Age	POD	Type of Casualty
Pomeroy, David Keith	PFC	Army	Lutesville	18Feb68	24	S.VN	H – Killed
Summers, Phillip Paul	SP5	Army	Marble Hill	01Dec67	22	S.VN	H – Killed

Iron County

Name	Rank/Service		Home	DOD	Age	POD	Type of Casualty
Buntion, Charles Wayne	SP4	Army	Ironton	31Mar72	19	S.VN	NH – Died – wounds
Firebaugh, Robert Anthony	PFC	Army	Annapolis	30Jan69	20	S.VN	H – Killed

Name	Rank/Service		Home	DOD	Age	POD	Type of Casualty
Middleton, Richard Wayne	PFC	Marines	Ironton	27Oct67	20	S.VN	H – Died – wounds
Stevens, Edward Howard	SP4	Army	Annapolis	19Jun67	20	S.VN	H – Died – missing

St. François County

Name	Rank/Service		Home	DOD	Age	POD	Type of Casualty
Cleve, Reginald David	WO	Army	Farmington	22Mar71	23	Laos	H – Died – missing
Ellis, Earl Wayne	SP4	Army	Bonne Terre	21Jun71	20	S.VN	NH – Died – other
Freeman, David Franklin	Sgt	Army	Farmington	15Sep70	24	S.VN	H – Killed
Isgrig, Dennis Edward	Cpl	Marines	Bonne Terre	15May68	21	S.VN	H – Killed
Johnson, Roger Lee, Jr.	Lt	Army	Flat River	28Sep68	19	S.VN	H – Died – wounds
Meador, Billy Ray	SP5	Army	Farmington	13May67	19	S.VN	H – Killed
Pipkin, Thomas Dewey, Jr.	PFC	Army	Farmington	11Oct67	20	S.VN	H – Killed
Suggs, John Fenton, Jr.	PFC	Army	Farmington	05Nov68	22	S.VN	H – Killed
Werley, Robert Wayne	SP4	Army	Desloge	13Jun68	19	S.VN	NH – Died – other

Perry County

Name	Rank/Service		Home	DOD	Age	POD	Type of Casualty
Ernest, Gary Joseph	PFC	Army	Perryville	16Aug66	33	S.VN	H – Killed
Lintner, Darryl Charles	PFC	Army	Perryville	20Apr68	20	S.VN	H – Killed
Loos, Thomas Walter	Sgt	Army	Perryville	04Feb68	20	S.VN	H – Killed

Ste. Genevieve County

Name	Rank/Service		Home	DOD	Age	POD	Type of Casualty
Seawel, Warren Paul	Cpl	Army	Ste. Genevieve	23Mar71	20	S.VN	H – Killed
Shuh, Frederick John	PFC	Marines	Ste. Genevieve	24Mar67	20	S.VN	H – Killed

Index

A Company, First Battalion, 5th Marines 169
A Company, First Recon Battalion 139
A Company, 7th Combat Engineers 158
Abright, Randell 54
Agent Orange 32, 33, 38, 39, 40, 41, 132
Agent Orange Veteran Payment Program 32
Albany, GA 79
Alexander County, IL 216
An Hoa, Vietnam 110, 112, 113, 116, 169, 174, 193
Anderson, Wiley 51
"Andy Griffith Show" 5
Apacalypse Now 212
Aragon, Joe 213
Arkansas River 70
Army of the Republic of South Vietnam 128
Australia 185

Bahamas 26
Barrett, Everette 54
Barrett, Gary 66
Barry, Donald C. 175
The Bataan Death March 1
Baylor University 97
Bauman, Dava Micheale Donze 28, 31, 36, 37, 38
Bauman, Ed 25, 26
Bauman, Mathew Michael Alexander 28, 46

Bauman, Patrick Norman Edwin 28, 46
Bauman, Wilma 25, 26
Beeler, Russell R. 216
Bennett, Jerry C. 213
Benton, Carroll J. 217
The Black Box 201
Blattel, David L. 217
Bloomfield, MO 83
Bloomsdale, MO 137, 158
Boardman, Michael J. 217
Bollinger County, MO 218
Bond, Major 194
Brazer, Corporal 99, 100
The Bridge Over the River Kwai 1
Brock, Terrance L. 217
Buatte, Carla 164, 165
Buatte, Dana 150
Buatte, Sgt. Donald 157, 162
Buatte, Sgt. John 157
Buatte, Michelle 164, 165
Buatte, Rose Lee 145, 146, 147, 150
Buatte, Vance 138, 150
Buatte, Victor 164, 165
Buntion, Charles W. 219
Burford, John S. 218
Burks, Virgil, Jr. 217
Burnett, Curters J. 217
Busch, Elwin H. 218
Butler, Legal T. 54

C Company, First Battalion, 5th Marines 203
Cairo, IL 19, 49, 169, 173
Cairo Baptist Church 51, 52
Cairo Evening Citizen 51

Index

Cairo Veterans Administration 20
California 12, 58, 125, 196
California Angels 143, 145
Camp Carroll 181, 182, 183
Camp Delmar Marine Base, CA 76
Camp Lejeune, NC 24, 106, 111, 113, 155, 179, 185
Camp Matthews 122
Camp Pendleton 2, 75, 83, 98, 105, 143, 151, 153, 158, 160, 164, 169, 179, 192
Camp Swab 152, 185
Cape Central High School 26, 110, 120, 192
Cape Girardeau, MO 3, 15, 25, 26, 37, 71, 79, 80, 107, 110, 111, 113, 117, 119, 121, 133, 138, 145, 192, 197, 211, 213
Cape Girardeau County, MO 217
Carlyle, Donald R. 217
Carrie 92, 93
Castor River 53, 68
Chaffee, MO 4
Charleston, MO 4, 46, 173
Chester, IL 12
China Beach 196, 205
Chu Lai, Vietnam 97, 201, 205, 126, 127, 139, 140, 143, 151, 152, 153, 154, 158
Clark, Ronald Dean 52
Clark Air Base 129
Clay, Charles E. 217, 218
Cleve, Reginald D. 219
Cobden, IL 133
Coeiler, Pat 164
Combined Action Program 115
Combs, Clifford D. 68, 70, 71, 218
Combs, Elizabeth 53, 55, 56, 63, 64, 65, 68, 69, 70, 71
Communications and Electronics Battalion 3
Con Thien, Vietnam 89, 90, 91, 101, 102, 103, 207, 213
Corona, CA 75
Corpus Christi, TX 153
Courtney, Chuck 193, 198, 199
Creola (Alabama) Police Department 133
Cross, Bennie L. 216
Cuban Missile Crisis 1

Da Nang, Vietnam 2, 10, 25, 76, 78, 79, 84, 89, 90, 92, 103, 104, 105, 106, 113, 116, 126, 127, 129, 143, 144, 155, 159, 160, 161, 162, 163, 164, 170, 171, 179, 180, 181, 182, 192, 195, 196, 205, 207
Da Nang Hospital 10, 11
Da Nang River 162
Darling, Buck 203
Davis, Doc 29
Davis, Don E. 216
Davis, Ray 59
The Deer Hunter 188
Dewlin, Al 107
Dewlin, Mike 97, 98, 107, 109
"Discovery Today" 208
Disneyland 58
District Intelligence Operations Coodinations Center 115
Ditterline, Cindy 15, 16, 17, 18, 19, 20, 21, 22, 23
DMZ (Demilitarized Zone) 2, 57, 58, 79, 87, 102, 126, 127, 162, 184, 207, 213
Dobbs, Ronald G. 217
Dobbs family 4
Doe Run, MO 177, 187
Dong Ha, Vietnam 84, 86, 102, 126, 127, 137, 143, 144, 177, 180, 181, 182, 184, 185, 207
Doyle, Doc 28
Dudley, Orville 54
Dusik, David 26

Ebaugh, Jeanne 120
Ebaugh, Kara 120
Ebaugh, Megan 120
Ebaugh, Paul, Mr. and Mrs. 113
Egan, Captain 100
Egyptian High School 51
El Toro, CA 6, 12, 106, 119, 155, 164, 196
Ellis, Earl W. 219
Ellis, George I. 81, 82, 83, 84, 85, 86, 87, 88, 89, 90, 91
Emrick, Sgt. Ervin 113, 114, 115
Ernest, Gary J. 219

Index

Farmington, MO 5, 177, 185, 187
Farmington State Penitentiary 187
Finley, Charles R. 218
Finley, Deborah 174
Firebaugh, Robert A. 218
First Armored Amphibious Company 105
First Battalion, First Marines 151
First Battalion, Ninth Marines 155, 207, 213
First Forced Recon. 192, 193, 194
First Marine Artillery Division 98
First Marine Division 105, 200
Flat River, MO 5
Fleet Marine Force West Pac 202
Flo's Cab 211, 212
Fonda, Jane 110, 117
Fortunate Son 82
Fourth Marines 2
Francis, Lindell 218
Fredericktown, MO 5, 81, 82, 177, 185, 186
Freeman, Bill 164
Freeman, David F. 219
Fulkerson, Ray 111, 117
Fulkerson, Sondra 108

G Company, Ninth Marines, Third Marine Division 53, 62, 85
Garwood, Bobby 196
Glass, Shirley Ann 164
Gonhoi Island 116
Graves, Teresa 79
Graves, Tony 157
Great Lakes 12, 83
Great Lakes Naval Hospital 11, 12
Gregory, Robert R. 218
Grenada 165
Griffon, John F. 54
Guadalcanal Diary 1
Guerin, Walter T. 216
Gulf of Tonkin 84

H Company, Second Battalion, First Marines 123
Hall, Keith 206
Harold, Sgt. 124

Hart, John 208
Hawaii 2, 57
Headquarters and Company, Twenty-Six Marines, Ninth Marine Amphibious Force 67
Headquarters Battery, Fourth Battalion, Twelfth Marines, Third Marine Division 24
Headquarters Marine Corps 125
Henderson, Rufus Q. 216
Henson, Normal H. 54
Hickam, Mo 177
Higgerson, Tommy D. 217
Hill, Alan, Jr. 217
Hill 22 160
Hill 52 159
Hill 552 99, 101, 102
Hill 689 83, 99, 101
Hill 861 207, 208
Hilton Head Island, South Carolina 146
Hinson, George 152, 164, 165
Ho Chi Minh Trail 142, 206
Hogan, Billy Jack, Jr. 218
Holiday Inn 15
Hollywood 117, 212
Homan, Bob 64, 68
Hope, Bob 79, 162
Horn, Maj. 104
Houston, Sam 121
Hovis, Charles W. 54
Huckstep, Albert 197
Huckstep, Carmen 197, 198
Huckstep, Gene 197
Huckstep, Holly 197, 198
Huckstep, Tara 197, 198
Huckstep, Zackary 197, 198
Hundley, Mose C. 52
Hungary 1
Hyde, Wayne 217

Inside Force Recon 198
Iron County, MO 218
Ironton, MO 5
Isgrig, Dennis Edward 219

Jackson, MO 37, 133, 200, 211
Jackson High School 133, 198

Japan 10, 76, 129, 130, 194
J.C. Penney Catalog 5
Jefferson Barricks 29
Jennings, Barbara 177, 179, 180, 185, 187, 190, 191
Johnson, George C. 54
Johnson, John R. 54
Johnson, Lyndon 121, 123, 145
Johnson, Marshall D. 216
Johnson, Roger L., Jr. 219
Johnson, William Joseph 52
Jones, Gunny 206
Jones, Leslie A. 54
Jones, Lt. 147, 150
Jones, Richard William 52, 216

K Company, First Battalion, Ninth Marines 182
K Company, Third Battalion, Fifth Marines 110
K Company, Fourth Battalion, Twelfth Marines 181, 183
Kadena Air Base 123
Karnes, Leslie L. 217
Kaskaskia, IL 158
Kemper Military School 83
Kennedy, Robert 3
Kensey, MO 158
Kentucky Lake 29
Khe Sanh, Vietnam 81, 83, 84, 97, 98, 99, 101, 102, 105, 180, 181, 182, 207
Killian, Sgt. James W. 195, 196
King, Martin Luther, Jr. 3
Kiss the Boys Goodbye 196
Kluck, Stanley B. 54
Koufax, Sandy 2, 3

L Company, Fourth Battalion, Twelfth Marines 177, 185
Lambert, Leo 193
Lanning, Michael Lee 198
Laos 107, 116, 140, 147, 192, 197, 206
Lavonia, MI 75
Lee, Gypsy Rose 79
Leslie, Phil 81, 86, 93
Lintner, Darryl C. 219

Little Company of Mary Hospital 13
Loyd, John T. 205
Loos, Thomas W. 219
Lorange, E.J. 54
Los Angeles Dodgers 2, 3, 126, 155
Louisa, KY 118
Lowes, Albert 212
Lowes, Jill 200
Lowes, Juanite 212
Lowes, Marilyn 200, 212, 213
Lutesville, MO 4

Madison County, MO 218
MAC 11 Marine Air Wing 76
McCall, Phillip G. 216
McCory, Daniel 190, 191
McCory, William 190, 191
McFall, Robert D. 218
Malaysia 143
Malley, Mary 11
Malley, Stephen M., II 6, 19, 21, 22
Marble Hill 4
Marble Mountain 10, 196
Marine Aircraft Wing Sixteen 10
Marine Corps Hymn 121
Marine Special Forces 16
Marion, IL 14, 117, 176
Mark Twain Forest 53
Marquand, MO 4, 5, 53, 64, 65, 66, 67, 68, 71
Marquand Funeral Home 68
Marshall, Larry H. 217
Marshall, William D. 54
Maryland 32
Maune, Lucille 93
MCRD San Deigo 2, 3, 24, 55, 56, 75
Mead River 113
Meador, Billy R. 219
Meadow Heights school district 80
Memphis, TN 6, 119
Menard Penitentiary 12
Merrill's Marauders 1
Meyer, Carl, Sr. 171
Meyer, Carl, III 173, 176
Meyer, Deborah 173, 176
Meyers, Harold 63
Middleton, Deanna 133
Middleton, Richard W. 219

Index

Miller, L/CPL 99, 100, 101
Mills, Clara 67, 68, 69, 71
Mills, Emmett 67
Mills, Harry 68
Mills, Lawrence S. 54, 218
Mississippi County, MO 216
Mississippi River 4, 156
Missouri Ozarks 147
Morrow, Vic 1
Mounds, IL 10, 169
Mounds City National Cemetery 4, 19, 49, 52
Mounds High School 6
Mounds Police Department 174
Mount Fuji 152
Mountain View Church 66
Mullen, Clifford T. 217

Nager, Margie 155
Neely, William M. 216
Neile, Thomas G. 216
Neill, Joe M. 216
New Madrid, MO 138
Newton, Wayne 201
Nixon, Richard 192, 197
Norfolk, VA 26, 32
Normandy Beach 1
NVA 83, 85, 101, 102, 103, 105, 106, 107, 113, 182, 183, 195, 196, 213

Oakland Naval Hospital 79
Okinawa 58, 98, 106, 119, 123, 138, 139, 140, 148, 152, 155, 158, 179, 200
Operations: Buffalo 207; Charleston 137; Colorado 137; Early 200; Hambolt 200; Hickory I&II 200; Kansas 137; Kentucky 137; Lancaster I&II 137; Mobile 137; Montgomery 137; Morgan 137; Napoleon 137; Neasho 137; Osceola I&II 137; Roachrider 200; Saline 137; Scotland II 137; Sierra 137, 200; Starlight 154; Stone 200; Sutter 137, 200; Tailer Common 115; Union I&II 200; Washington 137
Oran, MO 4

Osborn, Clyde S. 54
Ozark Airlines 211
Ozora, MO 151

Paducah, KY 13
Parker, Betsy 125
Patterson, Mike 98
Patton, MO 75
Patton High School 75
Peel, Steven B. 218
Pennington, Thomas J. 217
Pensacola, Florida 75, 122, 124, 130, 131
Pensacola Community College 153
Perkins, Cpl. William T. 209, 211, 214
Perry County, MO 219
Perryville, MO 191, 212
Persian Gulf War 33, 34, 146, 156, 157, 199
Philippine Islands 75, 200, 129
Phouma, Souvanna 192
Phu Bai, Vietnam 2, 24, 127, 128, 129, 144, 169, 182, 201, 208, 209,
Pinang, Malaysia 92
Pipkin, Thomas D., Jr. 219
Platoon 40, 188
Platoon 1056, First PT Battalion 56
Plumber, John D. 217
Poindexter, Lt. Col. 102
Pomeroy, David K. 218
Post–Traumatic Stress Disorder 132, 174, 175, 185
Potts, The Rev. Larry 50, 51
Profilet, Robert C. 216
Pulaski County, IL 216
Puller, Chesty 84, 85, 104
Puller, Lewis B., Jr. 81, 82, 84, 86, 87, 88, 89, 93, 94

Quang Nam Province, Vietnam 49, 50, 67
Quang Ngai 203
Quang Tri, Vietnam 98, 137, 140, 142,
Quantico, VA 97, 111

Reader's Digest 107, 109
Reagan, James A. 54
Repose (hospital ship) 79, 171
Riggs, Bill 112, 113
Robinson, Dewey W. 54
Roper Hospital 187
Russell, Clarence D. 217

Saigon, Vietnam 144
St. Charles, MO 178
St. François County, MO 219
Ste. Genevieve 5, 24, 25, 26, 27, 35, 36, 42, 46, 156, 158, 164
Ste. Genevieve County, MO 219
Ste. Genevieve High School 151
Ste. Genevieve Middle School 27
St. Louis, MO 24, 25, 28, 36, 46, 64, 119, 137, 138, 145, 155, 164, 177
St. Louis University Medical Hospital 28
St. Mary's Hospital 29, 32
St. Paul School 198
St. Vincent School 212
San Deigo, CA 138, 151, 158, 169, 178, 192
San Francisco, CA 145, 164
Sanctuary (hospital ship) 75, 76, 77
The Sands of Iwo Jima 1
Savannah, GA 146
Schemel, Gary L. 218
Schwarzkopf, Gen. H. Norman 146
Schweigert, Gail 155, 156
Schweigert, Julia 155, 156
Schweigert, Sgt. Lloyd 163, 164
Schweigert, Tony 155, 156
Scott County, MO 217
Seawel, Warren P. 219
Second Battalion, First Marines, First Marine Division 81, 83, 97, 98
Second Battalion, Fourth Marines 207
Second Battalion shore party 179
Second Marine Division 185
Second Platoon, Gulf Company 87
Sergeant Major of the Marine Corps 123
Shelley, Mr. 137, 145
Shetley Creek 63, 64
Shoemaker, Ronald E. 52, 216
Shuh, John F. 25, 219
Sides, Thelma 115
Sikeston, MO 4, 138
Simmons, Maj. Roger E. 193, 194, 196
Slayton, Ronald D. 217
Sommers, David 123
South China Sea 106, 137, 154, 162
Southeast Missouri 4, 107, 111, 113, 119, 120
Southeast Missouri Hospital 80
Southeast Missouri State College 26, 27, 46, 79, 93, 97, 111, 132, 165, 191
Southeastern Illinois Community College 6
Spiller, Chad 4
Spiller, Lisa 4
Spiller, Shirl 5
"The Star Spangled Banner" 38
The Stars and Stripes 154
Statesville Correctional Center 13
Stevens, Connie 79
Stevens, Edward H. 218
Stevenson, Monika Jensen 196
Stevenson, William 196
Stone, Oliver 115
Stover, Hazel 75, 76, 80
Stubbe, Ray William 198
Suggs, John F., Jr. 219
Summers, Phillip P. 218

Tate, Gary 153
Taylor, Robert L. Jr. 218
Teague, Olin 121
Templeton, Clarence W. 217
Terry, Gail 49, 51, 52
Terry, Jeanette 49, 50, 51, 52
Terry, John Francis, Jr. 4, 216
Terry, John Francis, Sr. 49, 50, 51
Tharp, Earl W., Jr. 218
Third Battalion, Eighth Marines 111
Third Battalion, Third Marines 151, 154
Third Marine Division 49, 98, 200, 206
Third Recon Battalion 137, 143, 145, 147
Thompson, James E. 217
Thompson, Penny 26, 27, 32, 46
Thompson, Sgt. 119

Thorpe, Chester E. 54
Tinsley, Steve 178
Tra Bong River 154
Tu Cau Bridge 89
Turner, Corporal 89
Twenty-sixth Marines 203
Tyner, Charles 87

Uncommon Valor 40
Underwood, Charles F.M. 54
University of South Alabama 132

V.A. Hospital 13, 17
V.A. Hospital, Poplar Bluff 27
V.A. Hospital, St. Louis 28
Vienna Correctional Center 174
Vienna High School 176
Viet Cong 14, 24, 25, 100, 105, 106, 140, 142
Vietnam Wall 21, 22, 33, 44, 71, 93, 94, 108, 110, 117, 213

Walker, David 133
Walker, L. Col. J.G. 10

Walker, Kimberly 133
Wallace, Thomas H. 54
Ward, Sondra 97
Warden, Sgt. Mike 202
Watts, General 140
Wayne, Cathy 196
Wayne, Dewey 66
Wayne, John 151, 192
Werley, Robert W. 219
Westbrook, Theodore 54
Weston, Tony 54
Wilkerson, Sgt. 80
Woods, Capt. 103
Woolf, Dwight D. 217
World War II 131, 158, 201
Wright, Maj. 102, 104
Wyatt, James E. 217

Yandell, Evelin 51
Yokosuka, Japan 10
Young, Jimmy R. 218
Young Cemetery 64
Youngstown, Ohio 193, 198
Yount, Edgar 75
Yount, Girdie 75

www.ingramcontent.com/pod-product-compliance
Ingram Content Group UK Ltd.
Pitfield, Milton Keynes, MK11 3LW, UK
UKHW041945140426
5217IPUK00014B/666